Music of the Middle Ages I

D1216899

MUSIC OF
THE MIDDLE AGES I

GIULIO CATTIN
III

TRANSLATED BY STEVEN BOTTERILL

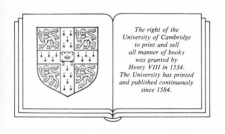

*The right of the
University of Cambridge
to print and sell
all manner of books
was granted by
Henry VIII in 1534.
The University has printed
and published continuously
since 1584.*

CAMBRIDGE UNIVERSITY PRESS

CAMBRIDGE

LONDON   NEW YORK   NEW ROCHELLE

MELBOURNE   SYDNEY

Published by the Press Syndicate of the University of Cambridge
The Pitt Building, Trumpington Street, Cambridge CB2 1RP
32 East 57th Street, New York, NY 10022, USA
296 Beaconsfield Parade, Middle Park, Melbourne 3206, Australia

Originally published in Italian as *Il Medioevo I* by
Edizioni di Torino, Turin, 1979 and © EDT 1979

First published in English by Cambridge University Press 1984 as
Music of the Middle Ages I

Printed in Great Britain at
the University Press, Cambridge

Library of Congress catalogue card number: 83-26316

British Library Cataloguing in Publication Data
Cattin, Giulio
Music of the Middle Ages.
1. Music – History and criticism
I. Title   II. Il medioevo. 1. *English*
780'.9'02   ML172
ISBN 0 521 24161 8 hard covers
ISBN 0 521 28489 9 paperback

CE

Contents

Contents

PUBLISHER'S NOTE

The publisher gratefully acknowledges the assistance of David Hiley
and Keith Falconer with the preparation of the text and biblio-
graphical additions for this English edition.

vi

Abbreviations

AcM	*Acta Musicologica*
AfMw	*Archiv für Musikwissenschaft*
AH	Analecta Hymnica Medii Aevi
AnnM	*Annales Musicologiques*
CCM	*Cahiers de Civilisation Médiévale*
CMPT	Colorado Music Press Translations
CSM	Corpus Scriptorum de Musica
EG	*Etudes Grégoriennes*
EL	*Ephemerides Liturgicae*
EMH	*Early Music History*
GkK	K. G. Fellerer (ed.): *Geschichte der katholischen Kirchenmusik*, vol. 1: *Von den Anfängen bis zum Tridentinum* (Kassel, 1972)
JAMS	*Journal of the American Musicological Society*
KmJb	*Kirchenmusikalisches Jahrbuch*
MD	*Musica Disciplina*
Mf	*Die Musikforschung*
MgB	Musikgeschichte in Bildern
MGG	*Die Musik in Geschichte und Gegenwart*, ed. F. Blume (14 vols. and supplements, Kassel, 1949–68)
MGH	Monumenta Germaniae Historica
MMB	Monumenta Musicae Byzantinae
MMMA	Monumenta Monodica Medii Aevi
MMS	Monumenta Musicae Sacrae
MQ	*Musical Quarterly*
MSD	Musicological Studies and Documents
NG	*The New Grove Dictionary of Music and Musicians*, ed. S. Sadie (20 vols., London, 1980)
NOHM	New Oxford History of Music
PL	*Patrologiae cursus completus. Series latina*, ed. J. P. Migne (225 vols., Paris, 1844–64)
PM	*Paléographie Musicale*
PSM	Princeton Studies in Music
RdM	*Revue de Musicologie*
RISM	Répertoire International des Sources Musicales
RQ	*Römische Quartalschrift*
SE	*Sacris Erudiri*
SM	*Studi Musicali*
SMUWO	*Studies in Music from the University of Western Ontario*

I

THE ORIGINS OF CHRISTIAN WORSHIP; LITURGY AND CHANT

1 The evidence of the early Christian sources

No musical material from the early centuries of Christianity has survived to the present day, with the exception of an incomplete fragment of a hymn in Greek alphabetical notation (*homoû pâsai* . . .) discovered in the Oxyrhynchus papyrus 1786 and attributed to the second half of the third century AD.[1] It is, therefore, impossible to gain a complete picture of the first developments in Christian chant from direct examination of sources.

It is the study of the earliest forms of liturgy which offers the only means of obtaining information on the distant origins of chant, and the broad outlines of such liturgy are familiar to us from the writings of the New Testament and the apostolic period, though in an incomplete and far from coherent form. Moreover, no other source can throw light on a phenomenon – that of primitive Christianity – which appears as such an anomaly in relation to the historical traditions of the Western world. The movement has often been called a 'graft', an image which expresses neatly the complete originality and novelty of a doctrine which arose and developed in the East according to cultural and religious traditions altogether foreign to those of the West, that is, to the synthesis of Greco-Roman civilisation. Past writers who have claimed that Christian chant derived in unbroken succession from Greco-Roman precedent were either unaware of, or else underestimated, the immense gulf created by the radical opposition between the Gospel (and the consequent new vision of God, man and the world) and pagan thought, even in its loftiest and most noble formulations, those of the philosophers.

Christianity – even if, at first, it was mistaken by the Romans for one of the many cults which flooded in from the East – carried within itself such a force for renewal that it brought about the bursting of the 'old wine-skins' (the image is Christ's: cf. Matthew 9, 17); and this was true even in comparison with Judaism, of which the new doctrine appeared to be an offshoot. The first missionaries of the Gospel, the Apostles, themselves all Jews, had their own individual methods of preaching and also brought with them new forms of worship, some deriving from Jewish practice, others previously quite unknown and modelled on the word and example of the Master. Those who had followed Christ from the beginning (John 15, 27), who had seen his works and heard his message, were in a position to become witnesses to his life and teaching. Their proclamation (*kérygma*) was concerned above all with the death and resurrection of Christ; but they went on to give a faithful account of his life, and repeated his words with a more perfect understanding of events which was bestowed on them after the resurrection of Christ and their illumination by the Spirit of truth (John 14, 26). 'Devoted to the service of the Word' (Acts 6, 4), they adapted its message to the understanding of their audience, owing a duty 'to Greeks as much as to barbarians, to the educated and the uneducated' (Romans 1, 14). And so in their preaching various elements can be identified: catechesis, narration, testimony, hymns, prayers and similar literary pieces which, at first handed on orally and later written down, were eventually incorporated into the four authentic Gospels. According to the prevalent modern view,[2] the Gospels and the Acts of the Apostles preserve the flavour of the Apostles' preaching, filtered through the experience of early liturgical congregations and arranged by the individual authors to suit either their own purposes or those determined by the needs of the communities for whom the written Gospel was intended.

What is most relevant to our subject is that the evidence of the Synoptic Gospels (Matthew, Mark and Luke, written in the period AD 65–80) and that of John (about AD 100) reflects customs introduced into the liturgy by the early Christian communities. Apart from material intended for use in prayer, readings and catechesis, it preserves certain rhythmical passages whose structure tends to suggest that they pre-date the Gospel text itself and may, at least on occasion or in certain places, have been sung. The celebrated 'canticles' which appear in the early chapters of Luke (*Magnificat*, Luke 1, 46–55; *Benedictus*, Luke 1, 68–79; and *Nunc dimittis*, Luke 2, 29–32, if this is not by the evangelist himself) may have originated in the liturgy of Jerusalem. But other, more obvious examples of hymnody (not in the technical sense applying to Western hymns) are to be found in the letters of Paul and Peter and in the Revelation of St John. Some texts are clearly associated with the rite of baptism and speak of the light (Christ) received by the baptised, for example Ephesians 5, 14; 1 Peter 1, 3–5 may have been chanted by the whole congregation at the end of the baptismal ceremony; and 1 Thessalonians 5, 16–22 was probably an opening hymn.[3] Other passages are short acclamations or doxologies, such as 1 Timothy 1, 17, while to the same letter (1 Timothy 3, 16) belongs a group of three distichs which the author has certainly drawn from a liturgical hymn. The primacy of Christ is the theme of the long composition inserted into the letter to the Colossians (1, 13–20), and frequent references to a prophetic text (Isaiah 53) make 1 Peter 2, 21–5 particularly interesting. A deservedly famous example is the hymn in the letter to the Philippians (2, 6–11) which is well suited to an Easter-night service. The president exhorts the congregation 'In your minds you must be the same as Christ Jesus', and those present reply with a chant.

As will be apparent, these are not strophic compositions following the principles of Greek or Latin metrics. The ground-rules of composition are those of Hebrew poetry (as in the Psalms), which will be further discussed below. Since we possess no evidence drawn directly from sources about the melodies which accompanied these texts, it will be useful to make the comparison with Hebrew precedent on this point as well.

The New Testament sources not only preserve fragments of chants taken from early Christian liturgy, but some of them, taken as a whole, display a structure which is clearly liturgical and sacramental. One such is the Gospel of John, in which the chapters which recount the conversation with Nicodemus, the cure of the cripple at Bethsaida and that of the man born blind would be catechisms used at baptism, the feeding of the five thousand would be an introduction to the liturgy of the eucharist, and so on. The letter of James is thought to be a homily and its content portrays a congregation of the years AD 56–7; the first letter of Peter is astonishingly rich in its treatment of liturgical and baptismal themes; and in Revelation, finally, the heavenly liturgy described in the various visions is built on the model of a Christian liturgy, not to mention the fact that its language is rich in allusions to the liturgical diction of early Christianity.[4] All this shows the liturgical practice of the Church in its earliest stages, the background against which Christian chant was heard for the first time.

2 The Jewish roots of Christian worship

The study of early Christian liturgy enables us to return to the concept of worship, and to the Jewish liturgy of the Temple and the synagogues which, ever more clearly, appear as the root of Christian liturgy. Certain characteristics which touch the very nature of Jewish worship are to be found, somewhat developed, in Christian liturgy. They include the sense of community, which before Christ had been confined to the Hebrew nation alone, but is now enlarged to take in all the peoples of the earth (universalism); the inward dimension of worship, once a theme of the prophets who urged inner purification and a conversion of the heart, and now carried by Christ and the preaching of the Apostles to make the most extreme demands (consider Stephen's declaration in Acts 7, 48: 'Even so the Most High does not live in a house that human hands have built', that of Peter (1 Peter 2, 4–5): 'so that you too . . . may be living stones making a spiritual house', or that of Paul (2 Corinthians 6, 16): 'We are the temple of the living God'); and thirdly, eschatological awareness which, based on God's promise to deliver his people and call them to communion with him, is offered again to Christians living out their worship in faithful expectation of the *parousia* or second coming of Christ.

So the early Church did not break with Jewish tradition, but introduced a new element into its worship: the Gospel as proclamation of the kingdom of God and of the death and resurrection of Christ.

From an objective point of view the nucleus of the faith shifted from the covenant of Sinai, on which were based the authority and efficacy of the Mosaic law (Torah), towards the new covenant realised by Christ, and from the old rites which were powerless to sanctify towards the unique sacrifice of Christ, accomplished once and for all (see the letter to the Hebrews). Subjectively the Christian life became the practice of 'the holy priesthood that offers the spiritual sacrifices which Jesus Christ has made acceptable to God' (1 Peter 2, 5). The religious vocabulary of the Old Testament could thus be used to express Christian spirituality through a change of meaning which adapted the rites of Jewish liturgy in a new direction, that of the redeeming act of Christ and of the Christian life as a glorification of the Father.

It will be understood that the message of Christ had great affinities with certain elements of the religious spectrum of Judaism. The

4

closest were the Pharisees (although Jesus often attacked their tendency to concentrate on the outward show of faith) and, especially, the Essenes, who lived in communities following a rule of strict asceticism, and with whom were connected the communities of the Qumrân caves on the Dead Sea where scrolls containing Biblical and extra-Biblical writings were discovered in 1947.

The outward sign of the spiritual relationship between Jews and Christians was found in the Christians' regular attendance at prayers in the Temple, where the Apostles themselves went to pray and to teach. 'They went as a body to the Temple every day' says Acts 2, 46, but adds immediately 'but met in their houses for the breaking of bread; they shared their food gladly and generously'. Although here the expression 'breaking of bread' may refer simply to a meal at which broken bread was offered to the guests, in Christian usage it very soon took on a more technical meaning, referring explicitly to the eucharist.[1] How long did Jewish worship co-exist with early Christian rites in this way? It had ceased to do so even before the destruction of Jerusalem (AD 70), as may be deduced from the clashes which took place between the two communities (such as the persecutions in the year 44) and from the decision of the Council of Jerusalem (49) not to impose the Jewish law on converts from paganism.[2] However, if direct contact between the two groups came to an end, the Palestinian Christians were mostly Jews and brought with them their own traditional inheritance; and they must have been mindful of Christ's declaration 'I have come not to abolish, but to complete' (Matthew 5, 17). It may be added that Paul and Barnabas, on their early missionary journeys, always headed first of all for the synagogues in the cities of the diaspora.

Any estimation of the debt owed by Christianity to Jewish tradition from a liturgical standpoint must include the following points: (1) baptismal rites, in the broad sense (in this case the mediation is due to John the Baptist, 'he who baptises'); (2) the first part of the celebration of the eucharist, including readings, prayers and chants on the model of Jewish services: this is what is nowadays called the 'liturgy of the Word' and corresponds to the didactic portion of the mass; (3) in the liturgy of the eucharistic sacrifice, certain prayers and the 'eucharistic prayer' itself (the *anaphora* or *canon* of the mass) are modelled on the Jewish *beracoth* or prayer of blessing, with the addition of the formulas of consecration of the bread and wine used by Christ (see the earliest accounts in 1 Corinthians 11, 23–6 and in the Synoptic Gospels); and indeed the structure of the liturgical sacrifice itself recalls the pattern of the Jewish sacrificial banquet, especially that of Passover which was the commemoration of the deliverance from Egypt and in the context of which Jesus chose to celebrate his own Passover (death and resurrection) and that of the disciples (liberation from the enslavement of evil); (4) the adoption of the Jewish calendar based on the seven-day week, with the gradual transference of the celebration of the Sabbath from Saturday to Sunday (*dies dominica*, the day recalling the resurrection of the Lord, the creation and the second coming) and with the beginnings of the annual celebration of Christ's Passover which formed the first focal point of the Christian liturgical year; (5) the practice of fasting in connection with worship (according to the rules of the early Church the days prescribed for fasting were Wednesday and Friday); (6) the complementary function of communal and personal prayer, following Jewish practice and the example of Jesus and the disciples; the Jews had special prayers for morning and evening which were to become the Lauds and Vespers of the Christian office, and were exhorted to make the day holy by praying at the third, sixth and ninth hours (compare the prayers in the Roman Office for the so-called minor hours: Terce, Sext and Nones) and even during the night (cf. Nocturns); (7) similarity between buildings used for worship; at Dura Europos the synagogue and the *domus ecclesiae* are two identical buildings differing only in their pictorial decoration and the symbols used in it.

There were of course influences from other sources on the developing liturgy of the Christian Church. The presence of hellenistic elements, for example, is undeniable; and this is due partly to the fact that Greek was the language used in the earliest liturgies, even in the West. The switch to Latin took place first in the African provinces and, naturally, affected catechesis and the didactic section of the mass. Towards the end of the third century Latin appeared in Rome as well, as an official language (used for such purposes as papal correspondence), but in the field of liturgy there was a long period in which both languages were used, a period which lasted, in such examples as the eucharistic prayer, into the fourth century and beyond. This survival forms the origin of the Greek lexical forms which remain in liturgical Latin (such as *kyrie eleison*). Other elements reveal their derivation from mystery-cults, such as the celebration of night-time vigils, the completion of baptism as an initiation rite (exorcism and unction), the *Disciplina arcani* (discipline of the occult), and so on. But such borrowings are not comparable in scale and scope with the inheritance drawn by Christian liturgy from its Jewish counterpart.

If these results emerge from the history of liturgy, what conclusions can be drawn from them for that of music? It has been widely assumed, understandably enough, that a large-scale transfusion took place, involving customs and melodies from Jewish tradition passing into that of Christianity. And yet – and this is an essential preliminary to any further discussion – the discovery of proof or even of clues in this field is very difficult, largely because the Jews, like the Christians (and this coincidence should not be overlooked), used no form of musical notation. They treated music as a solemn and privileged vehicle for the Word and the sacred texts, and considered the very function – or rather ministry – of the cantor to be sacred in itself. Furthermore, any melodic comparison of the heritage of Christian chant with that of the Jews must be undertaken with extreme caution, not only because the Jewish tradition was written down much later than the Christian, but also because of the possibility – which seems to have been verified in some cases – that it was the Jewish tradition which was influenced by the Christian in the course of centuries. Moreover, the dispersion of the Jews caused considerable diversification in the melodies of their ritual chants.

This is not to say that affinities and even coincidences between melodic fragments of Jewish and Christian chant are not to be found; every history of music[3] compares this or that passage to show their relationship (psalmodic intonations or similar recitatives such as the 'lamentations' are most often used). Too often, however, this involves literal quotation of Jewish models belonging to widely scattered communities, perhaps dispersed into the furthest reaches of the Western or Asiatic worlds; and there is always considerable scope for coincidence, given the basic nature, or rather the melodic poverty, of the cited texts.

Fortunately, direct comparison between the two repertories in their present form is not the only valid method of conducting this enquiry. Valuable help can be provided, for example, by an acquaintance with the development and the history of the Jewish repertory.[4] It is important to remember that it was only after the Babylonian exile, in the fifth century BC, that the ethnic and religious unity of the Jewish people was re-established around the figure of Esdras, and that neither the occupation of Palestine by Alexander the Great nor the vicissitudes endured under the *diádochoi* (Seleucids, Ptolemies, etc.) until the arrival of the Romans were able to damage significantly the sense of adherence to a unique community of religion and worship. This sense survived, to some extent, even among the Jews of the diaspora, resident in Rome and in almost every part of the Empire,

and in the richest commercial and manufacturing cities of the mediaeval and modern ages. In the nineteenth century and in the first
decades of the twentieth, several scholars devoted themselves to the
transcription of Jewish melodies,[5] though labouring under the dis-
advantage of having to imprison within bar-lines and tonal scales a
music which enjoyed an extraordinary rhythmic and melodic
freedom. Better results have been obtained from more recent
research,[6] thanks to recordings and to the application of the techniques of ethnomusicology. Even chants emanating from the most
distant areas reveal two types of relationship. The more important is
that they are related to each other, for beyond local differences there
exists a strong tradition which has preserved intact certain forms even
where the melodies are different; while the second connection – a
foreseeable one – is with the musical practice of the place where the
community has made its home. This evidence is much more interesting than individual and problematic melodic coincidences with Christian chant. And it is precisely on the level of form that the comparison
of the two traditions can show itself to be extremely significant.

3 The early forms of Christian chant

The same conception of the 'Word' in its sacred, mystical sense unites
Jewish and Christian spirituality; but among Christians its semantic
value is greater because the word (*logos*, *verbum*) is also the Son of
God, Christ. In both systems it is an essential part of worship, to the
point where – in Jewish ritual – the word is always chanted in order to
extract richness and solemnity from the musical sound; nor, indeed,
does Christian practice differ, in that the word is 'proclaimed' to the
congregation and not merely spoken or pronounced. This premise
explains why chanting, along with psalmody, is one of the universal
and distinctive traits of Jewish religious music. These are its essential
elements, according to Edith Gerson-Kiwi:[1] chanting is an amplifi-
cation of the word in a restricted number of sounds, governed by the
verbal rhythm, in phrases devoid of any metrical structure. It is not,
therefore, a melodic ornament, and still less a genuine musical
composition, since the text is pronounced rapidly, to the degree of
flexibility permitted by the nature of the language involved. In the
rabbinical schools future cantors (*hazam*, plural *hazamîn*) are taught
the recitative formulas (*ta'am*, *ta'amîn*) shown in their books by

conventional signs which have nothing to do with musical notation. *Ta'amîn* come in many different varieties, but each type has to be reproduced with absolute fidelity; and in them are found vocal passages, sometimes short and sometimes of reasonable length, based on an archaic musical scale familiar from other Middle Eastern sources and containing intervals of less than a semitone and frequent passages *glissando* from one note to another. In Christian practice the recitatives of the celebrant and the readings of the other ministers (Epistle, Gospel, Lamentations and so on) are based on this scheme. Differences include the disappearance of micro-intervals and other details (for example, in these Christian chants punctuation is more varied and more frequent), but the principle of construction is the same.

As for the psalms, the Old Testament and the tradition which survives today in Jewish communities reveal a considerable diversity in performance. H. Avenary[2] identifies the following variations: (1) single verses of the psalm are sung by the cantor and then repeated unchanged by the congregation (a simple teaching method); (2) the psalm is intoned by the soloist and sung as a whole by the congregation (rarely found); (3) the psalm is performed by the soloist, while the congregation responds with a given verse of the psalm as a refrain; (4) the psalm is performed by the soloist, the congregation singing *alleluia* after each verse; (5) the soloist chants the first half of each verse, and the congregation replies with the second; (6) the psalm is sung by the soloist, and the congregation joins in with certain verses only; (7) the psalm is sung with fresh text or music interpolated. In this variety of modes of performance (some of which presuppose rehearsal) one element is constant: the solo cantor who leads the congregation. He adapts the melodic formulas to the varying nature of the text, following that technique of variation which presided also over the formation of Western liturgical chant (the psalms follow the rules of a proper poetic form, but one completely different from those based on our metrical criteria of quantity or accent; the basic constructive principle is that of parallelism between the verses). In such chants, obviously, there is no room for polyphony, and the human voice, considered the most malleable and perfect of instruments, finds its fullest application in solo performance.

Was there unbroken continuity in the change from Jewish tradition to that of primitive Christianity? The unanimous opinion of scholars, especially of those who start from liturgical evidence, is that there was; they see in type 3 above the prototype of the responsorial psalm of the Christians, and in type 4 the model of alleluiatic psalmody, while type 6 is taken to be the precursor of antiphonal psalmody. It is true, however, that in recent years attention has been drawn to the absence of positive evidence for the existence of the responsorial psalm before the third century.[3] But the global scale of subsequent developments is such that the argument *e silentio* seems very weak, the more so because the Biblical precedents for psalms with a refrain are particularly notable (see Psalms 117 and 136 in the Vulgate numeration), even if their plan is not exactly that of the Christian responsorial psalm.

The *psalmus responsorius*, as it appears in Christian sources, obeys the following rules of repetition (where A indicates the refrain, B and C the verses of the psalm): soloist A, congregation A, soloist B, congregation A, soloist C, congregation A, and so on. In practice the response given by the soloist and repeated by the congregation is taken up by the congregation after every verse.

Evidence of the alleluiatic psalm is found as early as Tertullian (d. 220) and in the contemporary *Apostolic Tradition* of Hippolytus; as we have seen, it consisted of an acclamation (*alleluia*) after each verse chanted by the soloist. Traces of this kind of performance may be detectable in the ancient Ambrosian psalmody of Milan;[4] and it was re-introduced into the liturgy of the Hours as part of the reform ordained by the Second Vatican Council in 1970.

Antiphonal psalmody (formerly simply called antiphon) consisted of the alternation of the verses of a psalm between two semi-choruses, with or without a form of refrain, either taken from the same psalm or from elsewhere. Some scholars hold[5] that it was introduced somewhat reluctantly into the West and rather later than the responsorial psalm. In present-day usage 'antiphon' is the name given to the short phrase sung at the beginning and at the end of the psalm.

Another form which should not be overlooked is that in which the psalm is performed by a cantor without additions or verses used as a refrain. From this type of psalmody is derived the Gregorian *tractus* (called *cantus* in the Ambrosian rite), a meditative chant after a reading, originally performed by a soloist.

Another melodic form with its roots in Jewish tradition is the *jubilus*.[6] This consists of the joyful explosion of a vocal melisma, sometimes very long, without accompanying text. The fullest and most enthusiastic account of this musical form – a kind of contemplation – is given by St Augustine (354–430), who rarely misses an opportunity to discuss it, especially in his *Enarrationes in Psalmos*. He describes it as a chant much used in connection with the responsorial psalm, and thereby refutes the opinion of those who see in the *jubilus* no more than the direct ancestor of the *alleluia* in the mass. (It is noteworthy that the *alleluia* is compared by Augustine and others to the *kéleuma*, originally an oarsmen's song and therefore strongly rhythmical.) Furthermore, from certain other passages of Augustine[7] it might be inferred that the performance of the *jubilus* was not the exclusive preserve of the soloist, but that the congregation joined in; and one must therefore imagine simple or even standardised forms of *jubilus*. Among earlier authors, the *jubilus* is mentioned by St Ambrose (339–97) and by poets and other writers of classical Latinity (such as Varro, Silius Italicus and Marcus Aurelius) – a sign that the custom of performing the prolonged vocal passage was widespread even among the Romans, especially as the particular slogan of a given social or military group. This seems to be the meaning also of the Jewish *t'rû'āh*, a shout which in the oldest translations of the Bible is always rendered in words of similar etymology (*jubilatio, jubilare*). Given the evidence for its existence in the Latin world, it cannot be maintained that the *jubilus* is derived exclusively from the Jews; it is in fact a related phenomenon which the Christians, because of Biblical precedent, felt able to develop and thereby make more common.

A chronological list of some pieces of indirect evidence for ancient Christian chant forms a continuous testimony to what can be perceived clearly as a rich and multiform reality. Towards AD 50 St Paul, imprisoned at Philippi, sang with Silas during the night, perhaps a Jewish evening prayer, and the other prisoners listened (Acts 16, 25). In his writings St Paul refers to 'psalms, hymns and spiritual songs' (Ephesians 5, 19; Colossians 3, 16). Such words do not indicate a division of the repertory into three genres, as was once thought to be the case; and this is confirmed by the fact that in both cases an exhortation is accompanied by the words *in cordibus vestris* (in your hearts), which seem to act as a spur to inward adoration. If some kind of external reference is demanded at any price, it can only be to the melic forms of the Old Testament, certainly excluding hymns understood as strophic and metrical compositions.

It is certain that towards the end of the first century the *Sanctus* (*trisagion*) was sung, as can be seen from Revelation, from the letter of Pope Clement I to the Corinthians, and from the *Didaché* or *Doctrine of the Twelve Apostles*[8] (an invaluable little book which, among much else, contains the earliest description of a eucharistic gathering outside the New Testament). Indeed the *Sanctus* already had a place in Jewish ritual. The *Didaché* also provides information on prayers accompanied by a litany, and thus by acclamations from the congregation, after every intention pronounced by the celebrant. Among the rudimentary 'hymnodic' forms the *Gloria in excelsis* (*Laus angelorum* in the Ambrosian rite) should be mentioned, a doxology intended for use at morning prayer whose oldest version, in Greek, dates back to the second or third century.

In the year 112 Pliny the Younger, Governor of Bithynia in Asia Minor, sent a report on the Christians to the Emperor Trajan, requesting advice on the attitude he should adopt towards them. In the letter he writes that the Christians used to 'stato die ante lucem convenire carmenque Christo quasi deo dicere secum invicem' ('meet on a designated day [a Sunday] before dawn and sing among themselves a song to Christ as to a god': Letters x, 96). Ignoring the ambitious attempts made in the past to identify the *carmen* mentioned here, it is enough to note that the Christians sang among themselves (does *secum invicem* mean 'antiphonally'?) verses in honour of Christ.

The writings of the philosopher Justin, a convert from paganism, in his *Apologia* of about 150, are valuable for the history of the eucharistic liturgy, but on the present subject they reveal only that the congregation joined in the *amen*. More interesting is a passage from the *Apostolic Tradition* written in about 210 by a Roman priest, Hippolytus, in which all the elements that even today make up the preface are to be found. These include the dialogue between celebrant and congregation: 'The Lord be with you', 'Lift up your hearts', 'Let us give thanks to the Lord', 'It is right', etc., to which are added the common conclusion *amen* and the reference, mentioned above, to psalms sung by the deacon with *alleluia* as the refrain. Hippolytus and Clement of Alexandria (d. before 215) furnish information on the role of the *lector* and on the existence of formulas for the chanting of readings. Then for a long period there is discussion of the *schola lectorum* (the *lector's* ministry was a sacred one, which was conferred in a special rite of ordination), which was to be the forerunner of the *schola cantorum*. Originally *lector*, *cantor* and *psalmista* were almost synonymous.

In the light of this evidence certain opinions about the state of Christian chant before the Edict of Milan (313), in which the Church gained its liberty, can be critically evaluated. One common view[9] has it that certain gnostic currents of thought ('gnosis' was a heretical movement which tended to give a rationalistic interpretation to the Christian revelation) were responsible for the introduction of poetry and chant as a means of disseminating their own doctrines. The documents mentioned above compel a total reversal of this position; it was the gnostics who entered the battle with weapons which the

Church had been using from the beginning, as will be even clearer after the discussion below of hymns.

Equally extreme appears another thesis, which denies that Biblical psalms were chanted in the first two centuries of Christianity because – this is the argument of, for example, B. Fischer[10] – the so-called 'idiot psalms', compositions in free rhythm from private sources, were so widespread. The existence of such private compositions certainly cannot be denied, but this does not necessarily imply the exclusion of the Old Testament psalms.

Finally, the opinion of those (such as J. A. Jungmann[11]) who refuse to acknowledge any artistic value in the Christian chant of the early centuries can be shown to be based solely on a prejudice formed *a priori*. There is no explicit proof of this contention; why then should credit be given to such a reductive hypothesis, when Christian chant in its later development went on to reach what are by common consent the highest levels of art? Admittedly the first steps are always shaky, but they are indispensable if one is to walk confidently and eventually to run. Moreover, to maintain this view it would be necessary to ignore the weight of the Jewish tradition which stands so close to Christian experience.

4 Liturgy and chant after the Edict of Milan

Peace between the Church and the Roman Empire had a decisive effect on the liturgical life and musical practice of Christians. The chance to organise their own worship on a free and established basis (as had briefly been possible before the Edict of Milan) and to have available buildings large enough to hold the growing number of converts created radically altered conditions within the Church. Hence came the construction of ornate basilicas at Rome and in various parts of the Empire, along with the parallel and possibly consequent development of ceremonial, which was growing in splendour to match the increasing dignity of courtiers and Emperor alike. On 3 March 321, the *dies solis* (the Lord's Day for Christians) was recognised as a holiday for all workers; and this was the first step towards a calendar which, without abandoning the Roman holidays, opened the way for the demands of Christian worship. Two years later the ecumenical Council of Nicaea was summoned, at which the long-standing problem of the annual date of Easter was resolved (two different traditions had competed over a long period) and the ecclesiastical provinces presided over by Metropolitans were created at Alexandria, Antioch and, later, Byzantium. This provision had unforeseen consequences for the liturgical history of the East, as it laid the foundations for the autonomy of three great centres of influence, independent of each other and growing in stature even in comparison with Rome. Alexandria imposed its rite on Egypt and Ethiopia (though the Coptic and Ethiopian liturgies were subsequently to appear in the latter); Antioch took with it the churches of Western Syria, taking over important usages from Christianity in Jerusalem, but allowing the Maronite rite (named after the monastery of St Maron) to survive; Byzantium diffused its liturgy, very similar in many respects to that of Antioch, among the Slavs to the north and throughout Asia Minor to the south. However, in other regions, such as Eastern Syria and Armenia, the rites bearing those names continued to flourish independently. It may not be necessary to add that because each of these churches had and still has its own liturgy, they were able to bring to life their individual traditions of liturgical chant. Some of these have survived to the present day purely because their riches have remained intact, thanks to the conservatism which is a familiar phenomenon in ritual matters, and because they offer the possibility of comparison with the parallel aspects of the Western repertory.

In the new climate of liberty it was the task of the bishops, even in the West, to deepen knowledge and understanding of the initiation rites (baptism, anointing, eucharist); the period of Lent was given over to the final catechesis before baptism, which was conferred on Easter eve. The pagan festivals, which still survived, were replaced in AD 330 by the celebration of the birth of Jesus Christ which, along with Epiphany, came to form the second cycle of the liturgical year, after that of Easter and Pentecost. The memory of the ancient heroes was superseded in the Church by the cult of martyrs, which – especially in the fourth century – was intensified in order to combat the lethargy inevitably stealing over Christians after the declaration of peace.

Meanwhile, new difficulties were arising for the Church. Apart from the determined struggle against heretical movements, the greatest obstacles were the people's attachment to old superstitions and the incomprehension of intellectuals proud of ancient Roman tradition. Popes and bishops – such as, above all, the great pastors of the fourth and fifth centuries, Hilary of Poitiers, Ambrose of Milan, Rufinus of Aquileia, Jerome, Augustine, Popes Damasus and Leo the Great, to name only Westerners – combated these problems with an immense amount of activity in teaching, pastoral work and theological enquiry using, among other means, the opportunities offered by the liturgy. It was the golden age of the homily.

In the field of liturgy, it was precisely during the fourth century that the tendency to write down prayer-formulas, the order of readings and the texts of chants was spreading; the practice of improvisation was thus losing ground, although it had necessarily been the most striking characteristic of Christian rites in earlier centuries. The close connection between unity of faith and unity in prayer became apparent at this time, to the point where Prosper of Aquitaine (d. after 455) was able to state the famous principle 'legem credendi lex statuat supplicandi' ('the law of believing establishes the law of praying'). Now there existed a *lex supplicandi* (the liturgical structure) capable of expressing the *lex credendi*. Ambrose shows that he knew the Roman eucharistic prayer in almost exactly the same form as that which has come down to us. The first references to written formulas for the celebration of the eucharist (prefaces, etc.) and the administration of the sacraments appear in the rules laid down by various regional councils in the fourth and fifth centuries. The residence of *clerici* near the bishop and, above all, the establishment of the monastic system in the West favoured the full-scale organisation of the office (in the liturgy of the Hours), that is, of common prayer based essentially on the singing of psalms and arranged, as we have seen, at various hours of the day and even of the night. Also at this time the two cycles in which masses and offices would later be organised began to appear: the temporal cycle, including the feasts of the Lord and Sundays, and the cycle of the saints, including their feast-days. At the invitation of Pope Damasus, St Jerome (347–420) translated the Bible into Latin. This translation was the so-called Vulgate which more or less replaced earlier versions in liturgical usage.

As for the mass,[1] at Rome it began with a litany called the 'diaconal', which was imported from the East and spread rapidly through all the Western churches. The deacon articulated the intention of prayer and the congregation responded with a simple acclamation (*Kyrie eleison*, or *Praesta pater*, *Exaudi Domine*, etc.). The wide range of such prayers which developed led Gregory the Great to reduce the number of invocations, and his action seems to have been justified by the later appearance of an introductory chant, the introit, which required the performance of a whole psalm alternating with a refrain. In the time of Augustine the offertory and the communion chant were becoming widespread, both possessing the same responsorial structure as the introit. After the readings another responsorial chant, the gradual, was sung, followed by the *alleluia* modelled on the *jubilus*, the only passage of pure music allowed in the liturgy of all the Western churches. In the *alleluia* the human voice was treated like an instrument, and this called for professional skills on the part of the cantor. It is not known which of the popes was responsible for the deletion of the psalm which originally accompanied the *alleluia*.

The chants so far mentioned constitute what will later be called the *Proprium Missae*, that is, the texts which vary from mass to mass. The chants of the *Ordinarium* – those which, when the liturgy reaches its mature form, are present wholly or in part in every mass – are as follows: *Kyrie eleison* (the residual part of the primitive litany); *Gloria in excelsis*; *Sanctus*, whose derivation from Jewish ritual will be recalled; and *Agnus Dei*, introduced by Pope Sergius I in 701. The *Credo* entered Roman usage only in the eleventh century, but it was already being sung in Spain in the fifth century and in France in the Carolingian period. It should also be noted that all the intonations of the five chants of the *Ordinarium* which have come down to us are late, and mostly contemporary with the first manuscripts in musical notation, dating from the ninth and tenth centuries.

The establishment of a fixed repertory of prayers, readings and chants led to the use of particular books for each of the liturgical functions. The chief books used in the Roman liturgy[2] were the following. For the celebrant (Pope and bishops, and only later presbyters or priests) the first books to become commonplace were the *libelli missarum*, each of which had the prayer-formulas for certain groups of masses. Later all the celebrant's prayers were collected in the *liber sacramentorum* or *Sacramentarium*, of which three kinds are known to history: the Veronese, once wrongly attributed to Leo I (Pope from 440 to 461) and therefore also called 'Leonine', the Gelasian, so called after Gelasius I (Pope from 492 to 496: in fact the first version of the Gelasian, although it does include earlier material, dates from the end of the sixth century), and the Gregorian, attributed to Pope Gregory the Great. The book of readings was called the 'lectionary'; but in its place two separate collections could be used, the 'epistolary' and the 'evangel'. The texts of chants (notation did not yet exist) for the mass were collected in the *Antiphonarium* or *Antiphonale Missarum* (also called the Liber Gradualis), those for the Office in the *Antiphonarium Officii*. Other books of lesser importance were the *Psalterium*, the *Responsoriale*, the *Processionale*, the *Hymnarius* and, later, the *Troparium*, the *Sequentiarium*, etc. The complete missal, with texts of prayers, readings and chants, began to spread in the ninth and tenth centuries in Northern Italy and was called the Missale Plenarium. Finally the *Ordines Romani* contain the regulations for the rites, prayers and chants, mostly of the papal liturgy (a critical edition by Michel Andrieu of *Ordines* dating from before the eleventh century has now appeared).

Between the fourth and sixth centuries a new liturgical situation had developed. The consistent advance of Christianity through the old imperial provinces and the collision of Roman tradition with peoples coming from the East at the time of the barbarian invasions gave rise to new political and cultural relationships. Neither peremptory demands for liturgical uniformity nor severe impositions – perhaps ill timed and in any case unenforceable – came from the Roman pontiffs. At the end of the sixth century Pope Gregory the Great charged the monk Augustine, who was setting out to evangelise England, with the task of gathering the best from all the churches and 'placing it like a bundle (*fasciculum*) in the minds of the English'.[3] Such was the criterion used for centuries by Rome in working with local churches; it had allowed the most important churches to create their own liturgical traditions. None the less, from the end of the fifth century onwards there was a growing affirmation of the juridical principle of uniformity of discipline (and thus of liturgy) between all churches and their own Metropolitan. This encouraged the elimination of unduly fragmented rites, while enabling churches to arrive little by little at a local rite established on a regional basis. Understandably, this process reflected the differences in ethnic characteristics, cultural traditions and political situations, and resulted in an inexhaustible wealth of tradition expressed in liturgy and chant, to the rediscovery of which much modern research on the high Middle Ages has been devoted.

5 Hymnody

There is one musical form of Christian worship whose evolution spans the whole period, of several centuries, which has been discussed up to now: hymnody. The tradition of poetic compositions intended to be sung carries us back, as we have seen in various New Testament passages, to the earliest Christian communities. Such compositions, partly as an echo of St Paul's expression 'psalms, hymns and spiritual songs', were called 'hymns'.

The chief representative of hymnodic tradition in the East is usually taken to be the Syrian St Ephraim, deacon of Edessa (*c.* 303–73), a staunch opponent of the heretical writer Bardesanes (whom he cannot, however, have known). St Ephraim's compositions recall the pattern of the Biblical psalms, but are strophic in form and include, apart from a refrain, isosyllabic verses, alphabetical succession of opening letters (acrostic), and the use of pre-existing melodies, as was the case with many of the Old Testament psalms.

The variety of forms and attitudes to hymnody which appears in the Greek compositions of the early centuries leads us back to St Augustine's definition of a hymn:

> If you praise God and do not sing, that is not a hymn; if you sing and do not praise God, that is not a hymn; if you praise something contrary to the praise of God, even if you praise it in song, that is not a hymn. These, then, are the three requirements for a hymn: song, praise, praise of God. A hymn, therefore, is the praise of God expressed in song.[1]

It should be noted that there is no trace here of a reference to any strophic or metrical structure. Augustine was aware that compositions dating from before his day belonged to that genre which modern scholars usually call 'hymnodic psalmody', and he himself left a piece entitled *Psalmus contra partem Donati*,[2] written in an atmosphere of fierce anti-heretical polemic, which consists of passages of rhythmical prose containing assonances and alternating with a fixed refrain. And yet Augustine was himself an eye-witness of the birth of the hymn in the canonical form in which it was later to be recognised. His account (*Confessions* IX, 7) brings us to Milan, where in 386 Bishop Ambrose was holding out against the violent attacks of the Arian heretics backed by the Empress Justina.

In fact even before St Ambrose, St Hilary (Bishop of Poitiers, *c.* 315–67) had also composed hymns explicitly aimed against the Arians; but his excessively learned and complicated verses were never performed in a liturgical context. So it is Ambrose who merits the title of 'father' of Latin hymnody, since through his genius he was able to capture the faith and emotions of Christians with force and concision, in strophic sequences which presented the material in a fast-moving and accessible form. With Ambrose, hymnody took on a new and definitive shape; the short line of four iambs (each consisting of a short and a long syllable) is linked to 'quantitative' metrics, but already attention is being paid to the position of accent in the line, and a process of evolution is under way tending first to make long and accented syllables coincide, and ultimately to yield the complete predominance of the tonic accent as the constructive principle of versification.

Scholars[3] are not in agreement as to which hymns can safely be attributed to Ambrose, partly because all the hymns composed in imitation of the authentic pieces rapidly became widely known as 'Ambrosian'. Four hymns are known (unequivocally) to be by Ambrose, as they are quoted by Augustine: they are *Deus creator omnium, Aeterne rerum conditor, Iam surgit hora tertia* and *Intende qui regis Israel*. Opinions differ about a further fourteen, but in the present discussion the point is not a very important one. There are two statements in the passage cited from the *Confessions* which deserve closer attention: the innovations in the Milanese church took place 'after the manner of Eastern lands' ('secundum morem orientalium partium') and spread like wildfire throughout the West. Ambrose himself, in a sermon attacking the Arian bishop Auxentius, testifies to the extraordinary enthusiasm aroused among the faithful: 'They say that I have bewitched the people with the spell of my hymns; and indeed I do not deny it ... '[4]

Early Christian poetry reached its peak at the beginning of the fifth century with the Spaniard Aurelius Prudentius (348–413/24). He took over wholesale the legacy of Ambrose, but unlike his predecessor, who had created a genre which was extraordinarily vital because it was incorporated into the liturgy, Prudentius wrote exclusively literary works; only a few fragments of his hymns, not provided with original chants, entered the liturgy. Yet by the perfection of his art he managed to bring about the union between the pagan poetic world and the world of Christian ethics which others had sought in vain. But it is undeniable that his poetry belongs mainly to the past and remains no more than literature, albeit of outstanding quality.

In subsequent centuries there was no shortage of poets following in the footsteps of Ambrose and Prudentius: Paulinus of Nola, Caelius Sedulius, Prosper of Aquitaine, Sidonius Apollinaris, and others. Among these Venantius Fortunatus (*c.* 540–*c.* 600) is worthy of particular mention. A native of Valdobbiadene near Treviso who became bishop of Poitiers, he was a smooth and skilful versifier who wrote two famous hymns to the Cross which entered the liturgy: *Vexilla regis prodeunt*, in iambic dimeters (the metre used by Ambrose), and *Pange lingua gloriosi – proelium certaminis* in trochaic tetrameters, the so-called *versus quadratus* or legionaries' metre, named for its suitability as a march-rhythm. In the wake of these poets, many unknown versifiers devoted themselves to the composition of liturgical hymns; the tradition was to know a period of classicising revival, such as the Carolingian epoch, as well as lean years, but lasted unbroken up to and beyond the fifteenth century. Most of these texts are now gathered in the *Analecta Hymnica Medii Aevi*, and form an impressive body of work.

It has been mentioned above that the West was conquered by the innovations of St Ambrose. The singing of hymns rang out from Milan to the churches of France, Spain and North Africa. In Rome, the Ambrosian initiative does not seem to have been received with much enthusiasm; yet hymns were known there to some extent, if the story is true that Pope Gelasius (d. 496) wrote several 'in the style of Ambrose'. It was the monastic tradition which undertook the task of ensuring their diffusion; the rule of St Benedict (d. *c.* 547) prescribed the use of 'Ambrosian' hymns in all the hours of the office, and the later Rule of St Caesarius of Arles (d. 542) mentions fourteen hymns by name. Some limited resistance – such as that of the Council of Braga (563), at which the singing of any poetic composition in church was expressly forbidden – was soon overcome; the second Council of Tours (567) opened the gates not only to 'Ambrosian' hymns but also to any suitable text whose author's identity was known. Gregory the Great (d. 604) was probably a supporter of the hard line of the Council of Braga, since he aimed to exclude all non-Biblical texts from the liturgy; but his reforms did not affect monastic institutions (he himself had been a monk) and tradition even ascribes the authorship of several hymns to him. In the seventh and eighth centuries the hymnodic and liturgical tradition continued to grow apace in the French and Spanish churches; not even in the ninth century, when Gregorian books of the Roman liturgy had been available in Frankish territory for some time, did the performance of hymns become markedly less common. Evidence for this is found in a passage from Walafrid Strabo (840), the first liturgical historian,[5] and in the presence of hymnodic texts in liturgical books dating from before 1000, though not on a large scale and without notation, as the melodies would be familiar to all involved. Finally, from the eleventh and twelfth centuries onwards hymns re-appeared, this time to stay, in Roman liturgical books.

One significant fact reveals the uncertainties and fluctuations which affected hymnodic tradition in the West. Though the surviving liturgical repertory has come down to us without major melodic variants in the early sources, not only are such variants numerous in 'optional' compositions, especially hymns, but the melody for a given text changes from region to region, so that one melody may be used for several texts or one text for several melodies. On the other hand, the tradition of each individual church remains unchanged in such cases.

II

CHRISTIAN CHANT AT BYZANTIUM AND IN THE WESTERN CHURCHES

6   Greco-Byzantine chant

In the early centuries of the Christian era the comparative independence of individual communities encouraged, at the expense of any
tendency to centralisation, the uninhibited development of local
liturgies and their gradual coalescence in regional groups, distinguished further from one another by the use of different languages.
We have already considered the position of the liturgy in the Christian
East with its numerous rites. Each rite also developed its own musical
tradition, and the variety and richness of these traditions is visible
evidence of the extraordinary vitality of Christianity. Taken as a
whole, they not only have certain functional characteristics in
common – in that the several liturgies are variant forms of the same
worship – but also reveal a more or less striking uniformity in their
musical structure itself. Nowadays it is usual, quite rightly, to call
Christian chant 'plainchant'; and it is true that the name *cantus planus*
or *musica plana* does not appear before the twelfth century, and then
only in contrast to *musica mensurata*. But the expression has gradually
taken on a more specific and yet a broader meaning, so that, for
example, the French *plain-chant*, the Italian *canto gregoriano* ('Gregorian chant') and the English 'plainchant' cover the whole of
monodic church music. Since this latter name is used nowadays in a
more precise and technical sense, it is better to use the expression
'plainchant' ('plainsong') to denote the entire range of the music of the
Christian churches in West and East alike, emphasising thereby
certain common elements implicit in the name itself. It is a chant
which covers a limited number of intervals on the musical scale, in
which the unity of time is indivisible (which gives the impression of
a profound and immutable calm and gravity); no instrumental

accompaniment is used, and it exploits to the full its vocal qualities and singing potential in order to articulate liturgical prayer with remarkable simplicity and naturalness.

Within the very broad limits of this definition have arisen the various forms – like idioms or dialects of the same language – which Christian chant has taken throughout history: in the East, Greco-Byzantine, Armenian, Assyrio-Chaldean, etc.; in the West, Roman in its double form (Old Roman and Gregorian), Ambrosian, Gallican, Mozarabic and so on. Among the related chants of the Eastern rite Greco-Byzantine deserves the closest examination because it arose at the very heart of the Eastern Roman Empire, Constantinople, and for that reason wove a complex web of connections and relationships with Rome and the West during its evolution across the centuries.

Byzantium was not the birthplace of the rite which bears its name;[1] in fact the Byzantine rite stemmed from Antioch. Indeed, it is in the Syriac rite that it appears in its most primitive form, to be carried into Pontus and Cappadocia by the first missionaries, themselves of Syrian origin, and then to develop on the shores of the Bosphorus, especially after Constantinople became the capital of the Eastern Empire and, at the Council of Chalcedon in 451, was declared the seat of a patriarchate. From then on, the 'second Rome' enjoyed a steadily growing autonomy which manifested itself, in the liturgical field, in the composition of special rites, the adoption of a local calendar and the independent arrangement of liturgical feasts. The process of establishing this autonomy was completed between the eighth and the twelfth centuries.

One feature of the Byzantine rite is immediately striking: the growing tendency to use more than one language, in contrast to the unchallenged dominance of the Latin used in the West. Indeed, apart from Greek, which was employed in the provinces annexed by the Byzantine Empire and by the Greek communities in Sicily, Calabria, Apulia and Rome itself (such as the monastery of Grottaferrata), Armenian, Syriac, Arabic, paleo-Slavic (in Bulgaria, among the southern Slavs and in some branches of the Russian church), Georgian and others are also to be found. Two formulas, named after St John Chrysostom and St Basil, are used for the celebration of the eucharist. The singing of hymns is preferred in the divine office (unlike Western usage, which prefers psalms), and a 'canon' consisting of three, eight or nine 'odes' is sung. The discussion which follows is confined to ancient chant in Greek, which remained strictly monodic.

With regard to the relationship between present-day Byzantine chant and that which has come down to us in mediaeval liturgical manuscripts, it is generally accepted that the modern variety, which abounds in micro-intervals, has been heavily influenced by Arabian and Turkish music, while that of the Middle Ages was markedly closer to the chant of the Western churches. The suggestion that this chant may have been derived from the music of classical Greece has long since been abandoned. Originally Greek chant was probably a simple vocal device intended to expand on the liturgical texts which, from the third century onwards, were mostly taken from the Bible and the works of the Church Fathers.

The hymn to the Trinity preserved in Oxyrhynchus papyrus 1786 (mentioned above) shows already the characteristic style and cadences of Byzantine melody. After this example from the third century no more texts with musical notation are to be found until the ninth. This was the period in which the tradition of Constantinople was formed, and during which the legacy handed down by important centres such as Jerusalem and Antioch was moulded into shape as the expression of a liturgy which was no longer monastic, but took its character from the presence of the Imperial court and its splendours. It has an echo in the surviving acclamations which greeted the entry into the church of the Emperor and the Patriarch.

From the earliest days until the time of the Emperor Justinian (sixth century), the repertory cannot have been too large to be committed to memory with relative ease. Later a system of signs was introduced, based on the accents used by grammarians and intended to assist the memory of a reader who was already familiar with the repertory. This notation, called 'ecphonetic' (meaning 'declamatory'), appears from the ninth century onwards.

Some are prepared to attribute the absence of musical documents from this period to the depredations of the iconoclastic heresy; they see it as a consequence of the destruction of churches and monasteries that took place at the end of the twelfth century. Afterwards, there was a major flowering of ecclesiastical chant which brought about the need for written notation that could also indicate intervals. As a result many signs were added from the thirteenth century onwards as a guide to rhythmic interpretation. It is hardly necessary to add that this process affected liturgical music only (as was also the case in the West), because ceremonial chants and acclamations were only intoned, and secular melodies, however beautiful they may have been, were not considered worthy of being written down on expensive parchment. The evolution of Byzantine music came to an abrupt halt with the fall of Constantinople to the Turks in 1453.

For the reasons suggested above, the hymns of the Byzantine church were its most original and characteristic contribution to the poetry and music of Eastern Christendom. The key necessary for the deciphering of their notation was discovered by degrees in the first decades of this century, but facsimile editions and systematic transcriptions of source-material (cf. the various sections of *Monumenta Musicae Byzantinae*, 1935) began to appear later, thanks especially to the efforts of C. Høeg, H. J. W. Tillyard and E. Wellesz.

In order to understand the creative methods of Eastern composers, one universally accepted premise needs to be borne in mind: according to the *De caelesti hierarchia*,[2] the work of the author known by the name of Dionysius the Areopagite, an echo of the harmony and beauty of God is transmitted to the hierarchy of heavenly beings and thence to the earthly hierarchy of the Church. The music of the hymns sung in Heaven is revealed by the seraphim to those (prophets and saints) who are gifted with divine inspiration, and from them it is handed on to the inspired musicians who are the composers of liturgical hymns. Therefore the Church's hymns are nothing else than heavenly canticles conveyed from one order of beings to the next as far as the earth, and made perceptible to the human ears of the members of the ecclesiastical hierarchy. What, then, was the role of the artist? He was to follow the pattern of a pre-existing hymn which had been given to the Church by means of revelation. So the hymn-writer, author of words and music alike, found himself in exactly the same position as the icon-painter, who had to base his work exclusively on certain revealed archetypes. This conception of art means we can be sure that in the course of centuries no substantial changes will have taken place in the structure of a composition, although it may have been embellished with ornamental notes in order to make it match the growing splendour of the rites. One proof of such structural permanence is found in the analysis of Greek texts which entered the liturgy of Benevento (which spread throughout southern Italy and used both Greek and Latin for the major feasts) and remained intact from the time of the Exarchate of Ravenna (late sixth century) onwards. If the Beneventan version is compared with its Byzantine equivalent, dating from several centuries later, it is apparent that the melodic plan of the latter has remained identical, although it may be concealed by embellishments and flowery decorations. What is seen here is, basically, what in later Western music came to be called the technique of variation.

The repertory of Byzantine chant is divided, according to style, into three kinds:

(1) The 'hirmologic' style, named after the *Hirmologion*, a liturgical

book, and including the 'odes' of the 'canons'; each ode is sung according to a model strophe called the *hirmós*. In this style the melodies are short, remain within a limited range of notes, and either are syllabic or have only two notes per syllable.

(2) The 'sticherarchic' style, named after the *Sticherarion*, another liturgical book; the verses are called *stichi*. This is used for single-strophe poems, for tropes (interpolations between the verses of a psalm) and so on; it allows the use of melismas, but not so as to make the text incomprehensible.

(3) The 'asmatic' style, sometimes called 'papadic' or 'melismatic', which includes *cherubica*, alleluias, *kontakia*, etc. These richly ornate chants, to be performed by a soloist (*psaltista*), are difficult and fairly long; they appear for the first time in the thirteenth century, while 'hirmologic' and 'sticherarchic' chants are found, without changing their form, from the ninth to the fourteenth centuries.

From the point of view of tonal structure, the melodies are built up on the basis of eight kinds of scale called *échoi* (modes) which – contrary to the view once held – have nothing in common with the scales of classical Greece, but are of Syriac origin and, more distantly, are connected with the cosmological theories of the Jews, the Hittites and possibly of the Babylonians.[3]

The most solemn daily rites of the Byzantine liturgy were the *órthos* and the *hesperinós*, morning and evening offices respectively; mass was normally celebrated only on Sunday and on other feast-days. From this circumstance came the importance of the available corpus of hymns, which formed the larger part of the chants in the office. Among the most famous hymn-writers Romanus Melodus deserves special mention. A converted Syrian Jew, he was active at Constantinople under the Emperor Anastasius I (491–518), and invented the form of the *kontakion*, a kind of poetic homily. The celebrated hymn *Akathistos*[4] ('to be sung standing') may be the work of the Patriarch Sergius, who lived during the reign of Heraclius (610–41); it gives thanks to the Virgin for the successful defence of Constantinople against the Persians under Cosroe II.

The first flowering of the *kontakion* came to an end at the close of the seventh century, when it was replaced by the new metrical system of the *kanon* devised by St Andrew of Crete (*c.* 660–740) and perfected by St John Damascene and St Cosmas of Jerusalem. After the iconoclastic persecutions, the increased output of hymns also led to a renaissance of the *kontakion*.

During the period of Turkish domination, the Byzantine tradition survived in the Basilian monasteries of southern Italy and Sicily and, to the present day, in the Greek monastery of Grottaferrata, which has become a centre for the study and reconstruction of ancient Byzantine chant. The publication, now in progress, of thousands of texts and melodies shows that Byzantine chant was no less important, as regards expressive force in drama and contemplation, than the famous contemporary monuments of the architecture and mosaic art of Byzantium.

7 Old Roman (paleo-Roman) chant

Before 1891 no serious enquiry had been made into the direct origins of Roman chant or into the forerunners of that repertory which, under the name Gregorian, was considered to be a unique product of Roman genius. In that year a Benedictine monk, Dom Mocquereau, as part of his research into the manuscript tradition of Gregorian chant, published an account of three books of choral music discovered in the Vatican Library:[1] two Graduals (lat. 5319, from the eleventh or twelfth century, and Basilica di San Pietro F.22, from the thirteenth) and an Antiphonary (Basilica di San Pietro B.79, from the late twelfth century). Although the material in these sources covered the same liturgical feasts as did the Gregorian books, it was melodically distinct both from Gregorian and Ambrosian chant. Mocquereau was of the opinion that this third repertory, to which he gave the name 'Vatican', was a later corruption of Gregorian. A contrary view was expressed in 1912 by another Benedictine, Dom Andoyer, who concluded, after analysing the same individual sources, that they represented an earlier stage of musical development than that of Gregorian chant – a stage which he defined as 'antegregorian'.[2]

After this no new or authoritative conclusions were reached until 1950, when Bruno Stäblein declared that the three manuscripts were closely connected with the origins of Gregorian chant and were examples of what he called Old Roman chant (*altrömisch, vieux romain*).[3] From this time on the problem of Old Roman chant became the object of wide-ranging investigation, and to this day it not only claims the close attention of many scholars, but continually offers interesting new lines of research. Indeed, the point at issue is of considerable importance, for the existence of Old Roman and the process by which it passed into the Gregorian repertory at Rome

26

involve judgements which affect the traditional historical view of Rome as the cradle of liturgy and chant in western Europe.

Furthermore, an explanation was required for two inescapable questions arising from facts confirmed some time before. Among the hundreds of mediaeval books of Gregorian chant, Graduals and Antiphoners alike, there is not one which is known to have been written or used at Rome before the mid thirteenth century; on the contrary, the very few sources of definitely Roman origin which date from before that period contain material similar to that of the Gregorian manuscripts but different from a melodic point of view – and these are the sources indicated by Mocquereau.

In the years immediately following 1950 Stäblein published several articles containing the results of his research and the comparisons he had made.[4] The archaic elements to be found in Old Roman led him to conclude that, if the Gregorian and Old Roman repertories are two versions of the same chant, Gregorian is a revised form of Old Roman. Furthermore, basing his argument on the evidence of an *Ordo Romanus*[5] which ascribes an active interest in the revision of chant to eight Popes (from Damasus (366–84) to Martin (649–53)) and to three abbots of the Roman monastery of St Peter (Catolenus, Marianus and Virbonus), Stäblein held that it was to the three abbots that the credit for the reform, and thus for the movement from Old Roman to Gregorian, should be given. According to him the transformation would have taken place before 680, when Giovanni, the *archicantor* of St Peter's, was sent to England with the task of teaching the new repertory there. This dating, in Stäblein's opinion, is confirmed by what certain sources relate about the work of Pope Vitalian (657–72), during whose pontificate the chant in the papal liturgy was apparently performed by a group of cantors known as 'Vitaliani'. Finally, to explain how it came about that Old Roman was still in use in the period from the eleventh to the thirteenth centuries, Stäblein used as his point of departure the long-standing existence in Rome of two traditions: that of Old Roman, which remained unaltered in the monasteries of the Lateran, and that of Gregorian, practised in the Popes' Lateran palace.

The substance of Stäblein's argument remained largely unchanged in later years, though he was compelled by the criticisms of other scholars to make some slight modifications (for example, about the mission of the cantors to England). In brief, his hypothesis puts forward the idea of a transformation at Rome of Old Roman into Gregorian, and the coexistence of the two traditions (respectively, as papal liturgy and as that of other Roman churches) until the thirteenth century. This line of thought is developed in his more recent writings, such as the introductions to the first modern edition of an Old Roman manuscript (the Gradual Vat. lat. 5319 (1970)) and to volume III/4 of *Musikgeschichte in Bildern* (1975).[6] In the latter, having recognised the undeniable classical perfection of Gregorian monody, he sums up: 'It is the most valuable contribution which Rome has made to European music' (p. 25).

A position similar to that of Stäblein was taken up subsequently by Joseph Smits van Waesberghe, in whose view, however, Gregorian was the chant of the monastic institutions in Rome, while Old Roman remained the chant of the secular clergy.[7] He has been criticised by other scholars for an excessive dependence on the information contained in the *Liber Pontificalis* (a collection of papal biographies whose early portions – those dealing with the years up to 700 – are a highly unreliable source) and for making an over-strict and historically unfounded distinction between secular clergy and monks at Rome. His critics also draw attention to the absence of incontrovertible proof either that a reform of chant took place at Rome in the seventh century or that the two repertories survived side by side until the mid thirteenth century, objections which had already been raised against Stäblein's thesis.

Allowing for more or less personal emphases, other scholars (Ewald Jammers, S. J. P. Van Dijk, and others[8]) accepted Stäblein's view of the coexistence of the two Roman repertories, and also took into account a fact confirmed by liturgical historians, according to whom Rome had witnessed over a long period the coexistence of the papal liturgy (which was undergoing a continual, though slow-moving, process of reform) and the liturgy of the presbytal *tituli*, that is, of the parish churches served by non-Curial clergy.

Meanwhile, in 1954 Michel Huglo published an exhaustive and possibly definitive inventory of Old Roman sources, both direct (Graduals and Antiphonaries) and indirect, and demonstrated thereby that this chant was the official repertory at Rome towards the mid eighth century, in about 1140 and in the thirteenth century.[9] Old Roman was thus to be seen as a local repertory of specifically Roman origin (like Ambrosian at Milan or Beneventan at Benevento) which had none the less spread into central Italy and had left certain traces in the monastic centres of the Carolingian Empire (Stäblein has shown that in the ninth century it was in use as far away as St Gall) before Gregorian had definitively gained the upper hand. Although he came to no firm conclusion regarding the origins of Gregorian chant, Huglo was prepared to state that Old Roman was the only chant familiar to the entire Roman clergy; and this was a clear enough indication that the origins of Gregorian should be looked for outside Rome.

This was done by Helmut Hucke when developing, on various occasions, an alternative line of argument to that of Stäblein.[10] In Hucke's view, the point of departure for Gregorian is Old Roman, which underwent adjustment and modification in Frankish territory during the Carolingian era. This hypothesis may be supported by the reform promoted by the Carolingian monarchs from the eighth century onwards with the intention of making their peoples' liturgy conform to that of Rome; it is known that as a result of such edicts a new liturgy grew up, combining Roman elements with Gallic customs. A fate not dissimilar to that which overtook the rites and prayer-formulas would thus have befallen Old Roman. Entering the Frankish Empire on the heels of the Roman liturgy, it would have encountered the Gallic repertory and would have been transformed into Gregorian not only by an inevitable process of contamination (as when a foreign language adapts itself to indigenous speech-forms) but above all by being deliberately adapted for aesthetic reasons. Whatever the value of the latter motive, it should not be forgotten that musical notation did not exist at this time, and that the repertory was handed on by memory.

Hucke's thesis received support from Willi Apel and Robert J. Snow,[11] while Walther Lipphardt, although claiming that Gregorian was the Frankish version of a Roman original, maintained that the melodic material exported from Rome was accepted in France without undergoing modification; thus Gregorian would be nothing more than the Roman chant of the ninth century.[12] Apart from this detail, these are the broad lines of the second hypothesis: the birth of Gregorian in France as a result of the impact of Roman chant on the local Gallican traditions.

Recent studies,[13] rather than engaging in the sterile contrast of two contradictory opinions from a historical point of view, have rightly concentrated on minute comparative enquiry into the two repertories. This was perhaps the most neglected aspect of the question; for too long work had continued without taking proper account of these repertories, which were in fact the only ground where it was possible to reach conclusions unaffected by prejudice.

The characteristics of Old Roman chant about which scholars are agreed are as follows: its provincial character, in which it is no different from other regional plainchant repertories; the very small number of alleluiatic *jubili*; a notable dependence on stereotyped themes and formulas; the narrow limits of its melodic scope; the complete absence of the kind of repetitive phrases so typical of Gregorian alleluias; the preference for the melodic line to move almost always to the adjacent note rather than across wider intervals, as Gregorian, in contrast, often does. The comparison of individual pieces demonstrates that Old Roman adorns every syllable with more notes than does Gregorian (examples of the converse are rare) and that not only are the last notes of concluding phrases different, but so is the keynote of the melody. Furthermore, as far as liturgical rites are concerned, some (such as the special celebration of Vespers at Rome in Easter week) are typical of Old Roman sources, just as is the veneration of certain saints connected with the city of Rome.

In the search for a definitive solution to the problem, research into modal structure (that is, into the type of musical scale used in the two repertories) is proving particularly important. Even where this is not the intention, enquiries along these lines seem to confirm, to an almost decisive extent, the hypothesis of the non-Roman origin of Gregorian chant.

In the following example, taken from Avenary,[14] it is possible to compare in a short passage the differing melodic procedures of the two repertories. The two diagrams which appear at the end show, in percentages, the frequency of occurrence of the individual notes in the passage; in the Gregorian version the note which occurs most often is C, which forms part of a broken pentachord G–A + C–D, while in the Old Roman passage the most common note is A, which is part of a continuous pentachord G–D.

Since it appears that this result is a constant, the conclusion is

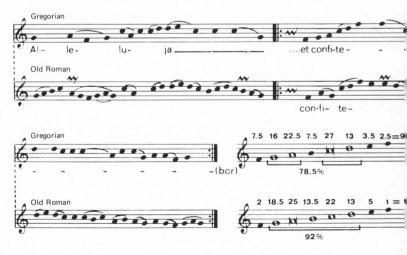

inevitable that two different conceptions of melodic movement and modal structure formed the basis of the two repertories, which means that the one (Gregorian) cannot be the product of spontaneous evolution by the other (Old Roman). But it is still more surprising to discover that the interrupted pattern of the scale in Gregorian and the continuous pattern in Old Roman correspond to the information given by the mediaeval theoreticians themselves about the musical positions and preferences of the 'Transalpine' peoples (for large intervals) and their 'Mediterranean' counterparts[15] (movement to adjacent notes). If this is indeed the case, it is highly unlikely that Gregorian chant was born on the banks of the Tiber.

8 Ambrosian (Milanese) chant

Among the local repertories created in the Western Church, only the chant of the Milanese – apart from that of Rome – has survived into modern times as part of an unbroken tradition. The reasons for this survival are to be sought partly in the political, administrative and religious role played by Milan in the late Imperial age and during the high Middle Ages, and partly in a series of eminent bishops, chief among them Ambrose, bishop from 374 to 397. His personality dominated the whole of northern Italy, and he was venerated by faithful and churches alike, who not only appreciated the vast range of his pastoral activity but considered him to be a master of doctrine and the spiritual life. His writings include many Biblical commentaries and dogmatic and ascetic treatises.

The Milanese rite, which took its name from Ambrose, owes him not a little, even if later accretions of varying origin have made it almost impossible today to identify with any confidence exactly what is to be attributed to the great bishop. Tradition has not hesitated to make him the inventor and architect of the whole liturgy and even of Milanese chant itself, but this is based – as will be seen in the case of Gregory the Great and Gregorian chant – on an assumption as audacious as it is legendary.

We have already examined the part played by Ambrose in the creation and diffusion of liturgical hymnody in the West. On the evidence of St Augustine and of Paulinus, the first biographer of the Milanese bishop, two other genres of liturgical chant are associated with the work of Ambrose: psalmody and antiphonal chant. Several passages in the saint's writings attest his fondness for the singing of psalms at liturgical services; as for the manner of their performance, the authentic Ambrosian tradition preserves very simple formulas for intonation, with no cadence at the end of the first hemistich, which some seek to date to the fourth century.[1] As far as antiphonal chant is concerned, Ambrose is said to have introduced the practice of singing psalms with a short refrain, or antiphon, inserted after each verse: this is, precisely, antiphonal chant. The performance of psalms and hymns had begun in the Milanese church not long before the conversion of Augustine (*Confessions* IX, 6); but this practice had rapidly taken on a character quite different from that of the church of Alexandria which had been its model. At Alexandria the psalm was intoned by the reader in such a way that he seemed 'pronuncianti vicinior . . . quam canenti' ('nearer to speaking than to singing'), while at Milan the delivery was a 'melos . . . cantilenarum suavium', a more ornate and varied melodic formula. This is confirmed by Augustine's reference immediately afterwards to singing 'suavi et artificiosa voce' ('in a sweet and artificial voice') and, further, 'liquida voce et convenientissima modulatione' (*Confessions* IX, 7).

Apart from this evidence, nothing can be added about the customs of the Milanese church in the Ambrosian period; and no historically reliable information on its musical heritage has been handed down by succeeding generations. It may, however, be assumed that Milan also shared in the store of material, at first uniform in character, which constituted the chant and liturgy of the Western churches in the fourth and fifth centuries. But, although some scraps of information are available about subsequent developments and the frequent reforms at Rome, an almost impenetrable silence envelops the history of the Milanese repertory. In any case the outdated view that saw Ambrosian rites and chant as a more ancient phase of Roman liturgy and chant can be set aside. Nowadays it is recognised that both traditions began from a common stock, and that exchanges undoubtedly took place, but that – as will appear below – the movement was more from Rome to Milan than vice versa. Furthermore it is now accepted that two other currents had an influence on Milanese chant: the first came from the East in the fifth to seventh centuries, and was of Greek or Greco-Syriac origin, while the second came from France in the eighth century.

The Greco-Syriac influence may have appeared at the time of the penetration of Christianity into Lombardy, with the church at Aquileia acting as go-between, a mediation which may be assumed even at this early date, but there are other significant clues: Eastern bishops at Milan, the presence there of Arian heretics, and so on. In subsequent centuries developments in religious history (the transfer of the capital from Milan to Ravenna; the exile of the Milanese hierarchy to Genoa, itself within the ambit of Byzantine and Ravennese influence; etc.) opened the way for other Eastern elements to enter, with the result that it is not difficult to detect with confidence the echo of Byzantine practice even in the modern Milanese repertory. It is evident not only in certain melodies (*transitoria*, antiphons *ad crucem*, and so on) whose texts are no more than translations of Byzantine originals,[2] but also in other chants whose tonal development does not coincide with that traditional in the West. This may appear either in the peculiarity of their modal patterns or in a preference for melodies constructed by movement to adjacent notes, especially in *jubili*, or, finally, in sudden switches from a strictly syllabic to a florid style.

Between the seventh and eighth centuries a new arrangement of the last part of the mass was devised at Milan, for which two series of chants were employed: the *transitoria* were borrowed from the East, the *confractoria* from the Roman repertory of the *communio*. A little later many Roman introits were also being used, and these came to form the Milanese *ingressa*; the same process seems already to have taken place with certain offertories.[3] Antiphons and responses for the office were also borrowed either from Byzantine sources or from Roman liturgical books. The comparison between the texts used in the Roman and Milanese repertories is highly significant in establishing the original version of their music: of the 245 Ambrosian chants preserved in sources dating from the tenth to the twelfth centuries, 131 are also found at Rome, while 114 are exclusive to Milan. Further, of the 131 shared texts, no fewer than 117 have an identical position in the two liturgies; and finally, of the 114 texts which are absent from the Roman repertory, only sixty-odd can definitely be assigned a Milanese origin. These facts combine to give an eloquent picture of the contacts between Rome and Milan: from a few samples (no large-scale comparative studies yet exist) it seems clear that there was a musical dependence on the Roman repertory (on Gregorian, not on Old Roman), even if this dependence was accompanied by a tendency to modify Roman models to bring them into line with the taste and expressive criteria of Ambrosian practice.[4] It should be added that the transfer of these Roman melodies to Milan must have taken place before the Roman repertory was imprisoned within the rigid confines of the *oktoechos* (eight modal scales), which means before the end of the eighth century.

It was also at this time that French influence made itself felt in the history of Ambrosian chant. At first it took the form of Charlemagne's attempt to absorb Milanese rites and chant into the wider liturgical uniformity which he wanted to establish throughout the Empire. Legend soon supplanted the facts, and it relates that the Ambrosian rite retained the title to its independence thanks to a miraculous portent.[5] Documentary evidence, however, is available to show the contribution which nearby churches of the Roman rite made to the Milanese repertory in the eighth and ninth centuries, to the extent that the appearance of the archetypes from which present-day Milanese liturgical texts are derived is generally ascribed to this period.[6] Unfortunately the perfecting of the melodies involved cannot be so clearly dated, since, as far as we know, musical notation only began to be used systematically at Milan from the twelfth century onwards, rather later than in other parts of Europe. The notation used at Milan was of the Italian style, but was closely related to that of St Gall, and remained unchanged for centuries.

The zone of influence of Ambrosian chant coincides roughly with the historic boundaries of the archdiocese of Milan, including certain valleys in the Ticino canton, but excluding Monza and a few other towns in the Milan area where the Roman rite is used to this day. None the less, the area which felt the influence of Ambrosian chant was a large one: it included adjacent and nearby dioceses (Bergamo, Brescia, Pavia, Piacenza, Vercelli, etc.) and even towns north of the Alps which had picked up certain elements at various times in the past. There is, however, no evidence for the penetration of Ambrosian into southern Italy, and although ancient sources speak of Ambrosian chant at Benevento and Montecassino, it is now accepted that in such cases 'Ambrosian' means no more than 'non-Roman'.

The most important sources of Ambrosian chant are the following manuscripts: London, British Library, Add. 34209 (twelfth century);[7] Oxford, Bodleian Library, lat.lit. a.4 (fourteenth century); Muggiasca (fourteenth century). Unlike those of the Roman tradition, the Ambrosian sources preserve chants for the mass together with those for the office. A performing edition of the *Antiphonale Missarum*, the work of the Benedictine Dom Gregorio Sunyol and commissioned by Cardinal Schuster, appeared in 1935 and was followed in 1939 by the *Liber Vesperalis*. This edition remains irreplaceable today because the long-awaited edition based on the manuscript tradition in its entirety has not yet been published.

Study of the present-day Milanese repertory, although it reveals a considerable degree of homogeneity in the chants, shows even more clearly the extreme tendencies to be found in them. For example, syllabic chants obey a syllabic principle far more rigid than that of equivalent Gregorian examples and, similarly, melismatic chants burst forth in unusual excesses comparable only with those of ancient Hispanic chant. It has already been suggested that every contribution made to the Milanese repertory seems to have undergone a process of adaptation, at least in its cadences, which made it part of a living tradition with its own rules to be observed. Other elements testify to the antiquity of Ambrosian, which underwent to a limited extent the transformations which also affected Roman chant. The first indication of this is that individual melodies were never allotted a 'mode', a tonal scale according to which they could be developed; the melodic line, therefore, unencumbered by the eight modes which will be encountered in the history of Roman chant, moves with absolute freedom up and down the diatonic scale. This same liberty is also attested by the possibility of tonal changes caused by the action of cadential formulas; by the total or partial transposition of melodic themes; by the arbitrary choice of the so-called 'dominant note' of each individual section of the melodic phrase (which produces a remarkable variety in the tonal system even within a given passage); by melodic formulas being fixed in certain modal combinations or wandering from modality to modality; and by 'leaps or, so to speak, daring ascents which appear as the expression of a primitive originality'.[8] The technique of 'verbal melody' occurs not infrequently; in this a stereotyped melodic pattern, which remains identical whatever the modal context, is invariably linked with a given word. The contrast mentioned above, between recited and copiously ornamented passages, is frequently found, not to mention the unexpected soaring upwards of the melodic line, with consequent dramatic effect, which follows a tranquilly repeated series of small intervals. As will be apparent, these last examples no longer concern the analysis of melodic or modal structure, but touch on the expressive possibilities of Ambrosian chant, which, coherent and irrepressible, transcend criteria which risk becoming too constrictive.

From a descriptive point of view, the individuality of the Milanese musical forms of the mass can be grasped by comparing them with the equivalent Roman chants, which pre-date the reforms of the Second Vatican Council (see the table on p. 36).

The Milanese tradition seems to have retained for many years a single intonation for the chants of the Ordinary: nowadays there are four melodies for the *Gloria*, one for the *Symbolum*, and four for the *Sanctus*: undeniably a smaller number in comparison with the Gregorian tradition. The most basic intonation is that for the *Symbolum*: it consists of a recitative formula with inflections which are repeated identically in each 'verse' of the text. Very similar to this is the intonation *simplex* for the *Gloria*, the other three versions of which are musically more advanced. Of the two basic melodies for the *Sanctus*, one is an expanded version of the other, while the remaining two melodies are adaptations of other chants.

The chants for the Proper of the mass, considered from the point of view of structure, may be divided into two groups: *ingressa, post Evangelium, confractorium* and *transitorium* are made up of only one section and may therefore be called antiphons; the other four (*psalmellus*, alleluia, *cantus* and *offertorium*) consist of two or more sections, that is, of a response with one or more verses. Lack of reference to a particular style is typical of Ambrosian antiphons; in each group examples belonging to every possible style are to be found, from the

Table I

	Roman		Ambrosian	
	Ordinary	Proper	Ordinary	Proper
Introductory rite		Introit		Ingressa (no psalm)
	Kyrie Gloria		Gloria (Laus) Kyrie (at the end)	
Liturgy of the Word				Reading from the Prophets Psalmellus
		Epistle Gradual Alleluia Sequence or Gospel		Alleluia Cantus Gospel post Evangelium
	Credo		Symbolum	
Sacrificial rite		Offertory		Offertorium
	Sanctus		Sanctus	
				Confractorium
	Agnus Dei			
		Communion		Transitorium

syllabic to the richly embroidered, and there are cases in which the intonation is formed by melodic patterns repeated insistently as if they were psalmodic formulas.

The *cantus* (which corresponds liturgically to the Roman tract) has, in certain cases, one or more verses, and replaces the alleluia not only in Lent but also in the week before Christmas, called *de Exceptato*. The alleluias are particularly interesting; in performance – as is, moreover, the case in the Roman rite – the joyful acclamation is pronounced twice, with a *versus* in between. The long *jubili* sung on *alleluia* are called *melodiae*, and differ from Roman custom in that the second is not an exact repetition of the first; sometimes the second *jubilus* is a new intonation, and then the two are called *prima melodia* and *secunda melodia*. Their performance, at least on the most solemn feast-days, required the participation of several singers (the soloist, the boys' choir, the readers, and so on) according to a lavishly organised plan of repetitions.[9]

In the case of the office (the liturgy of the Hours) many details distinguish it from the Roman tradition, even though the basic structure is still that of psalms and antiphons. Their intonation is simpler than at Rome; the psalms are devoid of median cadences and their tonal accord with the antiphon is subject to less strict control, since the keynote can be chosen from a wider range of possibilities. This flexibility in the Ambrosian psalmodic system is quite probably an echo of the tradition originally common to all the Western churches, before the doctrine of the eight notes was introduced into Roman chant. Forms peculiar to Milan include: *psallendae* (psalmodic verses with a doxology, used in processions), *antiphonae in choro* and various *responsoria* which are also found at Vespers and may be allotted to different performers (*responsoria cum infantibus, a subdiaconis, a notaro*, etc.). Their structure consists of the partial repetition of the refrain after the *versus* (ABA'). Some of the responses *cum infantibus* include a substantial melisma to be introduced into the repeat; this is a *melodia* (as in the case of the alleluia) which is 'well adapted to children, unconnected with the text and proceeding by small or adjacent intervals; a good example of pure monody in which the musical rhythm can easily be achieved with clarity and surprising effect'.[10]

Lastly, two other chants, unknown to the Roman repertory, deserve mention: they are the *lucernarium* and the *completorium*, which, respectively, come at the beginning and the end of Vespers. Most *lucernaria*, which take their name from the ritual of the lighting of the lamps, contain a reference to light, for example *Paravi lucernam* or *Quoniam tu illuminas*. The range of *lucernaria* amounts to about a dozen texts assigned to fixed days of the week or to a few solemn feasts. Smaller still is the number of *completoria* (this chant should not be confused with the Hour of the same name, the last of the day in the Roman office). Four of these may be chosen for Sundays throughout the year, with a very few exceptions.

To conclude, it must be admitted that the Ambrosian repertory enjoys a variety which is the equal of that of Roman chant; but it lacks stylistic uniformity within each category of chant and even within individual pieces, and shows a notable predilection for movement by small intervals. (It is significant that there is such a large number of occurrences of a group made up of four or five descending notes called the *climacus*.) Ambrosian chant is not, as it was once judged, prolix, nor does it show traces of the practice of improvisation, since the use of repetitive formulas, rhyme and other devices intended to create unity is too skilful for that. What sets it apart from Roman chant is its greater freedom, independent as it is of codifications and systems. In cases of parallel versions, once the assumption that Ambrosian is the oldest form of Roman chant has been abandoned, it may sometimes be found that it can be placed at a later stage of evolution, one characterised by a disposition towards ornamentation and expansion. Finally, it would not be proper to judge Milanese chant according to the aesthetic criteria established by and for Gregorian, as if it were a deviant and distorted branch of the latter; if it is taken at its own valuation, those same elements which are abnormal in Gregorian terms may constitute the most formally valid and aesthetically significant aspects of Ambrosian chant.

9   The ancient chant of Aquileia and Benevento

Towards the end of the fourth century, rites began to appear in the Latin West which were more or less visibly independent of the uniform tradition. Roman usage seems to have maintained its position as a standard against which new rites were to be measured, as Ambrose himself recognised: 'In all things we follow the precedent and forms of the Roman church.' Yet in his role as Bishop of Milan he claimed, at the same time, the right to adopt details of ritual which had their origins elsewhere: 'Things which have rightly been done elsewhere and which we have rightly preserved.'[1] It is clear from declarations of this kind that a liturgical pluralism was then developing, which, consequently, was to appear in chant as well. Moreover, although Pope Innocent I (402–17) wrote to Decentius, Bishop of Gubbio, complaining that some churches founded by Rome were no longer following the Roman tradition,[2] Rome itself, at the time, could only with great difficulty be seen as providing a complete and stable repertory of liturgical formulas and chants.

Apart from that of Milan, the northern Italian church which best deserves to be numbered among those which held a pre-eminent position in the fourth century is that of Aquileia, then the seat of a patriarchate. The name of a Bishop of Aquileia, Valerian, appears immediately after that of Pope Damasus (366–84) in a document sent to the bishops of Illyria between 369 and 372. To the same period belongs the evidence from St Jerome's *Chronicon* about the musical abilities of the clergy at Aquileia: 'The clergy of Aquileia are thought to sound like the choir of the blessed.'[3] As for the liturgy practised there, historians recognise in it traces of influence from Alexandria, from the churches of Africa and possibly from Arles. Indeed, the geographical position of the town, at the crossroads of the main routes joining North and South, East and West, clearly explains these influences, and also accounts for later connections with Ravenna and Milan. Traces of a Greek presence, mediated through Ravenna, are found in prayers invoking the Virgin as Mother of God, *theotokos*.

Unfortunately, the liturgical manuscripts compiled at Aquileia after the Carolingian age show signs of the movement towards uniformity which was inspired by the central authorities, and demonstrate the progressive elimination of the differences between liturgies. However, the study of these sources – now preserved at Aquileia, Cividale, Grado, Udine and Gorizia – while remaining useful for the identification of certain local peculiarities which were part of the so-called 'patriarchine rite', reveals that in some cases they came to Aquileia from various regions either of the peninsula or of lands north of the Alps. It thus becomes extremely important to check the provenance of any 'Aquileian' antiphoner or gradual, partly because this enables us to establish the origins of some of the oldest texts, performed for centuries in polyphonic versions in the churches subject to the patriarchate.

The musical repertory as a whole – apart from recitatives, a certain number of mediaeval chants associated with particular feasts or ceremonies, and later additions introduced into the Proper of the mass and the chants of the office (tropes, liturgical dramas, 'farsed' epistles (i.e. with textual additions), and so on) – seems to have been built up on the basis of Gregorian chant. This conclusion rests of necessity on the examples of Aquileian chant which have survived to the present day. For the earlier – pre-Carolingian – phase it is possible only to suggest that, in line with the creation of its own liturgical heritage, Aquileia seems to have inspired a musical repertory of its own, echoes of which may perhaps be detectable in some of the peculiarities which were present throughout the Middle Ages and survived until the disappearance of the 'patriarchine rite' in 1595. To learn more about this we shall have to await the completion of the patient and rigorous process of dating and comparing all the sources, with a view to identifying characteristic texts and melodies.

Geographical location and a certain amount of good fortune in the course of history also allowed the development and survival through the centuries of native rites and chants in the area of Benevento. As is well known, Benevento was for a long time the seat of the Longobard duchy of the same name, which was very closely involved with the Byzantine world as well as with Rome. This is also clear from its liturgical repertory, built up between the fifth and seventh centuries and preserved in many, admittedly late, manuscripts with their unmistakable script derived from minuscule cursive. Furthermore, the musical notation of Benevento is largely characterised by its resemblance to the later German 'horseshoe-nail-shaped' notation (*Hufnagelnotation*). The liturgy of Benevento, of an Italian type not devoid of points of contact with the Ambrosian rite, reached a peak of development as far as its basic outlines were concerned in the eighth century. At this time the first signs of decadence appeared, to be followed by the complete exhaustion of the creative impulse in the ninth. Some texts, however, were still being performed in the eleventh century, according to the sources and a prohibition issued by Pope Stephen IX in 1058. This suggests that it did not prove easy to establish Roman chant in a region whose musical tradition, at least in some of its basic features, dated back to the sixth century.

As with Aquileia, no purely Beneventan manuscript has survived. Those which we do have present a clearly Roman appearance onto which have been grafted a number of chants whose text or melody is otherwise unknown. (It is significant that this process of grafting should have taken place only from the eleventh century onwards). These chants can be divided into three groups. In a score or so of cases they follow Gregorian masses, as alternatives, especially on the most solemn feasts; this is certainly the most compact of the groups of ancient Beneventan chant. Other melodies are found scattered among the Roman chants for Holy Week, and are mostly Byzantine in origin;

in these cases both Latin and Greek versions of the text are present. Finally there are the chants for the feast-days of local saints; these mostly originate from southern Italy, but they do not preserve the typical characteristics of ancient Beneventan chant, as does the first group. Some of them are even of Roman origin, though they do not appear in Roman sources. From a formal point of view, it is worth noting that the introit (called *ingressa* at Benevento, as at Milan) and the communion-chant both lack psalmody.

As the number of surviving Beneventan chants is not very great, it becomes easier to identify some of their more distinctive traits. The most striking of these is their centonate character; in every piece one (or more) musical phrase at least is repeated, while identical melodic units are found in pieces of the same, or even different, genres. In 'imported' texts, those which have melodic parallels in Ambrosian, Old Roman or Gregorian chant, the Beneventan sections are frequently denoted by their preference for long series of *podatus* (a graphic sign consisting of two linked notes) on adjacent notes, which the melodic line follows, shifting one interval at most, to underline the verbal accent. Even cadences (in general, three kinds of cadence occur in Beneventan chant) are fairly characteristic, in that their pattern can be extended by the insertion of expanded melodic sections.

When subjected to stylistic analysis, Beneventan chant – apart from acclamations in the form of dialogue and the recitatives performed by the clergy (such as the Paschal proclamation and thus the *Exultet*, often preserved in the famous South Italian Exultet rolls) – is seen to be made up, on the whole, of ornate melodies, neither syllabic nor rich in melismas. Furthermore, as far as the organisation of melodic movement is concerned, it can be classed with the other Italian repertories (see the discussion of Old Roman chant), in that it shows a marked preference for intervals of a second and, in any case, a congenital reluctance to accept leaps between distant positions on the scale. Part of the same pattern is its tendency to proceed downwards in groups of three or four adjacent notes. There are very few syllabic melodies, while melismas, of which there are also comparatively few, are expanded only to a reasonable extent, without ever becoming excessive, even in solo passages. As for an aesthetic evaluation, that of Dom Hesbert will suffice: he describes Beneventan as a chant rich in emotive detail, supplicatory and often pathetic, and thus out of sympathy with the spirit of its Roman counterpart.[4]

10 Ancient Hispanic (Mozarabic) and Gallican chant

Outside Italy, there are three main strands which go to make up the thread of liturgical and musical development: the Celtic tradition, the Hispano-Mozarabic and the ancient Gallican. Almost nothing is known about the chant of the Celtic churches, which was found in Ireland, England and Brittany, largely because it was superseded, before the seventh century, by the arrival of Roman missionaries and as a result of successive invasions; nor, even later on, was it ever written down. It is possible that nowadays some traces might be found in some popular melodies or in Irish chants. Among surviving non-musical documents the Bangor Antiphonal, drawn up between 680 and 691, discovered at Bobbio and now in the Ambrosian Library at Milan, deserves mention, as does the Stowe Missal of the ninth century, now in Dublin.[1]

The name 'Mozarabic rite' refers to the type of liturgy which developed in about the sixth century in Visigothic Spain and which was practised by those Christians who remained 'among the Arabs' after the invasion, until the eleventh century. Spain had first absorbed the influence of Eastern liturgical customs imported by the invading Visigoths, as well as that of current usage in Gaul, especially at Arles. But very soon, at the end of the sixth century, a group of learned bishops helped to create the essential nucleus of the Hispanic liturgy, consisting of formularies and melodies. During the period of Arab rule, from 711/12 onwards, the local liturgy survived both in the occupied territories and in the provinces which had remained independent. From about the middle of the eleventh century there were strong representations in favour of the adoption of the Roman rite. Resistance was fairly weak, and in 1085 a council held at Burgos proclaimed the abolition of the traditional liturgy and the adoption of that of Rome. The national rite was retained in a few places ruled by the Moors, but in a state of progressive decline. Only in 1495 did Cardinal Francisco Ximénes de Cisneros, Archbishop of Toledo, produce an edition of the texts and order that the Mozarabic office be established on a permanent basis in one of the chapels of his cathedral. But then, as now, an unbridgeable gulf had opened in musical tradition; the ancient manuscripts containing the notation of the melodies were almost useless because it was impossible to read the neumes (notes), which had been written down without a stave until the eleventh century. The work of transcription had ceased in Spain long before the time when, elsewhere, ancient melodies were being transferred onto the lines of a stave and were therefore conveying the exact pitch of their sounds.

The Hispano-Mozarabic liturgy is of a typically popular stamp which made it possible for the congregation to take an active part in the rites. It also reflects the dramatic character common to Spaniards of all epochs and visible alike in their literature, art and music. A clear awareness of the distinctive characteristics of this autonomous liturgy appeared for the first time at the Fourth Council of Toledo, which took place in 633 under the chairmanship of St Isidore, Bishop of Seville (*c.* 560–636), whose instructions confirmed the uniformity of the 'ordo orandi et psallendi' ('order of prayer and praise') in the mass and the office.[2] Among the most important sources of Mozarabic chant is the Leon Antiphonary, produced in the tenth century but modelled on precedents dating back to the sixth and seventh.[3]

Mozarabic notation belongs in its essentials to two schools: one is that of Toledo, which sets the neumes out disjointedly and horizontally, and is not widely diffused; while the second, which is identifiable by the more vertical and elegant position of the neumes, includes some manuscripts originating from Silos and other centres, and most important, the Leon Antiphonary.

The table on page 44 sets out, in comparison with Roman forms, the chants used for the mass in the Hispanic and Gallican rites (the latter will be discussed below).

From a musical point of view[4] the most important chants for the mass were the alleluia (or *laudes*) which formed part either of the mass or of the office, where they respectively preceded and followed a psalmodic verse which was almost syllabic at the outset, but was then elaborated in lofty melismatic flights. The *alleluia prolixa* were examples in which the last syllable was sung in melismas of 50 to 200 notes, sometimes even reaching as many as 250 or 300; these melismas mostly appear in the *sonus*, the antiphons for Vespers, and in the *sacrificium*, the chant corresponding to the Roman offertory. The *psallendum* was a solo passage performed from the ambo, with portions reserved for the choir to join in; in its psalmodic form and melismatic style it was very similar to the Roman gradual. One typically Hispanic chant was the *clamor*, a kind of extension of the *psallendum*, which takes its name from its psalmodic form, with the insertion of an acclamation (*Deo gratias* or *Kyrie eleison*). The *threnos*, sung instead of the *psallendum* on certain days appointed for fasting,

Table 2

		Roman	Gallican	Mozarabic
Introductory rite		Introit	Ant. praelegendum (Gloria)	Praelegendum
		Kyrie		
		Gloria	Trisagion (Aius)	Trisagion (Aghios o theos)
			Kyrie (3 boys)	
			Benedictiones	
				Benedictiones (Benedictus es . . .)
Liturgy of the Word			*Reading from the Prophets*	*Reading from the Prophets*
			Hymnus trium puerorum	Psallendum; clamor
			Benediction or Sanctus	Versus or Threnos (= Lamentaciones)
				Preces
		Epistle	*Epistle*	*Epistle*
		Gradual	Responsorium	Laudes (Alleluia)
		Alleluia (Sequence) or Tract	Ant. ante Evangelium	
		Gospel	*Gospel*	*Gospel*
			Laudes	
		Credo	Preces	
Sacrificial rite		Offertory	Sonus	Sacrificium
		Sanctus	Laudes cum Alleluia Sanctus	
		Agnus Dei	And. ad confractorium	Ant. ad pacem Ant. ad confractionem
				Ant. ad accedentes
		Communion	Trecanum	
		(Ite missa est)	(Benedicamus)	

was made up of verses from the Biblical book of Lamentations (*threnoi*) or from the book of Job. The *preces*, used from the seventh century onwards, were a series of prayers collected in short phrases, which some consider to have been the prototype of the sequence. The name *trisagion* covered not only the *Sanctus*, which follows the preface, but also a particular chant which began with the words *Aghios o theos* and is clearly of Byzantine origin; indeed, the *Gloria* itself, for which some florid intonations survive, was sung in either Latin or Greek.

As for the office, the arrangement known as *cathedralis* (for the secular clergy) included only the chants for Lauds and Vespers; the *monasticus*, on the other hand, covered the whole series of the other Hours, as in the Roman rite. In Spain, as at Milan, hymns were always sung, and there are more than two hundred examples in the Spanish hymnary.

Today it is possible to read scarcely more than a score of pieces from the ancient corpus of Hispanic music, most of which have come down to us through the Aquitanian notation of a twelfth-century manuscript.[5] Not even the melodies reconstructed by Cardinal de Cisneros can be regarded as authentic, apart perhaps from a few recitatives which were preserved orally. Were the difficulties of transcription to be resolved once and for all, not only would the treasures of Mozarabic chant become accessible, but the way would be open to a better understanding of ancient Gallican tradition, which was connected to that of Spain by numerous reciprocal influences, to such an extent that the two liturgies may be thought of as twins.

The formularies, ceremonies and chant of the Gallican rite do not show any tidy uniformity, and for this reason liturgical historians prefer to talk of the 'Gallican family' and 'Gallican style' rather than of a unitary rite. The adjective 'Gallican', then, refers to the type of liturgy practised in Gaul, but with offshoots in Germany, Spain and northern Italy. The old suggestion that Gallican custom was a transplant from the East (specifically from Ephesus), or a borrowing from Milan, has now been set aside. Currently prevailing opinion holds that the point of departure is, once again, Roman chant, enriched subsequently by contributions from various sources and independently elaborated in accordance with the characters of the peoples involved, in a period stretching from the fifth to the seventh century.

The most fertile source of information on the chants for the mass in the Gallican style is the first of the two letters formerly attributed to St Germanus of Paris (d. 576) but now thought to date from the seventh century. The works of Caesarius, Bishop of Arles, are also rich in liturgical detail. The most important sources are the *Missale gothicum* (Autun, 690–710); the *Missale gallicanum vetus* (late seventh century); the eleven masses edited by F. J. Mone in 1850; various lectionaries, among them that of Luxeuil (seventh century); and the Bobbio Missal, which reveals interaction between Gallican customs and Roman usage as early as the beginning of the eighth century.[6] Since musical notation only became widespread at a time when the process of unification with the Roman tradition, imposed by the Carolingian monarchs, had already been going on for some time, no documentary evidence exists for Gallican practice in its pure state. Gallican melodies (as has already been seen with those of Benevento) are found in graduals and antiphoners with a Roman background, either as duplicates or as additions for use in particular rites unknown to the Roman tradition. Patient analytical research has now led to the compilation of a fairly sizeable catalogue of Gallican pieces and, above all, to the formation of certain criteria[7] in the light of which scholars can proceed to make further identifications. These criteria can be summed up as follows:

(1) The *liturgical* criterion: when Gallican and Celtic books not containing music (Sacramentaries, Lectionaries, *Ordines Romani*, etc.) mention chants which figure, with their music, in a Gregorian book, a Gallican origin can be assumed as long as one can be sure that it is not a case of mere coincidence. Further comparison is possible with the many pieces in Gregorian books which do not belong to the ancient Roman stock and for which a parallel text can be found in Hispanic or Ambrosian sources.

(2) The *philological* criterion: Gallican texts 'composed by the Church' (i.e. not of Biblical origin) can be recognised by their colourful diction, by the prolixity of their style, and sometimes by the choice of unusual expressions or phrases. For example, the repertory which has survived in Aquitanian notation, if exposed to the scrutiny of textual criticism, reveals its non-Gregorian origin.

(3) The *musical* criterion: though for Walafrid Strabo (825/30) Gallican pieces were recognisable 'by the words and by the sound' ('verbis et sono'),[8] it is difficult for us to identify the 'sound' of Gallican melody. In practice the musical criterion can be applied where certain formulas of intonation or melisma, and some cadences, have been used in pieces which have already been identified as Gallican by their texts; it should be borne in mind that Gallican melodies can break out in luxuriant elaborations just as readily as their Ambrosian or Mozarabic counterparts. Furthermore, even in these cases a certain amount of prudence should be used in musical analysis, since it is always possible that one is dealing with late pieces, written when Roman chant had already been introduced officially into France. Notation also offers a clue to Gallican ancestry; it has been established that a characteristic symbol of two notes, the *pes stratus*, occurs only in melodies of 'Western' origin, that is, in Gallican or Franco-Roman examples[9] (the latter are so called because they appeared after the encounter between the Roman tradition and that of the lands north of the Alps).

The plan of the chants for the mass mentioned above throws into relief the similarities between the Mozarabic liturgy and the liturgies of the Gallican family. After the entry-chant made up of the *antiphona ad praelegendum* with its psalm, the *Aius* or *trisagion* was sung, which was followed by the triple *Kyrie eleison* recited or chanted by three boys, and the canticle *Benedictus*. The first two readings were separated by the 'Song of the Three Young Men' (Daniel 3, 52 et seqq.) and followed by a responsorium sung by the boys (compare the *responsoria cum infantibus* of the Milanese rite) and by the *antiphona ante Evangelium*. After the reading of the Gospel the *trisagion* was repeated and the *preces* were sung, the latter being a kind of litanic prayer of which numerous examples have survived in the Aquitanian manuscripts.[10] The liturgy of the sacrifice opened with the offertory procession and the performance of the *sonus*, an artistically elaborate piece which ended with an alleluia in a fairly florid style. A special antiphon was sung during the *fractio panis* (compare the Ambrosian *confractorium*), which preceded the *Pater noster* and a blessing by the celebrant, to whose prayers the faithful replied *amen*. (In the Mozarabic rite *amen* was said after the separate petitions of the *Pater noster* itself.) Finally, during communion the *trecanum* was sung, consisting perhaps of the antiphonal chanting of three verses of a psalm.

The information which has come down to us about the liturgy of the Hours is scantier, but these were probably arranged differently in different churches. The main forms of chant were the same as in the other liturgies: antiphonal psalmody, antiphons, readings, extended responses and, in some churches, hymns; all churches, however, were acquainted with the prose hymns *Te Deum laudamus* and *Gloria in excelsis*. The Gallican tradition also included the *lucernarium*, a responsorial piece with a metrical hymn. As is well known, certain celebrations in the Gallican style, with their chants (consecration of churches, conferring of holy orders, blessing of oil, and so on) passed *en bloc* into the Roman tradition.

III

GREGORIAN CHANT

11 Gregory the Great

The traditional iconography of Pope Gregory I (590–604), as it appears in the miniatures decorating innumerable liturgical manuscripts of the Middle Ages, shows him clad in papal vestments, with stylus and *volumen* in hand, while a dove, symbolising divine inspiration, suggests the texts and melodies of the liturgy to him. The image sums up the centuries-old belief that Gregory had played a central and active role in the formation of the liturgical heritage of the West, to the point where the name 'Gregorian' had been given to the chant of the Roman church.

The accuracy of this traditional view was first questioned in the seventeenth century, by Pierre Goussainville, and from the nineteenth century onwards the problem came to seem increasingly urgent and indeed fundamental.[1] Historians were forced to make their choice among contrary positions. Even today the controversy awaits a complete and definitive solution, but historical researches presented in support of the various hypotheses make it easier to form a balanced judgement which corresponds more closely to the truth.

Born in 540 into a noble Roman family (probably the *gens Anicia*), Gregory had the most thorough education available in the society of his time.[2] It was one of the darkest periods in Roman history, when the city, taken and retaken by Ostrogoths and Byzantines during the Gothic war, was in danger of destruction at the hands of King Totila. After administrative and educational order was re-established by the *Pragmatica sanctio* of Justinian in 554, Gregory was able to embark on the career of public office for which his family had intended him. He had reached the rank of *praefectus urbis* when, on the death of his father, he decided to abandon his secular activities and live the life of an ascetic. To this end he transformed the family home on the Caelian hill into a monastery and, very probably, began to observe the Benedictine Rule there. His retreat into the cloister did not last long.

48

His experience of conditions in Rome and of the city's relations with the Byzantine government was too valuable for Pope Pelagius II to be able to leave him in the silence of his monastery, and he was chosen to be sent as papal ambassador (*apocrisarius*) to Constantinople, where he stayed from 579 to 585 or 586. He did not speak Greek (a detail worth noting in the light of his liturgical reforms), but he won the respect of everyone at court. Recalled to Rome to be appointed papal secretary, he experienced an agonising conflict between his contemplative vocation and the arduous duties of his office, which were only a foretaste of the still heavier burden he was compelled to bear on being elected pope, despite his reluctance.

He threw himself at once into a formidable programme of work. First of all he turned to Rome, laid waste by war and the plague which was raging there. To cleanse the city of the epidemic he organised the *litania septiformis*, in which the faithful were required to assemble in seven solemn processions and converge on the basilica of S. Maria Maggiore. To counter the growing menace of famine he arranged for shipments of grain from Sicily, and meanwhile devoted himself to the renewal of religious life at Rome and the restoration of clerical discipline. His letters reveal the wide range of his involvement in various Italian churches (whose metropolitans were based at Ravenna, Milan, Aquileia and Cagliari) in settling disputes, encouraging the doing of good works, and exhorting and correcting the faithful. The chief aim of his political policy was the settling of the Lombard problem in Italy. Even the churches of Africa, Illyria and the barbarian kingdoms of the West (Visigoths in Spain, Franks in Gaul, and so on) had their share of his attention. He ordered the first missionary expedition in the recorded history of the Roman church, sending the monk Augustine with some forty companions to preach the Gospel in England. In his relations with the Eastern churches, while affirming the *principatus* of his see, he made sure that his authority did not become burdensome to the patriarchs.

Gregory paid particular attention to the management of the lands owned by the Church, aware that this was at that time one of the tasks given to a bishop. Finally, his literary output (homilies, Biblical commentaries, dialogues, etc.) was prodigious, especially in view of the countless demands of his ministry. Understandably enough, its chief feature is its practical, exegetical and moral character. If Gregory's poor health, mentioned by contemporary sources, is taken into account, the amount of work he undertook has something miraculous about it. The liturgical practice of the only mediaeval pope whom posterity was to call 'Great' must be seen against this background.

Gregory's experience of the religious life cannot have left him insensible to the problems of liturgy. Following in the footsteps of several of his predecessors, notably Gelasius, he compiled a Sacramentary, a collection of the prayers recited during mass by the celebrant. This kind of Sacramentary, called 'Gregorian' after him, can be reconstructed using later copies which have survived into modern times (one of the oldest is a reproduction of the copy sent to Charlemagne by Pope Hadrian I in about 785–6).[3] Generally it opens with the words 'Here begins the book of the sacraments set forth in the cycle of the year, edited by St Gregory the Pontiff of Rome' (*Incipit liber Sacramentorum de circulo anni expositus, a S. Gregorio papa Romano editus*). It contains the formulas used by the pope at the masses for the most solemn feasts of the year, for certain Sundays and for a few saints' days, particularly those with Roman connections, and refers explicitly to the so-called *stationes*, the Roman churches where the pontiff celebrated mass.

It is not impossible that Gregory rearranged the Antiphoner for the mass, a book which at that time contained only the texts of chants, at the same time as he was compiling his Sacramentary. But it is precisely in defining the scope of his involvement that scholars have taken up contrasting positions.[4]

To avoid merely regurgitating preconceived notions, it will be useful to examine briefly the evidence of the ancient sources. The *Vita* which explicitly attributes to Gregory the creation or reform of the chants in the Antiphoner ('... antiphonarium centonem, cantorum studiosissimus, nimis utiliter compilavit. Scholam quoque cantorum ... constituit': 'most zealous on the singers' behalf, he compiled a collection of antiphons, of the utmost usefulness. And he founded the song school') was written by John the Deacon (Johannes Hymmonides) between 872 and 875.[5] It is thus later than Gregory by about three centuries; three hundred years in mediaeval Rome, wracked by calamities and disorder! In contrast, the documents most nearly contemporary with Gregory have nothing to say either about chant or about the *schola*. A *Vita* dating almost from the saint's lifetime and the *Liber pontificalis* (638) are equally silent; while doubtful references appear in the epitaph composed by Pope Honorius (625–38) and a text of Bede (who died in 735).[6] Only in the time of Hadrian I (772–95) do manuscript Antiphoners begin to appear, prefaced by a verse introduction which praises Gregory as the architect of the liturgical repertory:[7]

Gregory the Great

Gregorius praesul . . .
composuit hunc libellum musicae artis
scholae cantorum anni circuli . . .

(The leader Gregory . . . composed this little book of the art of music, the music of the song school through the circle of the year.)

A similar attribution is found in a source dating from the same period as this preface (*Ordo Romanus* xix), but Paul the Deacon, writing in about 780, says not a word about chant or the *schola* in recording the many traditions which had come down to him.[8]

Some of the great pope's strictly liturgical activity is known to us from his writings, such as his tendency to simplify rites and prayers. He put a severe limit on the length of the litany, reduced to ten or so the number of prefaces to the Proper, moved the *Pater noster* to the end of the canon, deleted the alleluia from the rites for the three Sundays before Lent, allowed the use of two readings instead of the traditional three in his reform of the Lectionary, and so on. This, then, is a set of ordinances which justifies his reputation as a liturgical reformer.

Some have seen a reference to the foundation of the *schola cantorum* in a famous canon of the Roman Synod which took place in 595;[9] but this text only lays down that clerics and monks should be brought into the papal palace instead of laymen, so that they might be a good influence on each other. It may well be that the desire to establish more edifying conditions for ascetic and, perhaps, liturgical life is behind this edict; but in no way can the opening of the *schola cantorum* be linked with this passage. Nor should another text – in which Gregory condemns an established abuse at Rome, the conferring of the diaconate on candidates gifted with good voices but leading far from exemplary lives – be taken as a sign of the presence of a permanently constituted group of singers.[10] If anything, Gregory's words prove that the opposite was the case, since in the same text he allots only the singing of the Gospel to the deacons, ordering that the chanting of psalms and other readings should be performed by the sub-deacons and, if necessary, by clergy in minor orders.

It must, however, be acknowledged that although these two passages do not offer conclusive proof of the existence of the *schola cantorum*, several archaeological discoveries (such as those at the basilica of S. Marco Papa and the lower church of San Clemente in Rome, as well as other churches outside Rome, at Alvignano near Caserta, Castelfusano near the ancient Laurentum, and others) have produced evidence that groups of singers (*psallentes*) existed in the fifth century and were positioned in an enclosed area in front of the sanctuary. In addition, some indirect literary evidence tends to confirm these archaeological clues.[11]

To sum up: as far as Gregory himself is concerned, none of his own writings and no other source roughly contemporary with him testifies to his direct involvement in musical matters. If he did have any influence in this field, it came about indirectly, through his liturgical initiatives. The development of the tradition in which Gregory is presented as the composer of Gregorian melodies took place gradually, and found its most coherent expression in the late *Vita* of John the Deacon. It took three centuries to create the myth of Gregory, in line with a practice familiar in other cultural contexts, the placing of a prolonged and varied process under the patronage of a particular celebrity. On the other hand, it should be stressed that Gregory's Antiphoner – assuming that he did compile one – cannot have contained any musical material, since at the time no system of notation had yet been devised.

After Gregory there was a period of fairly rapid evolution at Rome. Inscriptions on tombs and passages from the *Liber pontificalis* bear witness that his successors (Deusdedit, Honorius, Leo II and Benedict II) were known for the quality of their voices. In 678 the archicantor John was sent to England; he died in 681. The Venerable Bede, writing about him in 730, gives us to understand that a hierarchy had grown up among the subdiaconal cantors at Rome, with whom Gregory had been concerned. Then it was the turn of Sergius I, who became pope in 687, the first of a series of popes of Eastern origin, who were to introduce Greek texts and festivals into the West. Coming to Rome from Sicily, he entered the urban clergy and, in order to receive a thorough training in the chant of his church, was entrusted to the 'prior of the cantors'.

A later document brings us into the Frankish period.[12] Some time before 760, Bishop Remedius (Rémi), the brother of King Pepin, had received Simeon, sub-prior (*secundicerius*) of the Roman *schola cantorum*, at Rouen. The information is to be found in the letter which Pope Paul I wrote to Rémi asking that Simeon should be sent back to him. The pope's letter also contains an invitation to send to Rome, where they would be properly taught, those monks who had not learned the performance of psalmody from Simeon. In this passage there is an obvious reference to a Roman tradition, but Gregory is not mentioned, and neither is Gregorian chant.

The information in *Ordo Romanus* xxxvi is naturally more explicit.[13] Though written towards the end of the tenth century, it seems to reflect the situation of an earlier time when it states that at

Rome musically gifted boys were educated in the *schola* and then became *cubicularii* (that is, were allowed to share in the life of the papal household). Furthermore, it will be recalled that Paul the Deacon (Warnefrid), writing his life of Gregory towards the end of the eighth century, does not yet speak of 'Gregorian chant'. It is thus probable that the decisive step was taken between the end of the eighth century and the beginning of the ninth. This is the period in which the prologue to the *Antiphonale Missarum*, attributing the composition of melodies to Gregory, begins to appear in Switzerland and northern Italy.[14] Thereafter the way ahead is open: the name 'Gregorian chant' becomes more and more common, and the Roman *schola* adopts Gregory as its founder and patron. In 873 John the Deacon's *Vita* gives official blessing to the new situation.

12 The liturgy of the Western churches in the Carolingian period: Franco-Roman chant

As we have seen, the Merovingian church practised the ancient Gallican rite. For a long time the popes remained unperturbed by the discrepancies between the Roman rite, subject as it was to a continuing process of reform, and the practice of the Frankish churches; although they did intervene occasionally to ensure that Roman discipline was respected. This was the intent of the reply sent by Gregory II (715–31) to Boniface, the apostle of Germany.[1] Moreover, political conditions, especially the growing pressure from the Lombards on the Church's territory, did not allow the popes to gain direct experience of the position in countries north of the Alps. It may perhaps have been the Lombard encirclement itself which made the establishment of direct contact with Frankish circles so opportune.

Appeals to the Byzantine *basileus* by Popes Zacharias and Stephen II went unheeded. The latter, driven by the desire to save Rome, turned in 753 to Pepin the Short, who did not fail to see the importance of adding a sacral character to his kingly authority, and realised that he would acquire considerable prestige throughout the West as the saviour of Christian Rome. Terms were soon concluded by the Abbot of Jumièges, who had quickly been sent to negotiate. The pope decided to betake himself to France, and Chrodegang, Bishop of Metz and a relative of the king, came to Italy to escort him on his journey. We do not know the details of the sixteen months which the pope spent in France, but it is easy to imagine that he must have been surprised when confronted with the difference in texts and rites, and that he may have suggested a return to uniformity. It is equally understandable that Chrodegang should have felt himself personally involved and committed to a policy of conformity with Rome. In a letter of 794 Charlemagne makes direct reference to Pope Stephen's arrival in Gaul as the first step in the revision of the liturgy.[2]

The consequences were not long in appearing. Simeon, *secundicerius* of the Roman *schola*, visited Bishop Rémi at Rouen and was recalled to Rome in about 760. Meanwhile, at Metz, Chrodegang (who died in 766) had set the process of reform in motion. Paul the Deacon, who died in 799, wrote of him in his *Liber de Episcopis Mettensibus*:[3] 'The clergy there being abundantly imbued with divine law and Roman chant, he directed that they should preserve the custom and ceremonial of the Roman Church' ('Ipsum clerum abundanter lege divina Romanaque imbutum cantilena, morem atque ordinem Romanae Ecclesiae servare praecepit': note the phrase 'Romana cantilena', destined to have a great future). As a result of this reform (which was disciplinary as well as liturgical, since it introduced communal life among the clergy) Metz was considered throughout the ninth century as one of the centres from which the tradition of Roman chant was diffused, and it was to Metz that men went to study it.

Charlemagne continued and perfected his father's work; his *Admonitio generalis* of 789 is well known. In it he urged upon clerics 'that they should sing Roman chant in its entirety' ('ut cantum romanum pleniter discant'), following the lines laid down by his father, Pepin, with the abolition of the Gallican rite 'for unanimity within the apostolic see and for the peaceful concord of the holy Church of God' ('ob unanimitatem sedis [apostolicae] et sanctae Dei ecclesiae pacificam concordiam').[4] In a series of legislative acts (those of 802 and 803, for instance) Charlemagne unequivocally imposed the Roman rite for the mass and the night-office. Various Roman books are known to have been sent into France; the dispatch of the Gregorian Sacramentary by Pope Hadrian between 785 and 790 has already been mentioned. This work was completed by Alcuin (who died in 804), the sacred palace's 'minister' for worship and culture, who was also responsible for a *Comes*, a complete Lectionary for the mass. In subsequent decades other clerics sought to follow his example by devoting themselves to a rearrangement of the Antiphoner; among them were Amalar, Bishop of Metz and author of a *De ordine Antiphonarii* (831–2), and Agobard, Bishop of Lyons, who wrote a *De correctione Antiphonarii*. These were attempts to modify

Roman books to suit the needs of the Frankish churches, and as such led to recastings and additions. The outcome was the appearance of a composite liturgy born of compromise, Roman in its basic structure, but shot through with strong Gallican influences.[5]

This liturgy, which spread beyond the Alps and the Rhine from the ninth century onwards, set out on the way back to Rome in the wake of the Imperial invasions in the era of the Ottos. Full and significant testimony to this is found in the so-called *Pontificale Romano-germanicum*, compiled at Mainz towards 950 and later carried into Italy by German bishops in the Emperor's train. There it was gradually accepted by the Italian churches and by the papal see itself. Some final alterations were made at Rome, understandably, but in its broad lines the liturgy, then said to be 'according to the usage of the Roman court' (*secundum consuetudinem Romanae Curiae*), derives from the impact of the encounter between local and Old Roman traditions which had taken place in France and Germany in previous centuries.

As has been suggested above, the course of events is by no means so clear from a musical point of view. It is more difficult to establish facts accurately because no fully notated books exist anywhere in Europe between 750 and the first decades of the tenth century; it has been held that early forms of neumes appear from about 820 or 830 onwards, but they are exceptional.[6] For this reason the body of the repertory was still entrusted to the memories of singers. Try to imagine what the learning by heart of a new repertory meant to the cantors of the Frankish era, what effort it must have required and what overlaps and borrowings were the price that inevitably had to be paid! Musical disagreements, between individuals and whole schools, must have existed on an enormous scale. In a word, it must be conceded that considerable contamination occurred between the Gallican musical tradition and that of Rome, just as it did in the case of texts and liturgical arrangements. According to what is still the most acceptable hypothesis, the repertory which we now call 'Gregorian' sprang from this contamination, and so it comes to form, from a musical stand-point, the exact counterpart of the Franco-Roman liturgy.[7]

Later, when the Franco-Roman liturgy (which had spread throughout Europe under the name of 'Roman' liturgy) actually returned to Rome, it found there the Roman liturgy as practised in the city itself, and this was a fresh pretext for reaction and interference in the liturgical sphere – and even more in the musical. The liturgy of Rome itself, in fact, had not changed at all, at least in the arrangement of its liturgical calendar. In consequence the antagonism of the two traditions became obvious and intolerable. If, for example, the pope went to his own cathedral, the Lateran, to celebrate pontifical mass in the first half of the twelfth century, the canons of the basilica, who came 'from the ends of the earth' ('ex diversis terrarum partibus') and did not know how to sing 'in the manner of the Romans' ('more Romanorum'), had to give way to the native canons (relates canon Bernhard of the Congregation of San Frediano of Lucca[8]). No doubt this is an extreme example, but it is legitimate to suppose that the coexistence of the two repertories must also have caused confrontation, exchanges and perhaps friction elsewhere. So did further contamination take place? In the opinion of some scholars,[9] incontrovertible evidence exists for the stages and the different degrees of the resistance put up by the Romans against the growing influx of Gregorian (i.e. Franco-Roman) chant. At first Gallican melody was confined, quite simply, to Franco-Roman texts. Later it was accepted, but was subject to transposition to a scale more traditional in the Roman repertory;[10] and eventually Gallican melodies were employed without any alteration. The evidence for this process of assimilation is supposed to be found in two Antiphoners of Old Roman chant (London, British Museum, Add. 29988; Rome, Vatican Library, Arch. S. Pietro B79).[11] These are the most recent conclusions of specialists in the field; but the complexity of the problem leads one to expect fresh results, and possibly fresh solutions, from research currently under way.

13 From oral tradition to neumatic notation

Western Christian chant developed in a world where the secret of notation was unknown. The exhausting effort of memorising the repertory and handing it on from one singer to another, from one generation to the next, was carried on across the centuries. According to contemporary accounts, ten years were not enough to master the required technique. The study of surviving melodies has uncovered traces of this process, which have been analysed scientifically by Ferretti.[1] It appears that there was hardly any composition which could be called completely original; the singer, instead of indulging his personal inspiration, is closely bound to a tradition founded on melodic formulas. These have the potential to form vital elements of structure; they are combined, expanded and contracted in apparently infinite variety, though in fact they follow precise and pre-ordained rules. The singer learned to handle them and place them in a proper relationship one to another, depending on their function as introductory, median or concluding 'cells'. This is why recourse was constantly had to the great schools at Rome and Metz in the Carolingian period; they possessed the secret of perfection in composition, handed down by a school of outstanding quality. It was a secret which made it possible to reproduce the required piece on any occasion, while respecting the basic identity of a tradition perceived as a living thing. This attitude was also sustained by the universality of character of tens of thousands of pieces performed for centuries throughout Europe. There is, however, a third element in the transmission, whether written or oral, of liturgical chant: its sacral nature. This comes either from the role of chant as an integral part of the liturgy (which protects it from alteration) or from the view that chant is the inspired work of Gregory the Great. The name of this saint was, in a sense, a seal of authenticity for liturgical chant, and guaranteed that it would be preserved with the utmost care. Paradoxically, more than one systematic revision of the melodies of the liturgy (such as those of the Cistercians and the Dominicans) was undertaken because Gregory was thought to have been too learned a man and too gifted an artist to have composed chants which did not obey the rules laid down by theorists.

The invention of neumatic notation was also, obviously, intended to encourage a more effective transmission of the repertory, but at first notation remained linked to the oral tradition and did not aspire to replace it. It was simply an aid to the singer's memory. The 'notator' attempted to write the cheironomic gestures down on parchment[2] (*chironomia* is the name given to the hand-movements which indicate in space the two basic motions of a melody, its rise and fall). To do this he used accents and punctuation marks, which took on a purely musical significance and were called *neumes* (meaning 'signs' in this context; elsewhere *neuma* can also refer to a melodic interpolation[3]). This happened towards the mid ninth century, at a time when certain pieces were being written down because they were only rarely performed and therefore ran the risk of being forgotten. Sometimes this also applied to secular songs or chants foreign to the repertory with which the scribe was familiar from daily liturgical use.

The extension of neumatic notation to the whole of the repertory came about gradually, and not without challenging the customs of centuries. For example, familiar contractions in the texts had to be abandoned to make sufficient room for melismas. But the problem which the first practitioners of notation, all unawares, were called upon to resolve was of an exclusively musical nature: was it more necessary to indicate precisely the pitch of sounds – the melodic line which had already been committed to memory – or to express in writing all those details of interpretation which give life and expressiveness to Gregorian monody – changes in tempo, light or staccato notes, rhythmic stresses, and so on? The reply varied in different regions. Paleo-Frankish notation, for instance, followed by the notations of a whole swathe of Mediterranean lands (Aquitaine and others), seems to give greater importance to the *diastema* of the individual notes (the interval, or distance between two sounds of different pitch), while the notation of Laon and of the monasteries in the area of Lake Constance and Zurich (St Gall, Einsiedeln, Reichenau) sought to define even the most minute details of rhythmic movement and expression. Thanks to a whole series of graphical conventions (modifications in the design of notes, the use of additional signs such as the dash or *episema*, abbreviations such as *t* (*tenete*) and *c* (*celeriter*), etc.) the singer was able to call the melody and tempo of the piece to mind with perfect ease, when refreshing his memory before the service by consulting a volume which could be of modest size. Large choir books begin to appear only later on, after the adoption of a fully diastematic system.

As far as melodic line is concerned, it is inconceivable that singers remained committed to early forms of neumatic notation. At the end of the ninth century Hucbald of Saint-Amand had already complained that those forms gave no precise indication of intervals and suggested that alphabetical notation, like that used in schools for the teaching of the *ars musica*, should be used as well as neumes.[4] But experiment led to a different outcome. The diastematic system appeared almost simultaneously in several countries when it was noticed that a larger space could be used to indicate an important interval, such as a fifth, on the parchment. The next sign of attention being paid to the *diastema* is the appearance, in the second half of the tenth century, of the *custos*, a small note at the end of a line at a height corresponding to that of the note with which the melody continues on the next line. Lines traced on the page were also used; irregular lines for the neumes, regular ones for the text. At the beginning of the eleventh century it became possible to indicate semitones by using coloured lines (red for F, yellow for C) and key letters: C = ▮ ; F = ⅄ = ℈ . Finally, the second half of the eleventh century saw the appearance throughout the West of a more complete diastematic system, and of the tetragram (a four-line musical stave), which was devised by adding two black lines to the two coloured ones. Thus for the first time in the Middle Ages it became possible for a singer to 'read' music and learn it *sine magistro* (without a teacher).

The tetragram, by its very nature, made it much more likely that certain groups of notes in neumatic notation would revert to the exact plan of the diatonic scale, which assumes intervals of a whole-tone except in the semitones E-F and B-C. Originally these groups could also describe much smaller intervals, such as the quarter-tones of Eastern chant. For this reason Gregorian chant became completely diatonic from the beginning of the twelfth century, except in a few regions (such as Switzerland and Bavaria) where the mixed tradition survived into the thirteenth and fourteenth centuries.

It will now be clear that Guido d'Arezzo, the famous monk of Pomposa and Fonte Avellana (*c.* 992–1050), did no more than collate and popularise a skilful synthesis of experiments being made in various countries, when he set out his own system of notation in the *Prologus in Antiphonarium*.[5] Yet the credit for another important innovation, described in the *Epistola ad Michaelem de ignoto cantu*,[6] may well be his; it is a mnemonic device for recalling the exact intonation of notes, based on syllables taken from the first strophe of a liturgical hymn in honour of St John the Baptist, whose hemistichs begin in such a way as to form an ordered succession of tones and semitones. The first syllable of each hemistich forms a hexa-chord (an ascending series of six notes), and these give their names to the notes of the hexachord itself. The text runs:

Ut quaeant laxis *Re*sonare fibris
*Mi*ra gestorum *Fa*muli tuorum
*Sol*ve polluti *La*bii reatum
*S*ancte *I*ohannes.

Si (*S*ancte *I*ohannes) was introduced in 1482 by Bartolomeo Ramis de Pareja, while the change from *Ut* to *Do* in Italy is said to have been the work of Giovanni Battista Doni (1640), using the first two letters of his surname.

In order not to break up Guido's later teaching into unconnected fragments, it may be useful to discuss the hexachord and its impor-tance in the context of mediaeval and later theory.[7] The notes taken from *Ut quaeant laxis* fixed precisely the position of the semitone E-F (the semitone by definition), and this was a decisive response to the lively questioning of contemporary research. The intervals thus appeared in the following series, which was called the 'natural hexachord':

Ut	Re	Mi	Fa	Sol	La
T	T	ST	T	T	

Leaving the series of intervals intact, the 'hard hexachord':

Sol	La	Si	Ut	Re	Mi
T	T	ST	T	T	

and the 'soft hexachord':

Fa	Sol	La	Si	Ut	Re
T	T	ST	T	T	

were produced if the first note was any other than *Ut* and, therefore, the position of the semitone was altered correspondingly.

Before writing out the notes of a melody, it was essential to identify its range, which meant working out beforehand the position of the upper semitone. The hexachord was then sung thus:

```
                                  ↗ Mi  Fa  Sol  La  (hard)
Ut   Re   Mi   Fa   Sol   La        ♮         (natural)
                          →Mi  Fa         Sol  La  (soft)
                                 ♭
```

This diagram explains why all intervals of a semitone came to be called *Mi-Fa*, and why the whole system of these 'mutations' (passage from one hexachord to another) should have acquired the name of 'solmisation'. Passing from the natural to the soft hexachord one does indeed pass from *Sol* to *Mi*.

The hexachord represents the transitional phase between the tetrachord of Greek music and our own musical system, based on the heptachord and hence on the octave.

14 Notation: problems of derivation and regional variation

After the initial phase in which liturgical chant developed a manuscript tradition, neumes – the constituent elements of chant notation – evolved according to certain genetic relationships, and in a variety of forms which partly reflected regional peculiarities in their design. The diagram on p. 61, a simplified version of the reconstruction made by Bruno Stäblein,[1] gives an overview of the development of notation.

With all the usual limitations of a schematic design, the diagram still gives a sufficient idea of the various reciprocal derivations and

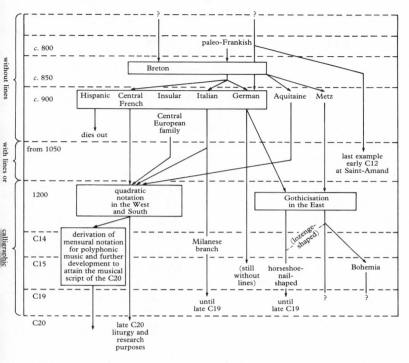

relationships involved. None the less it must be pointed out at once that the appearance of a type of notation in a given country was governed by a large number of sometimes unforeseeable factors. These included varying political fortunes, the reform of monastic orders and their movements, and emigration by monks, such as that of the Irish missionaries who founded great monasteries which were to be the homes of famous *scriptoria* (for example, Lérins; Luxeuil; Bobbio, founded by the monk Columbanus in 612 and responsible for the preservation of the Celtic 'Bangor Antiphoner' drawn up towards the end of the seventh century;[2] St Gall, founded in 614 by the monk of the same name, a companion of Columbanus; and so on).

This is not the place to reproduce even samples of manuscript pages in the various regional scripts. However, no one who is at all interested in this period of music history should miss an opportunity to enjoy the incomparable experience of studying some examples of the ancient manuscript sources directly, even in reproductions. Manuscripts in neumatic notation are the only evidence available to us which can bring ancient music fully alive today. The eye guides the voice, while the latter in its turn gives the ear a chance to enjoy its listening. 'Knowing how to read prepares one for the pleasure of listening',[3] especially – as in our present case – when reading pages on which the scribe, writing 'by ear', has preserved every detail of the melody with the strokes of his pen.

Once scholars were content to identify the large 'families' among the thousands of surviving manuscripts; these form the main threads of the tradition, and were for all practical purposes the same as those shown in Stäblein's diagram. Today, however, paleographical science has considerably refined its criteria of research and identification. One elementary method of differentiation starts from the overall form of the neumes: thus we have 'point' notation from Aquitaine, 'accent' notation from St Gall, Germany and France, with some overlap into England and Italy, and mixed notation, with 'linked points', from Brittany, Metz, Milan and Catalonia. Mixed notation prevailed in the end because it was better adapted to being written down on a stave.

In considering those forms of notation used in Italy alone, it is usual to distinguish the following varieties of 'national' notation:[4]

(1) primitive Northern Italian notation (up to the eleventh century, with some overlap into central Italy)
(2) the notation of Nonantola, which spread from that monastery to numerous other centres
(3) Central Italian notation (Tuscany, Umbria, Lazio)
(4) Cassino–Beneventan notation (southern Italy, with influence as far as the Dalmatian coast)

Others, meanwhile, are imported from other countries:

(1) the notation of Novalesa and Vercelli, of Franco-German origin
(2) that of Monza, derived from St Gall
(3) that of Ivrea, derived from Brittany
(4) that of Como, originating in Metz
(5) that imported by the Normans into Calabria and Sicily
(6) that of Aquitaine

But even this sub-division is by no means satisfactory. Taking Northern Italy as an example, the following list of centres suggests itself: Novalesa, Vercelli, Novara (Ivrea), Pavia, Milan, Monza, Como, Modena, Piacenza, Bologna, Nonantola, Padua, and Lucca. It is clear that paleographical science has succeeded in establishing the characteristics of the principal *scriptoria* with reasonable accuracy. A highly significant contribution to this process was made by the facsimile edition of the major sources prepared by the monks of Solesmes in vols. II and III of *Paléographie Musicale*, as well as by other scholars. However, although this is undoubtedly cause for some satisfaction, there remains a long way to go before we arrive at a full classification and thorough study of the vast mass of material handed down to us in the liturgical books of the Middle Ages.

15 Neumes and their classification

In the context of notation a neume is defined as the note or notes sung to a single syllable. If a neume is made up of more than one sign, these are treated as neumatic elements; so every syllable has one neume, which may be made up of one or more neumatic elements. The use of neumes began long before any attempt was made to define or classify them[1] (this became necessary only from the eleventh and twelfth centuries onwards). For this reason no list can be completely successful in classifying all the signs used in notation, especially if regional variations are taken into account. Even the usual terminology of the subject is no more than conventional, as becomes clear when one realises that, according to the notation used, the same sound may be indicated by signs with different names. On the other hand, classification of some sort is an indispensable necessity, for information and teaching alike.

To begin with we will take quadratic notation, which was used to translate neumatic notation in late manuscripts and in the liturgical books of the *Editio Vaticana*.[2] Its constituent elements are these. As is well known, a four-line musical stave (tetragram) is used for this notation; the clefs of C and F indicate the lines on which the respective notes are read and, according to their position on the lines of the stave, determine the position of the other notes to be placed on the lines and in the spaces between them. The signs used for musical punctuation (which have nothing to do with the bar-lines used to measure time in modern notation) are

(1) the quarter-bar on the fourth line of the stave, which usually indicates a slight breath;

(2) the semi-bar on the two middle lines, indicating a prolonged breath, but not one long enough to interrupt the broad rhythm of the melodic and verbal phrase;

(3) the whole bar, which is the approximate equivalent of a pause of one beat;

(4) the double bar, usually found at the end of a piece, though in the body of the melody it can indicate alternation between the semi-choruses.

Fourteenth-century antiphoner with quadratic notation. Short responsories for Pentecost.

Naturals and flats are used as signs of modulation, though only in front of B. A very few pieces have a B flat placed on the clef. In the course of a piece the flat is retained until the first change of word, or until the first sign of melodic articulation (at a bar-line).

The following model suggests one of the possible classifications of neumes:[3]

(1) *Neumes indicating melodic movement* (formed in the St Gall notation by the three basic signs: acute accent, grave accent, point):

   (a) Neumes of one note:

      Virga ⸙   (never found on its own in the
                            Editio Vaticana)

      Punctum ▪   (the lozenge-shaped note ◆ used in
                            the *Editio Vaticana* occurs only in
                            late manuscripts)

   (b) Neumes of two or three notes:

      Clivis ⌐▪   *Pes* ▐
      Porrectus ◥◣   *Torculus* ▪▪▪
      Climacus ⸙▪▪   *Scandicus* ▟

   (c) More extended neumes:
      The two- and three-note neumes are used, with the addition of other signs which transform them into *resupinus*, *flexus*, *subpunctis* (see below the diagram of the St Gall neumes, sections 9–12).

(2) *Neumes involving unison* (the *Editio Vaticana* reserved no specific sign for these, which are derived from the ancient signs of elision):

      Apostropha ▪
      Distropha ▪▪
      Tristropha ▪▪▪

(3) *Neumes of conduction*: apart from the *quilisma*, these are distinguished by the presence of the *oriscus* (rendered by the *punctum* in the *Editio Vaticana*), which leads on to the next note in certain situations which there is no room to specify here. They are:

      Pressus ▪⌐▪   *Pes quassus* ▐
      Virga strata ▪▪   *Quilisma* ▟▪
      Salicus ▟   *Pes stratus* ▐▪

The above neumatic groups can become liquescent neumes, identified in the *Editio Vaticana* by a note printed in smaller type. This little note indicates that the articulation of the syllable is somewhat complex. Details like these reveal that originally the literary text and the melody translated into written signs formed an indivisible unit.

Unfortunately we have already come across cases in which the quadratic notation used in modern editions of liturgical books has shown itself incapable of expressing some of the peculiarities of neumatic notation. This fault appears even more serious when the symbols of modern notation are compared with a diagrammatic summary of the signs used in neumatic notation. For this purpose the classification of neumes proposed by Dom Eugène Cardine[4] has been used. It is an exemplary work among the many attempts at classification which have been carried out in the past, both for its observation of historical reality (in deliberately confining itself to the St Gall notation) and because it displays, even to the non-specialist, the unsuspected variety and expressive richness of one of the most perfect neumatic styles.

In order to read and understand the table its twofold arrangement should be borne in mind.

(1) *Vertically* three sections, corresponding to the diacritical signs which were the origin of neumes, are placed one above the other. They are: neumes derived from accents (nos. 1–12 and 17); neumes derived from signs of elision (nos. 13–16; no. 17 is the opposite of nos. 14–15); neumes derived from wavy lines of contraction (nos. 18–22) as well as the *quilisma* (no. 23), derived from the question-mark. The *pes stratus* (no. 24) is considered separately because of the different implications of its tradition.

(2) *Horizontally* the table is divided into a series of columns, each given a letter of the alphabet (a-h). Starting with the simple form of the neume (a), the written forms which express details of rhythm are laid out. This may be done by adding letters of the alphabet (b) or an *episema*, a dash at the upper end of the sign (c), or by modifying the shape of the neume itself (d), or by grouping the signs together differently (e). These four columns (b, c, d and e) include the most important results of the paleographical research carried out in recent years. Thanks to the explanation of the letters in (b) given by Notker, a monk of St Gall who died in 912, it became possible to explain the episemas in (c) and the angular, twisted and elongated dashes in (d). This led to a fuller understanding of the value of the 'neumatic pauses' in (e), which will be discussed below. Finally, the signs in the last columns add further melodic (f) or phonetic (g and h) details.

The 'significative letters' explained by Notker are a peculiarity of the notation of St Gall[5] (those of the system of Metz are slightly different). They give an expressive quality to the neumatic sign which ultimately enriches the value of the neumes from the point of view of melody, rhythm or volume. They are almost always taken from the initial letter of a word; to indicate a melodic detail, for instance, there

Neumes and their classification

Table of St Gall Neumes

name of neume	basic script	scripts differentiated by				scripts indicating particular detail		
		addition		alteration		melodic	phonetic	
		of letters	of episemas	ot design	of grouping		liquescence	
							inc.	dec.
	a	b	c	d	e	f	g	h
1	virga								
2	punctum et tractulus								
3	clivis								
4	pes								
5	porrectus								
6	torculus								
7	climacus								
8	scandicus								
9	porrectus flexus								
10	pes sub-bipunctus								
11	scandicus flexus								
12	torculus resupinus								
13	apostropha								
14	distropha								
15	tristropha								
16	trigon								
17	bivirga et trivirga								
18	pressus								
19	virga strata								
20	oriscus								
21	salicus								
22	pes quassus								
23	quilisma								
24	pes stratus								

Forms shown in parentheses are those used only in combination with other neumes

Gradual (from an antiphoner for the mass) with non-diastematic notation of the St Gall variety; eleventh century. Proper of the mass for the feast of St John the Baptist. Unpublished fly-sheet, marked D. magg. I.15, in the Biblioteca del Seminario, Vicenza.

are such as s(ursum), a(ltius), l(evare), i(usum), and i(nferius). The letters t(enete) and c(eleriter) require a change in tempo such as 'allargando' or 'accelerando'. Those which refer to volume are less straightforward; the most common is f(ragor) or f(remitus), but this means f(astigium) in the Laon script. Some are taken from adverbs and render the indications above even more subtly: m(ediocriter), v(alde), b(ene), len(iter) (sweetly), con(jungatur) (legato), etc.

The one immediately urgent observation to be made about such a mass of material must concern the striking disproportion between the countless neumes of the St Gall script and the few used in modern quadratic notation. The consequence of this today is that to acquire even a non-specialist acquaintance with the Gregorian heritage it is imperative to become aware of the manuscript sources, which contain the secret of a faithful and strictly accurate interpretation. Fortunately the most important sources have been published in facsimile already, or soon will be.

It seems useful, therefore, to list here a small number of manuscripts, chosen from those which are best able to contribute to the critical reconstruction of the Gregorian repertory:[6]

St Gall 359 (Cantatorium; from St Gall, ninth or tenth century); St Gall 390–391 (office antiphoner; notated by the monk Hartker in about 1000);

Einsiedeln 121 (mass antiphoner; Einsiedeln, tenth or eleventh century); Bamberg lit. 6 (mass antiphoner; St Emmeram, Regensburg, tenth or eleventh century);

Laon 239 (mass antiphoner; Laon, tenth century);

Chartres 47 (Brittany, tenth century); Paris, B.N. lat. 903 (Saint-Yrieix, eleventh century); Paris, B.N. lat. 776 (Gaillac, eleventh century);

Benevento VI 34 (Benevento, eleventh or twelfth century); Vatican, lat. 10673 (Benevento, eleventh century);

Rome, Angelica 123 (Bologna, eleventh century);

Piacenza, B.Capit. 65 (Piacenza, thirteenth century).

An eleventh-century manuscript from Dijon, H.159 in the Ecole de Médicine at Montpellier, played a vital role in the deciphering of neumes written without stave-lines (*in campo aperto*) during the nineteenth century.[7] Above the neumatic notation it carries an alphabetical notation which precisely fixes the intervals of the melody.

16 Neumes and words

In undertaking the analysis of liturgical monody it seems appropriate to stress a basic principle which governed the very birth of Gregorian melody: the inseparable unity of neumes and words, which is also an indispensable requirement for a proper performance. The musical phrase was composed to adorn the text, and in this function it lives and shows its full beauty. This is true even of the relationship between syllable and neume, because the syllable determines the length of the neume, which itself remains a single entity even if drawn out in a prolonged series of signs. It is also the syllable which affects the quality of the melody, because – in most cases – the tonic syllable is higher than the unstressed syllables. If there are exceptions to this rule, they are fully justified by more general musical practice, which gives priority to the movement of single units; but they may just be cases of clumsy adaptation of texts to suit existing melodic formulas. Even the volume and the rhythmic position of the syllable within the word affect the value and interpretation of the neume. For example, take the paroxytone pronunciation of the majority of Latin words (where the accent falls on the penultimate syllable). The tonic syllable is the climax of the phase of movement, while the final syllable represents the harmonious dissipation and eventual disappearance of tension. This is verbal rhythm. Furthermore, the synthesis required for accurate pronunciation of any pre-tonic syllables and the final syllable can be constructed around the accent.

In the case of proparoxytone accent (falling on the antepenultimate syllable), a weak transitional syllable forms a space between the accent and the final syllable, the two poles of the rhythm. In short, it is normal in Gregorian chant for neumes to conform, to a certain extent, to the rhythm and natural intensity of the syllables. The verbal context is thus an important factor in determining the value of neumes and of quadratic notation, which means that respect for the verbal rhythm is the most obvious and essential requirement for a good performance. The greater one's respect for the text, in punctuation, rhythmic arrangement of syllables and articulation, the more the performance of the music will gain in naturalness and fidelity.

The same principles apply to individual words in their relationship with the melody. In this case also the unity of words and melody must be identified and expressed, as the arrangement of the neumes itself suggests and demands. Indeed it is known that in one and the same melodic phrase the neumes are constructed differently according to the syllabic consistency of the words. In this context the phenomenon known as *emboîtement*[1] ('jointing') takes on a new importance. It consists of the elision of a word with the following word, and thus the immediate succession – or, better, interpenetration – between the end of a rhythmic unit (and a word) and the beginning of a freshly accented unit based on the first syllable of the following word (for example: mirabi-*lis Fa*-cta est; quoni-*am Ni*-hil). Sometimes, in contrast, the verbal rhythm seems to lose its independence, to the advantage of the melodic line; but it is understandable that this should happen, especially in syllabic pieces. These examples are taken from Agustoni, *Le chant grégorien*, p.243.

Easter sequence (4th strophe):

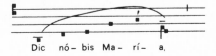

Dic nó – bis Ma – rí – a,

Antiphon *Veni, Domine, visitare* (Saturday before the Second Sunday in Advent):

Antiphon *In pace* (Third Nocturn for Holy Saturday):

Although they are not common, passages do exist in which the melody 'describes' the inner meaning of the word in an appropriate way, for example with an obvious upward movement on the verb *ascendere* or with long melismas on *jubilare*:

Offertory *Ascendit* (Ascension):

This feature should, however, be interpreted with some caution. It is clearly not part of the intention of Gregorian melody, always so sober and linear, to indulge in mere outward description or an anachronistic search for 'affect'.

Similar observations could be made about the connection between the textual phrase and the melody. It is an essential part of Gregorian music, in which there is almost always a perfect correlation between textual and musical cadences, for example. On this point, in any case, manuscript tradition makes a less direct contribution, since at the time of the earliest manuscripts our system of literary punctuation was not yet fully in use. The following equivalents are generally used in the *Editio Vaticana*: quarter-bar = comma, half-bar = colon, whole bar = full stop. There are, of course, exceptions, due either to the inadequacies of the punctuation system or to the adaptation of the text to an existing melody.

The remarks made so far presuppose a vision of the act of composition as a unitary whole; but this is a vision foreign, at least to an extent, to the practice of mediaeval composers. It is known, in fact, that they did not share the entirely modern preoccupation with appearing original, but preferred to work on traditional themes, upon which they expanded in order to create new chants. This procedure was wholly normal, especially during the period when the repertory was transmitted orally and, as has been explained above, melodic formulas had to be learned by heart. Is it then possible to speak of a creative unity between words and music?

The answer cannot be other than 'yes', at least if certain limits are observed – which may also help to clarify the issue. In the classical period of Gregorian composition, years of practice and a hard-working apprenticeship put the solo singer in an ideal position to recreate the melodies of liturgical texts in an artistic form, even if he used stereotyped formulas in the process. His talent was displayed in his ability to transform isolated formulaic groupings into a creative unity. This remains true even in the era of the written tradition. The ancient basis of the Gregorian heritage developed from the brilliant and inexhaustibly varied elaboration of a set of traditional formulas into a new and perfect art-form. The less obvious and irritating the join between shapeless pieces of material learned by heart, or taken from existing chants, the greater was the degree of a piece's perfection. However, even in the use of this method of composition, usually called 'centonate' ('patchwork'), there was ample scope for the genius of the composer, whose creative interpretation was irreplaceable and whose stamp of originality cannot be effaced. Furthermore, in the long story of the development of the repertory of Gregorian chant there are some examples of compositions which are quite independent of formulas and models. There can be no doubt that in such cases the melody depends heavily on the text, to which it adds interpretation and commentary.

Compositions resulting from belated and inept adaptations of texts to existing melodic models reveal the other side of the coin. It is precisely in these cases that clashes and contradictions between the demands of the words and those of the music are found, examples of which are mentioned above. But these are only a few in number, mostly now discovered and analysed, and are cases in which even the ancient manuscripts – in contrast with the assured compactness and uniformity of the rest of the tradition – offer a variety of versions of the melody as proof of their belated insertion into the classic repertory.[2]

17 Neumes and Gregorian time

The reading of mediaeval music from the point of view of the duration of notes is a crucial problem which has engaged scholars for very many years, and still continues to do so. (The expression 'mediaeval music' is left deliberately vague because, as will become clear, the problem is not confined to Gregorian monody.) The reason for this is very simple. We have lost the sense of continuity with an interpretative tradition which would link us to the golden age of Gregorian chant in composition and performance. Even in the great abbeys which saw the birth and the splendour of chant as performed each day by the choir, the practice slipped into disuse from the eleventh century onwards. Nor did theoretical treatises on music play a decisive part in the reconstruction of the ancient tradition. Such works, written at a time when familiarity with liturgical monody was very nearly universal, seem inadequate or ambiguous today, to the extent that they are sometimes quoted in support of contrary arguments. Among the causes of this decline – which will be discussed in detail below – may be listed the advent of the practice of polyphony, which often took liturgical melodies as the basis of its polyphonic structure. In this way it imposed upon such melodies extended time-values which were completely alien to their original nature. (It may be noted that the term *tenor*, as denoting the plainchant-bearing part in polyphony, derives directly from *tenere*.)

Factors like these led to a total misunderstanding of Gregorian monody, and, still worse, to entirely aberrant and intolerable practices in performance. One proof of this is the fact that attempts to reform Gregorian chant always included the aim of removing melismas to cut down on the supposedly unbearable longueurs with which – in the opinion of the 'reformers' – they had become ruinously encrusted over the centuries.[1]

It is not surprising, then, that when the attempt was made in the nineteenth century to find new ways of performing chant, scholars should have made a fresh start and turned to the ancient sources in a way that would enable them to rediscover certain basic principles. One of these, and by no means the least important, was the rediscovery of the intimate connection between the music and the Latin text, about which, as we have seen, the study of the sources leaves no room for doubt. It was then possible to define the nature of the Latin used in the intonations of Gregorian melody. It is a very free form of prose (the question of hymns need not concern us here, since they are, as has already been suggested, an entirely independent musical genre), which no longer observes the classical rules of quantity of syllables (long and short), and whose pronunciation is based on the tonic accent of the words. This premise was of great importance in drawing the conclusion that, if Gregorian melody is essentially an expression and decoration of a literary text, it is precisely in the form of that text that the basic unit, to which corresponds the music's basic unit of duration, will be found. Every piece of music develops in time and must therefore be capable of being related to a simple unit of duration. Now the simplest constituent element of a text is the syllable; so it is to the length of a syllable that the basic time of Gregorian chant is linked. Hence it is called 'syllabic' or 'median' time. Like the syllable it is simple and indivisible. Further, just as the pronunciation of a syllable can be freely lengthened or shortened according to the requirements of its function or position within a word, so the length of syllabic time can be adapted with complete freedom to such requirements. This happens not only when text and melody are proceeding together and are expressed in their simplest elements (syllabic melodies), but also in the most ornate and melismatic passages, where the textual support of the syllables is lacking. In such cases it is the script used in the manuscripts, with its choice among the various forms of neume, which indicates both the value of the neume (weight and function) and the duration of the corresponding unit of time. In other words, even in purely melodic passages, there is a clear and significant relation between the *form* of the neume and its *value* and *duration*. It would, however, be wrong to detach the individual neumatic signs from their melodic and verbal context, or even from their melody alone. Their value is governed, as has already been made clear, by their melodic context *as well*. Evidently, therefore, the term 'isochronism' can and must be used only in a very elastic sense, even if the fundamental simplicity and unity of syllabic time are taken for granted. Syllabic time is not measured with a metronome, nor is it increased or diminished by fractions formed in proportion to the basic time (halves, thirds and so on). Instead it contains gradations whose extent is defined both by proper pronunciation and by a precise observation of the neumatic signs which, in the best manuscripts, will show different characteristics in each of the three following cases. Take the three expressions (1) *Veni domine*, (2) *non confundentur*, (3) *dii eorum – filii tui*. As they are pronounced a different syllabic time corresponds to each of these as follows: (1) normal time, (2) augmented time, (3) diminished time. In short, though a suitable degree of flexibility is necessary in the basic time of any kind of music, it is all the more essential in Gregorian, which is purely vocal music, takes its form from its text alone, and rejects a concept of time which was quite unknown to the composers of the Middle Ages.

Yet the diversity of neumatic scripts is such that some scholars (and their disciples) have claimed to detect in it the basis of a mensuralist interpretation of Gregorian chant. For this reason they have attributed proportional values of duration to the various signs. This is the 'mensuralist theory', a convenient label which covers several different positions adopted by schools and scholars. Roughly speaking, one group, associated with the ideas of Dom Jeannin and represented more recently by J. W. A. Vollaerts and his disciple Dom G. Murray, assigns single or double values to neumes.[2] Others, meanwhile, each for their own reasons or according to different schemes, attribute multiple proportional values to them. Among these are G.-L. Houdard, the Swiss Jesuit A. Dechevrens, H. Riemann, P. Wagner and, more recently, E. Jammers and W. Lipphardt.[3]

In the ancient theoretical treatises there are indeed passages which seem at first sight to justify the mensuralist thesis, but the very disparity of the conclusions reached entitles us to be somewhat circumspect about the validity of the hypotheses which have been put forward. If the practical results of research are taken into account, no one can deny that mensuralism weighs down the movement of Gregorian melody with the obligatory imposition of bar-lines and, worse, applies a theory of tempo and rhythm which is completely foreign to the authentic basis of Gregorian chant. This last assertion requires us to distinguish between eras and centuries, each of which may have seen the use of its own modes and customs; not to mention the fact that the same principles cannot always be adapted to all the genres which make up the repertory customarily called Gregorian. It would, in fact, be absurd to claim that there is no trace of mensuralism in hymns and sequences, precisely because these chants form a separate genre, or are later than the earliest Gregorian material.

In recent decades continuing work on the sources of the classical repertory (especially the Proper of the mass and the office, but also on the various sections of the Ordinary) has seemed to give decisive support to the non-mensuralist thesis. For example, there have been comparisons between the signs for the tractulus and virga in syllabic passages, from a paleographical standpoint, which reveal beyond doubt that there is a total rhythmic equivalence between the two notes.[4] Their different functions are determined, in fact, entirely by melodic factors. In addition, the absolute freedom with which the ancient scribes used the episema when marking a cadence 'is difficult to reconcile with the mensuralist concept, which suggests a strict doubling of the simple rhythmic value when a neume in the form of an episema is used'.[5] The frequent use of the episema to pick out monosyllabic words or accented syllables in a psalmodic formula leads to the same conclusion. According to mensuralist criteria the flow of the intonation should be expanded unnaturally to include doubling of the notes marked with an episema, whereas in fact the use of the episema is intended to do no more than stress the need for clear enunciation of the word or syllable – an enunciation which would certainly have been observed in a non-musical reading.

18 Neumes and Gregorian rhythm

This is a subject which must be considered without recourse to preconceptions, and above all without being obsessively concerned with measurement, a mentality to which we have become accustomed, thanks to the polyphonic music of recent centuries. Such an approach will help in overcoming the fairly widespread reluctance to accept the argument that Gregorian is organised according to a so-called 'free rhythm'. It would be a grave mistake to assume that a melody, if it is not enclosed within bar-lines which determine its movement in fixed and immutable periods, is no more than an amorphous fluid, lacking both coherence and points of reference and support. 'Free rhythm' means the arrangement of the indivisible cells of a melody or of its phrases in an order which has no obligatory or symmetrical cadences; but it does not mean the absence of rhythm. After all, if, in Plato's words, rhythm is 'the ordering of movement', there can be no music where there is no rhythm.

A more exact definition is that rhythm is the relation or synthesis between sounds which refer mutually one to another. It is tension and relaxation, movement and repose. As in a word the movement which originates in the first syllable reaches a climax in the tonic and then dies away at the end, so in every group of sounds there is a kind of vital flow which co-ordinates them, unifies them, puts them in a hierarchical order and thus creates an autonomous musical unit. It is essential that the unifying role of rhythm be properly understood. It requires that each forward movement (also called *arsis* or *protasis*) should lead to repose in a cadence (*thesis, apodosis*). This function of rhythm remains the same whether it involves a short word to be intoned on two or three notes (*Dé-us*; *Dó-mi-nus*), or when the melodic design is broader in scope. The number of subordinate elements does not affect the nature of the rhythm, even if it must be allowed that in the second case it results from the interrelation of two phrases organised around one or more notes which constitute the climax or the unifying centre. Thus the different levels on which the workings of rhythm are perceptible are already becoming clear. If a melody is accompanied by a text, it will be a matter of working out the exact movement of the syllables, words, parentheses, terms and phrases (this is called 'macro-rhythm', and is stressed by the punctuation marks in the text). Consider the following example,[1] where *a* corresponds to the forward movement, *b* to the climax, and *c* to the relaxation which flows into the cadence at *d*.

mi– se– ri– cor– di– a *

Although it is easier to comprehend the rhythmic sense of a passage as a whole, before descending to consider its constituent parts (and this, indeed, must be the basic criterion of any attempt at analysis), from a historical point of view it was the rhythmic value of the short neumes which was identified first. When this involves no more than two or three notes spread over different syllables, the last note (and not the first, as was thought at one time) is normally the principal element, because it coincides with a syllabic articulation. It has thus been customary to consider the pes and the clivis (neumes of two notes) as binary groups, and the porrectus, the torculus, etc. as ternary groups. The problem became more complex when it involved the rhythmic interpretation of longer neumatic sequences, such as melismas. At first it was thought that each written unit kept, as part of a composition, the same value which it had on its own. It was understandable that this view should be taken, given the prevailing illusion that this was a way of respecting a traditional rhythm represented in the neumes. However, it soon became clear that the musical sense of this or that passage contradicted such an interpretation. Two differing schools of thought arose in consequence. One remained blindly committed to the older theory, and continued to divide rhythm into binary and ternary groups (this is the so-called 'Solesmes' method,[2] to which we shall return). The other, meanwhile, preferred to adapt its practice to the evidence of the music in its context. This was the better path to follow, but it seemed to lead inexorably to an unlooked-for discovery, namely, to a declaration that neumes had no rhythmic significance. Such a position would be basically illogical, since it was thought valid to use neumes to determine elementary rhythms, and yet they were to be set aside whenever their interpretation seemed to offer some difficulty.

Research in recent decades has shown that more and more obvious anomalies arise from the rigid application of the binary and ternary principle even to syllabic melodies,[3] above all when attempts are made to define such groups using purely mechanical criteria, without taking proper account of the nature of accent in Latin, and allowing, for example, a scansion like *justificátio* instead of *jústificátio*. (It is inconceivable – though the suggestion has been made – that one should start from the last note of the passage and mark out the *arsis* every two or three notes.) The systematic division of a Gregorian phrase into two or three beats is thus a hypothesis which does not correspond to the facts (the nature of its melodic and verbal units), and which may let in through the window an obsession with measurement very similar to the detested predecessor which was thrown out by the door.

As for more ornate or purely melodic passages, the apparent divergence between neumes and rhythm has gradually come to seem less profound, thanks to a deeper understanding of neumes and their written expression. Indeed, it is foreseeable that patient analysis and comparative study of sources will eventually lead to a complete understanding of the evidence and the full resolution of what, at present, are taken to be anomalies. One alone of these extensions of knowledge, the discovery of the rhythmic significance of the 'neumatic pause', has already proved to be most useful in clarifying certain points.[4] This pause consists of a particular form taken by the neume in which either the first, the last or an intermediate note is isolated on the page (these are, respectively, initial, terminal and median pauses). Examination of the manuscripts has revealed that deliberate isolation – especially in its median form – has an immediate effect on rhythm, because it draws attention to the importance of the note which it follows, or, in other words, the note on which the scribe's hand rested. It would take too long to specify here the various subtleties of interpretation, including those used in performance, which are due to this discovery; but it is clear that today no student of Gregorian chant can ignore its existence or its expressive power.

We have already noted that one result of the relative isochronism of Gregorian syllabic time is that the characteristic movement or repose of a rhythmic element is independent of the corresponding sound, however closely prolongation is normally connected with relaxation. Indeed the rhythmic function of a sound or series of sounds is determined not by any physical characteristic of the sound itself, but by its position in the rhythmic unit. (Musical rhythm employs various physical properties of sound – duration, pitch, volume, timbre – without corresponding exactly to any of them.) If a note is the initial point of a rhythmic curve, for that very reason it is a point of dynamic focus and must be sung in a way which leads on to the note with which the period of repose begins. It does not matter if the two phases are made up of several notes or whether the destination is a simple or a compound cadence, or in the upper or lower register.

As well as the position of the cadence, verbal accent and other written details, the modal structure of a composition can offer useful guidance to the location of rhythmic stresses and the internal foci of a piece, as will be discussed in the next chapter. Indeed, in the range of sounds some are more important than others, which appear to be purely ornamental and should be treated as such. Once again, however, there is no place here for strict and mechanical rules which would unnecessarily limit the infinite variety of possibilities.

In order to grasp the indivisible union between neumes and rhythm, as well as the richness of movement and the vast wealth of detail conveyed in Gregorian notation, it may be useful to recall that neumatic script has also been called 'cheironomic notation'. The copyist's hand followed the undulations of the melody faithfully, rose and fell along with it, freely dividing the lower curves, even where these were joined together. But when a note stood out from the rest because of some detail of movement, punctuation or expression, then the hand paused and so interrupted the graphic flow. This helped the singer to work out the exact rhythm of the melisma; the *ductus* followed precisely that of the voice. This is a genuine mimesis: the projection onto parchment of the very gestures of the choir-master.[5]

19 Modal theory and structure

While the process of creating liturgical music was continuing through the early centuries of Christianity, no theorists of the art appeared. There is an explanation for this apparent lacuna. According to Greco-Roman tradition, the theorist occupied himself essentially with research into two questions: verbal rhythm (prosody and metrics)[1] and the nature of interval. This was the subject of the *ars musica*, the discipline which was later incorporated into the educational system of the Middle Ages as organised in the Trivium and Quadrivium. If at first the Church was content to allow its wealth of chant to come into being without encouraging the teaching of theory (a task which was, after all, not really its concern), when the time came to take on this responsibility it did so by turning to pagan tradition.

The doyen of Christian scholars in the field was, as far as we know, Augustine (354-430). It seems that he intended to write two works on music, but completed only one, the *De musica libri sex*, which deals with the metrics of language. As he himself tells us, he did not have time either to write or to research the second book, which was to have been concerned with intervals. Augustine's most original trait is his elevation of music to the point where it becomes a principle of divine knowledge: the soul is purified by *numerositas*, which is the profound essence of music and transforms it into a relationship between celestial numbers.

Augustine's theoretical position, strictly in line as it is with the legacy of classical treatises on the subject, forms the link between the past and the new musical practices which came in from the East and were modified in Western Europe. It was the first stage in revealing to the Christian world a theory which no cultivated man would henceforth be able to ignore, and also the premise necessary to prove that theory and practice could and should advance together (though it took centuries to convince some people of this). A century after Augustine, Boethius (480-524) wrote his *De institutione musica* with the evident intention of translating the Greek theoretical tradition into Latin. It is interesting to note that he, unlike Augustine, allows himself, for example, some actual description of the various chants, and mentions three vocal styles: speaking voice, singing voice, and recitation by 'chanting'.[2] This last is presumably a reference to liturgical chant. Cassiodorus (468-552) turns out to be less well informed and less original. However, having written his books with the practical aim of instructing the young monks of his monastery (Vivarium, in Calabria) in the performance of chant, he stands on the one hand in the moral and religious tradition already developed by the Fathers of the Church (especially Augustine), while also deriving his technical material from various writers of classical antiquity. Yet he does not fully understand their teaching, and thus contributes to the diffusion of erroneous interpretations which is to be a burden through the Middle Ages and beyond.

Isidore, Bishop of Seville (*c.* 560-636), was guided in his works by an even more direct experience of liturgical chant. In the famous *Etymologiae* and the *De ecclesiasticis officiis* the theory of the seven arts is expounded along traditional lines, but the author is more urgently interested in practice, as even his choice of words reveals. Isidore is the first to define music in relation to *peritia* as well as to *scientia*. Furthermore, he discusses rhythm in its proper place, as an adjunct of grammar and prosody, a clear sign that for him there was no connection at all between the rhythm of ecclesiastical chant and the quantities of classical Latin. A phrase of his on another subject shows us beyond doubt just how far distant he was even from the beginnings of notation: 'Nisi enim ab homine memoria teneantur, soni pereunt, quia scribi non possunt' ('Unless sounds are remembered by man, they perish, for they cannot be written down').[3] Finally he describes musical instruments, more out of a desire for comprehensiveness than out of real interest, as if instrumental music did not really exist.

After Isidore musical theory is enveloped in a great silence. As far as we know, we have to wait till the Carolingian era to encounter other theorists. But in the meantime, although we cannot document the phases of its gradual development, a radical process of codification and re-ordering of the total structure of liturgical melody was coming to fruition. Melodies were adapted – sometimes on the bed of Procrustes – to accord with the canons of the Byzantine *oktoechos*, a system of eight 'modes' used in church music.

The origin of modes is a very complex problem to which contradictory solutions have been put forward. Although Byzantine theory claims to reproduce structures and definitions taken from classical Greece, the notion of a 'mode' as a form of octave is unknown in Greek theory – as is the term *echos* itself, at least when used to mean 'mode'. If anything, the appropriate terms were *tonos* and *tropos*, which indicated the different pitches at which the Greeks wrote their own basic scale (two octaves in the minor). It was to these different pitches that the names Dorian, Hypodorian, Phrygian, Hypophrygian, and so on were given. Not even the Latin authors mentioned above use these Greek terms to include the modes peculiar to church music. Moreover, it is only after Aurelian of Réomé (first half of the ninth century) that there is discussion of the eight tones used for the psalm (as a recitation-formula) and of the *modus* or *tropos* of the antiphon which is closely connected with it: the initial melodic impulse of the antiphon has in fact to relate to the conclusion of the psalmodic intonation. This is repeated by Regino of Prüm, Hucbald of Saint-Amand and the anonymous treatises *Musica Enchiriadis* and *Commemoratio brevis*. Then the unknown author of the *Alia musica* (perhaps of the early tenth century) goes on to misunderstand Boethius: it is clear that he understands the tones – which in Boethius were only those arranged in ascending order according to traditional Greek teaching – as referring to liturgical modes. From this stems the 'imbroglio of modes', to borrow a well-known phrase from J. Chailley, a confusion in order and terminology with the tones of the ancient Greeks. One conclusion is immediately apparent: we should banish the still-widespread habit of using Greek terminology to refer to the modes of Western music from the musical vocabulary. To call a Bach toccata Dorian or 'in Dorian style' because it is written in D minor without a flat in the clef is a historical heresy which denies the true nature of modes.

What, then, was meant by 'modes' in the church music of the Middle Ages? The term refers to a method of composition according to a diatonic scale, characterised by its basic sound and the differing positions of tones and semitones. At first the teaching was that there are four kinds of mode, whose basic notes are the equivalent of Re, Mi, Fa and Sol (though they had not yet been given these names), and each of these is extended upwards in a series of four notes without sharps or flats. In a kind of supplement, another series of four notes is added going upwards to obtain the authentic modal scale (*modus authenticus*), while if the series of four is added downwards, the result is the plagal mode (*plagalis, collateralis, subiugalis*). Thus emerge the eight ecclesiastical modes. Later they were given Latinised Greek names: *protus, deuterus, tritus, tetrardus*, each of which may be authentic or plagal; but they are also listed in continuous numeration, *primus, secundus* and so on. In the diagram on p. 83 the modes are arranged according to their names (the pseudo-Greek ones are included for completeness' sake), their *tonica* or *finalis* and their context (range of the octave), which in the plagal modes always starts a fourth below the tonic.

The four authentic modes were sometimes called *ambrosiani* and the four plagal ones *gregoriani*, with an implicit reference to their 'inventors'; but it goes without saying that such attributions are wholly unfounded, if only because the Ambrosian and Gregorian repertories, taken as a whole, do not differ greatly in their tonal structure.

Reducing the range of each mode to an octave is a little simplistic, since many melodies require at least one extra note below the tonic, especially at the point of the final cadence.

Modern expositions of modal theory usually stress the so-called 'dominant' note as well. This is a second tonal focus which some claim to identify a fifth above the tonic in the authentic modes and a third above in the plagal. In reality this view of the dominant as characteristic of a mode cannot be maintained, as the mediaeval treatises do not mention it, and in many melodies it is hard to find anyway. It does,

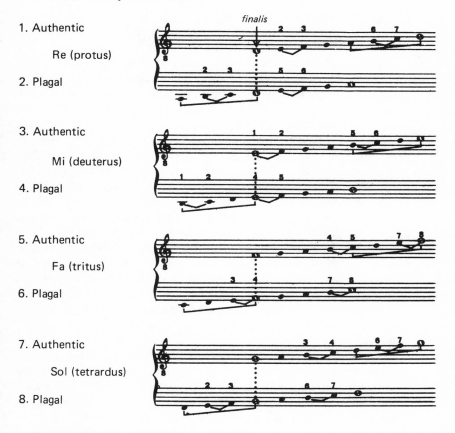

1. Authentic

   Re (protus)

2. Plagal

3. Authentic

   Mi (deuterus)

4. Plagal

5. Authentic

   Fa (tritus)

6. Plagal

7. Authentic

   Sol (tetrardus)

8. Plagal

NB: figures above the notes indicate semitones

however, play a prominent part in certain special melodies associated with a particular mode, such as the psalmodic formulas, where the dominant coincides with the key-note of the recitation, also called *tuba* or *tenor*.

The mediaeval singer, before musical notation was introduced, found one great advantage in modal classification: it made it easier for him to memorise the repertory, as he found melodic formulas arranged according to mode. It did not take long to devise a still more functional classification, in which pieces themselves were arranged in the same fashion. Thus the tonary (*tonale* or *libellus tonarius*) was born, more a textbook than a liturgical work, which none the less was soon combined with an antiphoner, a gradual or another book of chant. In it are found antiphons collected around one of the eight psalmodic tones (at first in liturgical order, later alphabetically), but graduals, offertories, responsories and so on soon appear too. Evidence for the tonary in its oldest form is found in the so-called 'Charlemagne Psalter' (MS Paris, B.N. lat. 13159), which dates from the end of the eighth century and may be (in the opinion of the leading specialist in the field, Michel Huglo[4]) one of the earliest existing editions anywhere. In the tonary the cantor would find the genre and the verbal *incipit* of his pieces, as well as the intonation-formulas expressed in syllabic forms, such as *Noannoeane, Noeagis*, etc., which clearly had a mnemonic function. Their origin can be traced to the Byzantine *epechemata*, which were in fact used as models in teaching and in the study of psalmodic intonations.

We have already pointed out that not all compositions from the early Gregorian stock can be confined within the pattern of the *oktoechos*. Although modern liturgical books indicate the mode to which a melody belongs by placing a figure before each individual piece, in some cases these attributions are not altogether certain. Analysis of the repertory, especially of tracts and responsories, seems to confirm Peter Wagner's suggestion that the *protus* and *tetrardus* should be considered the primitive modes of Christian music.[5]

The difficulty of establishing the modes of some Gregorian compositions with any precision has suggested new solutions for the problem to some modern scholars. According to Dom Jean Claire,[6] for example, the oldest portions of the office (remnants of responsorial psalmody, like short responses) postulate the existence of a single-element archaic modality (where the end of the antiphon and the beginning of the psalm are at the same pitch), which contrasts with the double-element evolved modality of tonic + first note and therefore dominant. This ancient modality is based on three related notes separated by a tone: F-G-A in the pentatonic system D-F-G-A-C, C-D-E in the system A-C-D-E-G. The transition from archaic to evolved modality took place thanks to an expansion of range due at once to the raising of the first note of the psalm and the lowering of the final note of the antiphon. Others have put forward the theory of the 'three modal groups' (so-called), based on the hexachordal scale known to Guido d'Arezzo. The three hexachords (natural, hard and soft) with which we are already familiar are used in this theory too.[7] It will be recalled that each is distinguished by its particular semitone: E-F in the natural, B-C in the hard and A-B flat in the soft. In this theory the prevalence of one of the three semitones determines to which of the corresponding modal groups the piece should be assigned.

Still on the subject of hexachords, the importance of their connection to the basic scale obtained from mathematical computations of the monochord should not be overlooked. We know already that the Middle Ages inherited from the Greeks the scale of two octaves in the minor (possibly from baritone A to A above middle C), in which the notes were at first named after fifteen letters of the Latin alphabet (A–P). Later on this alphabetic nomenclature was limited to the first seven letters (A–G), which were made to coincide with the notes of the diatonic scale:

A	B	C	D	E	F	G
Ut	Re	Mi	Fa	Sol	La	Si

With the Odonian notation of the tenth century (named after Odo of Cluny, or possibly Odo of Saint-Maur-des-Fossés) there was a return to the application of the alphabetic series to the Greek two-octave system, in which A was the equivalent of La. Capital letters (A–G) were used for the lower octave and small letters (a–g) for the next.

It was also Odo who introduced the Greek capital letter *gamma* (Γ) to denote the sound below the first La, from which came the name 'gamut' as applied to the whole scale. Later Guido d'Arezzo gave doubled small letters (aa, bb, cc, etc.) to the other notes above the scale, but nowadays these are usually indicated by a superscript figure. Thus the system of nomenclature was completed, and it remained unchanged. It was used at first in the teaching of the *ars musica*, but turned out to be of immense practical significance when Guido named the notes of the ascending series of the natural hexachord after the syllables of the hymn *Ut quaeant laxis*. Guido's method became so popular that in the thirteenth century each of the seven sequences which reproduced the order of tones and semitones in the hymn (T T S T) and was restricted to the basic scale was considered to be a hexachord. Because of the partial overlap between these sequences it was inevitable that, for example, the same sound would be La in one hexachord, Sol in another and Re in a third. This can be understood by studying the diagram on p. 86, which reproduces the final form of the hexachordal system, superimposed on the basic scale.

To find the full form of the name for any note in the basic scale, start from the bottom line (letter of the alphabet) and work upwards, gradually adding the names acquired by the sound within each

HEXACHORD

7. *Hard*   Ut Re – Mi Fa Sol La

6. *Soft*   Ut Re Mi Fa – Sol La

5. *Natural*   Ut Re Mi Fa Sol La

4. *Hard*   Ut Re – Mi Fa Sol La

3. *Soft*   Ut Re Mi Fa – Sol La

2. *Natural*   Ut Re Mi Fa Sol La

1. *Hard*   Ut Re Mi Fa Sol La

Γ A B C D E F G a b♭ b c d e f g a¹ b♭¹ b¹ c¹ d¹ e¹

soft hexachord → b♭

hard hexachord → ♮

hexachord. One example: the full name of the sound corresponding to G would be G Sol Re Ut.

We have already explained that the transition from one hexachord to another was called 'mutation', and that the point selected for this transition was usually determined by the desire to keep the name Mi-Fa for the semitone of the new hexachord, so that the name 'solmisation' is given to the system of mutations as a whole. A guide to mastering the technique of solmisation was offered by the so-called 'Guidonian hand', wrongly credited to Guido d'Arezzo. In this the different levels of the basic scale were distributed across the left hand, but the evidence of the sources is not in agreement about the details.

20 Classical forms of the Gregorian repertory

By 'classical forms' of Gregorian chant is meant the repertory as it appears in the ninth century, with the addition of the chants for the Ordinary (*Kyrie, Gloria*, etc.), although these are of later date. The most readily available reference work for the earliest repertories of mass chants is the *Antiphonale Missarum Sextuplex*, edited by R.-J. Hesbert.

The Gregorian repertory can be sub-divided in various ways and studied according to these divisions: style (syllabic, neumatic, melismatic); liturgical usage (chants can be for the mass or the office, those for the mass are used in meditation or processions, and so on); and form (recitatives, free compositions, responsorial psalmody, antiphonal psalmody, etc.). Chants will be discussed below according to an essentially practical criterion – their use in the liturgy – and starting from the form they take in modern liturgical books.

It is not possible here to enter into a detailed analysis of recitatives (the formulas used for the interventions of the celebrant (prayers, preface, *Pater noster* etc.) and the other ministers (readings, Epistle, Gospel)). As for the tones of psalms, we may mention the constant recurrence of psalms throughout the early centuries of Christianity and their role as guide in the application of the *oktoechos* to the Western repertory (the eight tones are called 'regular' and are heavily dependent on the eight modes of the antiphons). Their structure includes the intonation (*initium*), the tenor (key-note or dominant of the recitation), a median cadence halfway through the verse, and a final cadence, which may have several *differentiae* to join it as smoothly as possible to the antiphon. In liturgical books the text given to the *differentiae* consists of the letters *e u o u a e* (the vowels of *seculorum. Amen*).

Antiphons, in their present form, are short, simple compositions which introduce or conclude the chanting of a psalm or canticle. In the mass, antiphonal psalmody is found in the introit and the communion-chant. The former includes a highly ornate antiphon, reserved for the *schola* and alternating with one or more verses of a psalm, which accompanies the entry of the celebrant. It is, in fact, the introductory chant which sets the theme of the feast or the liturgical season. The communion, performed as its name implies during the administration of the eucharist, had remained in the form of an antiphon lacking its psalm; but after the reform ordained by the Second Vatican Council, liturgical books began to list one or more psalms which can be alternated with the antiphon, as was the practice originally. Introit and communion alike usually have a neumatic melody which, in most cases, is original, not composed by the 'patchwork' method or modelled on common melodic stereotypes. Of the two categories the melodies for the communion are the less uniform, having a high degree of modal instability.

We know already that the tract, uniquely among the surviving chants of the mass, is associated with 'direct' or 'continuous' psalmody, and takes its name straight from this style of performance. It was sung after the gradual, instead of the alleluia, in the period before Easter and on other days of penitence. Musically it is a very ornate piece, a meditative chant, which may have come down to the Christians from the chants of the synagogue. Because of its nature its performance is confined to the soloist. The early stock of Gregorian chant includes only a few examples, almost all composed in the plagal *tetrardus* mode (a few are in the plagal *protus*), and built up on a basic melody which varies only in the length and accentuation of the text. It offers an interesting field for the examination of compositional technique by means of the juxtaposition and adaptation of melodic formulas.

The oldest and most typical meditative chant is the gradual, perhaps so called because it was sung on the steps (*gradus*) of the ambo or the sanctuary after a reading from the Old Testament. It was also called *responsorium* and, as such, is made up of two sections, a choral response and a verse for the soloist. This is all that remains of the earliest responsorial form abandoned centuries before. From a stylistic angle, it is the most elaborate composition in the Gregorian repertory, melismas of from ten to thirty notes being quite normal.

Standard melodies occur frequently, and they in their turn are built up from standard phrases, which are especially common in the verses. Their modal structure is sometimes of the expanded type (which uses extra notes). It sometimes seems that the intensity of the various texts used for this chant manages to find its expression in stereotyped formulas which force the melody out of its usual range; it is not uncommon to find notes an eleventh above the tonic of the piece. One related group of graduals belongs, in its modality, to the *tritus* (the fifth mode) and often produces the effect of the modern major chord F-A-C, which gives it a light and lively character. The nineteen graduals belonging to the *Justus ut palma* group deserve separate consideration. They have so many elements in common that they form the most uniform group in the whole heritage of Gregorian chant. Their endings on A have led some to suggest that they are transcribed a fifth above D, which is assumed to be their original end-note, but it is not impossible that A is the correct form.

As an independent composition the alleluia is the chant of acclamation, or *jubilus*, which precedes the announcement of the Gospel in the mass. It appears in liturgical books interspersed with a verse of a psalm, undoubtedly a more recent addition, given that the oldest sources do not include it or at least do not give reliable lists for it. The performance of the alleluia is associated with the joy of Easter, and also celebrates the 'passover' of believers into the bliss of eternity. According to tradition, the reduction in the number of melismas can be attributed to Gregory the Great. Until the reforms carried out after Vatican II the plan of the alleluia's performance was clearly responsorial, and took the following form:

Singer: *Alleluia* (intonation only)
Choir: *Alleluia* (intonation and melisma)
Singer: Verse
Choir: End of the verse (often with the same melody as the melisma)
Singer: *Alleluia* (intonation only)
Choir: −*a* (melisma)

Verse melodies for the alleluia are distinguished by their frequent adaptation to different texts and their close connection – as far as melodic formulas are concerned – with the alleluia. Out of 125 versicles, in fact, 115 use the same material as the alleluia. As for melodic range, some of the oldest examples confine themselves to moving up and down within a fifth, but other, more recent examples go beyond the limits of their mode, especially in descending scales.

The offertory, a chant performed in the mass during the procession which brings the sacrificial offerings to the altar, was originally made up of a whole psalm with an antiphon, but later it was clearly distinguished from the other processional chants (introit and communion) by developing a more melismatic style similar to that of the graduals. Until the twelfth century it retained a certain number of verses (two or three), with the antiphon repeated after each. This transformation from antiphonal to responsorial chant seems to be unique in the history of Gregorian chant. Other elements, however, are also unique to the offertory: an enormously extended melodic range, and the repetition of individual words or phrases in the text. The ultimate development of this technique is reached in the fourth verse of the offertory *Vir erat* (from the book of Job), in which the first word (*Quoniam*) is repeated three times and the closing phrase (*ut videant bona*) is taken up no fewer than seven times; but this composition is quite exceptional in its subjective and dramatic power. Other pieces are much admired for their splendid melismas and the classical qualities of their conception; one such is the famous *Jubilate Deo universa terra*. No model phrases which can be transferred to other pieces are found in the repertory of offertories, though there are some among tracts, graduals and responsories, but repetitive structures do occur (identical verse-endings, echoes between verse and response, and so on) within separate pieces. Many specialists believe that Gregorian art reaches one of its highest points in the offertory, thanks to the harmony of the various elements, the elegance of the melodic lines and the originality of the formulas used. It is regrettable that the ancient verses are omitted from modern liturgical books.

Among the chants of the office, the responsories (referring to the *responsoria prolixa*, not the *responsoria brevia* of the lesser Hours) are the only pieces in which the vigorous creative impulse of Gregorian composers shows itself to best advantage. They form part of Matins, where they have a function corresponding to that of tracts and graduals in the mass, as meditative chants after a reading. The Roman liturgy includes nine responsories (the nine readings are split up into groups of three, one for each of the night-hours), while the monastic (Benedictine) liturgy includes twelve for each feast. This has produced a large number of these chants, exceeded only by the number of antiphons. As the name implies, the formal structure of responsories derives from early responsorial psalmody. Today it consists of a first section (the response) and a *versus*, after which the response is repeated in whole or in part (A B A').

The music of section A belongs in a large number of cases to the *protus* or *tetrardus* modes, and uses standard formulas which are found in many examples, although the 'patchwork' process is less wide-spread and striking than among the tracts. Enough room is left for individual enterprise to enable it sometimes to bring out the express-ive and even dramatic features of the liturgical text. The melodies of the verses, as they appear today, are an elaborate expansion of one of the eight psalmodic tones. The study of these melodies is useful in exploring the primitive design, and above all the *tenores*, of ancient psalmody.

The five chants of the Ordinary of the mass, whose texts do not change, appear comparatively late. The only variety in these is achieved through the large number of melodies on which they are intoned. *Kyrie, Sanctus* and *Agnus Dei* are used in every mass, *Gloria* and *Credo* on feast-days, though the *Gloria* is omitted in Advent and Lent. Originally sung by the congregation, they at first followed simple melodies, but from about the ninth century onwards the *schola* took them over and embellished them, a process which reached its peak in the fifteenth century and beyond. During this period a vast *corpus* of melodies was created, of which only a tiny proportion is reproduced in modern liturgical collections.[1]

Such collections, unlike older sources (where the chants are grouped separately, *Kyrie*s, *Gloria*s and so on all together) contain eighteen schemes, for each of which a *Kyrie, Gloria, Sanctus* and *Agnus Dei* are chosen, along with a selection of *ad libitum* chants. Even today the *Credo* forms a section on its own. These schemes were mostly devised by modern editors, and are not based on thematic relationships between their constituent forms although complete cycles, *Kyrie – Gloria – Sanctus – Agnus Dei*, are found in some sources from the thirteenth century onwards.[2]

More than two hundred melodies for the *Kyrie* are known to exist. In the invocation the words *Kyrie eleison, Christe eleison, Kyrie eleison*, are repeated three times, according to various melodic patterns of which the most common are:

    a a a, a a a, a a b
    a a a, b b b, a a a'
    a a a, b b b, c c c'
    a b a, c d c, e f e'

From simple, almost syllabic examples, which are presumably very old, the melodies range to highly melismatic structures in which elements unfamiliar to the classical Gregorian repertory are some-times found. They include extended range, unusual intervals, long descending scales and a marked tendency to expressivity. In an attempt to encourage dialogue between *schola* and congregation, recent liturgical reforms have prescribed that the triad of invocations should be repeated only once.

As we have seen, the text of *Gloria* can be traced back to a psalmodic design, which is also clearly reflected in the melody of what, in P. Wagner's opinion,[3] may be the oldest example to come down to us (it is classed in liturgical books as *Gloria XV*). In fact this intonation can be reduced to a repeated psalmodic formula adapted to the differing length of the verses, as is shown in this partial transcription by W. Apel.[4]

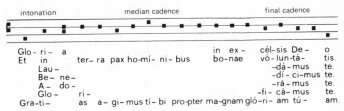

Sources have provided us with fifty-six intonations, which may be arranged in three groups according to their form: free compositions; melodies with partial correspondence in the verses, caused by repetitions in the text (the largest group); and melodies with complete correspondence between verses, where the text is fitted to a single formula.

The *Credo* entered the Roman liturgy rather late. Tradition suggests that it was introduced to Rome by Pope Benedict VIII in 1014, at the insistence of the German Emperor, Henry II. This explains its absence from the ancient sources, and the fact that in modern liturgical books the intonations for the *Credo* are grouped separately from the cycles for the Ordinary. A recent study by T. Miazga lists over seven hundred melodies, but this cannot be a definitive total, since new intonations continue to crop up, even in eighteenth- and nineteenth-century sources. From this vast supply, official books take only four melodies, plus two *ad libitum*. The oldest of these is the so-called *Credo I* or 'authentic' *Credo*, found in manuscripts from the twelfth century, but probably older and possibly of Byzantine origin. The melody is constructed in a similar way to *Gloria XV*, in a psalmodic recitative-pattern. Among the other intonations, *Credo IV* should also be mentioned; also called *Cardinalis*, it was already widespread in the fifteenth century and was used in many polyphonic compositions.[5]

The *Sanctus*, placed at the end of the preface in the mass, comes immediately before the great eucharistic prayer. It was sung by the congregation until the late eighth century, when it passed into the choral repertory. Western tradition has left us at least 231 melodies (according to P. J. Thannabaur), whose composition reached a peak in the eleventh, twelfth and, later, fifteenth centuries. On the whole the melismatic style is most commonly found in these pieces, especially in the triple repetition of *sanctus* and in the *hosanna*, while from a formal viewpoint melodies with internal thematic reminiscences are very common. More common still are melodies which repeat the music exactly to match textual repetitions (*hosanna I* repeated as *hosanna II*, and so on). Modern liturgical books contain a selection of eighteen intonations, of which number XVIII is perhaps the oldest, given its obvious psalmodic origins.

The *Agnus Dei*, introduced into the Roman liturgy by Pope Sergius I (d. 701), had entered usage some time before in several Western churches, as had the *Kyrie*, with which the *Agnus Dei* has some features in common. At first the invocation was repeated throughout the rite of the *fractio panis*, but in the eleventh or twelfth centuries the number of repetitions was restricted to three. Also in the twelfth century, the third *miserere nobis* was replaced by *dona nobis pacem*. Many of the surviving intonations repeat the same melody three times (A A A), while others conform to the pattern A B A, or sometimes A A B. Stylistically, only a few display archaic features; the most linear, and perhaps the oldest, is number XVIII in the liturgical collections, which is used in the mass for the dead and at the ends of litanies.

Although the singing of hymns goes back, as we have seen, almost to the dawn of Christianity, they were accepted officially into the Roman liturgy only at a comparatively late date, towards the ninth or tenth century. The means of their entry was provided by the Benedictine monastic tradition, whose hymnary (originally the liturgical book which contained the hymns) was transplanted into Roman practice after various individual churches had been using it for some time. This did not hinder the formation of an immense wealth of texts and melodies in the Western tradition, whose chief strands – as Bruno Stäblein's copious anthology demonstrates – can be identified as stemming from regional customs, certain religious orders (Cistercians, Dominicans, Franciscans) and the role of hymns in liturgical contexts (the mass, the liturgy of the Hours, processions, and so on).

21 Decline and revival

In strictly chronological terms the remarks made in this section should be postponed until the end of the book, partly because some symptoms of the decline of Gregorian chant will be discussed in the next chapter. It seems appropriate, however, to bring forward this treatment of the progressive decline of liturgical chant and the efforts made in recent years to ensure its recovery, because it is exclusively concerned with the classical Gregorian repertory, to which the pages immediately preceding this section were devoted. It is impossible to ignore the fact that, in the whole panorama of mediaeval music, only Gregorian chant (along with Ambrosian, which shared its destiny) can boast of a reconstructed, if not actually uninterrupted, tradition, because it was for centuries and remains today the official chant of the Catholic liturgy. Later additions to this heritage (new offices; and, still more, new musical forms arising within or outside the liturgy after the ninth and tenth centuries: tropes, sequences and so on) cannot be approached and rediscovered in the same spirit as can a repertory which is still alive today. For this reason it seems proper to sketch that repertory's history as far as the final stages, which brings it into our own time.

We have already seen that, up to the ninth and tenth centuries, liturgical melodies were handed down with some care; the earliest notated manuscripts reveal a definite uniformity of tradition. Later, although the repertory for the mass underwent no major alteration, that for the office was enlarged by more or less successful adaptations used for new feasts (especially in the 'sanctorial' cycle). On the other hand, the diastematic system and, later, the appearance of the stave secured an exact representation of the melodic line at the cost of making the indication of rhythm more difficult. The sense of rhythm became more and more feeble, except in the centres connected with the monastery of St Gall. Tropes and sequences (see the next chapter), with their syllabic, rhythmically more regular melodies, were thus easier to understand, and caused a move away from ornate and melismatic melodies and, consequently, from free rhythm. So marked was this move that in the manuscripts the melodies begin to appear interspersed with frequent bar-lines and with their neumes broken up, a sign that a new method of performance was becoming fashionable, a method in which the style of Gregorian chant called *fractus*, measured in beats, has its unhappy origins. Furthermore, at an even earlier date, in the time of Guido d'Arezzo and Hermannus Contractus (d. 1054), various modal adjustments had taken place: for example, the dominant of the *deuterus* had shifted from B to C.

Between 1134 and 1140 the Cistercians worked on the reform of their choral chant, following principles laid down *a priori* by St Bernard, who was under the mistaken impression that this was the way to return to authentic Gregorian chant. On the whole his instructions caused serious damage to the traditional repertory, demanding a single mode for every composition, the exclusion of the flat, the restriction of every melody to a range of ten notes, the avoidance of authentic and plagal modes in combination, and the abbreviation of those insufficiently austere frivolities, melismas. Unfortunately, in 1256 the Dominicans also adopted the Cistercian repertory.

After the appearance of 'figured' music the notes of Gregorian chant served to render proportional units of duration: the virga had the value of a long, the punctum that of a breve, and the lozenge-shaped note that of a semibreve. Singers of church music transferred the proportional values of figured music to Gregorian monody as well, especially when early polyphonic forms (*organum* and *discantus*) began to spread; and, worse still, when Gregorian chant, its rhythm now completely wrecked, was used note by note (hence the name *cantus firmus*) as the basis of more elaborate polyphonic constructions (*motetus*, etc.). In the bull *Docta Sanctorum Patrum* of 1322, Pope John XXII sought to re-assert the honour and integrity of traditional chant, but his efforts were largely in vain. Polyphony advanced triumphantly, in equal measure with the progressive disappearance into obscurity of the theory and practice of Gregorian chant.

Against this background of decline there took place, in 1577, after the Council of Trent had left the problem unresolved, the unfortunate attempt of Pope Gregory XIII to improve the traditional chants by a process of radical reform, involving particularly the removal of melismas, which no one any longer understood or was able to perform. The task was entrusted to Palestrina and Annibale Zoilo but was never brought to a conclusion, thanks to the strenuous representations made to the pope by the Spanish musician Don Fernando de las Infantas and his sovereign, Philip II. The problem arose again some thirty years later, when Raimondi, chief printer of the Medici firm (named after the cardinal who was its protector), requested permission from the pope to print the *Graduale*. In 1611 Paul V agreed, and ordered Cardinal Del Monte to choose a commission which would edit the chants. Felice Anerio and Francesco Soriano were chosen and, with an alacrity worthy of a better cause, prepared the material for their edition, of which the first volume appeared in 1614. This was the origin of the 'Medici edition', regrettably famous because – chosen over more than two centuries as the model for numerous other editions – it was declared official by the ecclesiastical authorities in the last decades of the nineteenth century.

In it the Gregorian melodies appeared much curtailed and irremediably re-ordered according to the aesthetic criteria of the sixteenth and seventeenth centuries, applied in a pernicious and arbitrary manner. Pustet, a publisher at Ratisbon (Regensburg), reprinted it in 1868–9, and obtained the rights to it from the pope for thirty years, at a time when the anti-historical and anti-aesthetic character of the 'Medici edition' was becoming more and more obvious.

The eighteenth and nineteenth centuries saw the aberrant practice of Gregorian chant reach its nadir. A few impressions recorded in 1830 by Mendelssohn, after hearing a performance by the choir of the Sistine Chapel, will suffice as evidence:

> The intonation is entrusted to a soprano soloist, who hits the first note with some vigour, loads it with appoggiaturas, and rounds off the final syllable with an extended trill. Then sopranos and tenors sing the melody as it stands in the book, more or less, while altos and basses sing on a third . . . The whole piece is sung in a sprightly rhythm.

None the less, the foundations of a renaissance were also being laid in the nineteenth century.

The movement for the reform of liturgical chant, which appeared in several European countries in the second half of the nineteenth century, is not seen in its proper light unless account is also taken of parallel developments aimed at the refinement and reform of the liturgy. In both cases the initial requirements were the same, which explains why the first supporter of the movement for liturgical reform, the Benedictine Dom Prosper Guéranger (1805–77), was also the promoter of the renewal of Gregorian chant. At the former monastery of St Peter at Solesmes, which he acquired in 1833 with the intention of re-establishing the Benedictine Rule there, he found himself face to face with a very concrete problem: how was the new community to be given a genuine repertory of chants for the monastic liturgy? Guéranger's intuition helped him to solve the problem. Under his guidance the choir of monks managed to give its chant a character which had been unknown till then, and which Canon Gontier rendered in theoretical terms in his *Méthode raisonnée* of 1859. In essentials the book anticipates the principles of rhythm which were to make the 'Solesmes school' famous.

In the same year, 1859, Joseph Pothier entered Solesmes; he was to be one of the architects of reform. Shortly afterwards, on becoming instructor in chant to the novices, he was bold enough to have them perform melodies taken from manuscripts as part of the course. After undertaking, in collaboration with Dom Jausions, the study of neumes *in campo aperto*, he was the first to devise a comparative method of examining sources, and prepared a report which – not without delays and hesitation, as these were still the years of the privilege granted to the Pustet edition – appeared under the title *Les mélodies grégoriennes* in 1880, an important date in the history of the restoration of chant.

This work was soon followed by a transcription of the *Graduale* or *Antiphonale Missarum*, which, none the less, was only allowed to appear in 1883, and then only for the exclusive use of the Benedictine congregation at Solesmes. The previous year, during an international congress at Arezzo, the monks of Solesmes had sung the mass for 15 September with the new melodies, and had thereby inspired an almost unanimous vote in favour of reform of the liturgical books in accordance with the new discoveries. The authorities at Rome declined to accept the motion passed at Arezzo and re-asserted the official status of the Ratisbon edition.

Dom Pothier's *Graduale*, although it marked an unmistakable advance on the other editions available at the time, was still a product of compromise, perhaps compiled with pastoral rather than scientific intentions. A solid basis of scientific exactitude was given to Pothier's work by a young monk who entered Solesmes in 1875, Dom André Mocquereau (1849–1930). Gifted as he was with greater teaching abilities, he gradually replaced Pothier in the running of the choir and – much more important – almost simultaneously, in 1888, devised a plan for the publication in facsimile of the oldest sources of Gregorian chant. The result was the birth of the monumental *Paléographie Musicale*, the first instalment of which appeared in 1889. In the following years Mocquereau travelled round the major European libraries, tracking down and photographing manuscripts, so that by 1904 the archive at Solesmes possessed more than 250 complete examples.

In the meantime, liturgical chant had ceased to present itself as a problem simply for Solesmes or for only a few bishops: it had become a problem for the whole Church. In 1887 Leo XIII summoned the Triestine Jesuit Angelo De Santi (1847–1922) to Rome, with instructions to write about liturgical chant in *La Civiltà Cattolica*, an official organ of the Holy See. His presence at Rome was invaluable for the cause of reform, because – despite the delicacy of his position and the numerous attacks made on him – he was able to ensure that his ideas percolated to Solesmes. Leo XIII showed himself more and more determined to embark on a serious revision of liturgical chant and, with this intention, organised in 1893 an important conference of the most significant personalities in the contemporary Church, among them Cardinal Giuseppe Sarto, the future Pope Pius X. This had no more original idea than to turn to De Santi, who sent a report which Sarto presented to the Congregazione dei Riti (the papal office responsible for liturgical matters) in the form of a *votum*. The conference then issued a communique in 1894, which, though disappointing for the reformers, at least enlarged the boundaries of action within the rules: the use of the Ratisbon edition was recommended, but each individual bishop was free to use the edition he preferred in his own diocese. As a result, the melodies as restored by Pothier became much more widespread.

In 1899 an incident provoked, it has been suggested, by Monsignor Lorenzo Perosi, the director of the Sistine Chapel, further weighted the scales in favour of Solesmes. He inserted several Gregorian chants into a service and was consequently reported to the pope, but was able to show that the melodies mentioned in the accusation came from the Vatican's own archives and were thus part of the Sistine's repertory.

Finally, on 17 May 1901, shortly after the Pustet edition's privileges expired, the pope sent a letter of praise and encouragement to the abbot of Solesmes. This was the seal set on the approach taken by Solesmes in its liturgical initiatives, but its difficulties were not over yet. In the same year the French monasteries were suppressed by governmental edict, and the monks were forced to leave the country. The community of Solesmes went to Appuldurcombe, on the Isle of Wight, while the monks of Saint-Wandrille, including Dom Pothier, took refuge in Belgium.

In August 1903 Cardinal Sarto became pope, and a mere two months later he requested Cardinal Vicario to prepare texts for the reform of sacred music. Once again he turned to De Santi's report, and the new text was prepared and signed by the pope on 22 November, the feast of St Cecilia. Now recognised as the *magna carta* of the process of renewal, Pius X's *Motu proprio* declares, among much else, that Gregorian chant and classical polyphony are accorded a special place in the Catholic liturgy; that new compositions are not to be excluded, but must conform to very precise requirements; that the organ is the only instrument normally permitted in ritual usage; that Gregorian chant is to be a subject for study in seminaries; and so on.

The papal declaration was the first stage of the reform; there remained the problem of an official edition of the melodies. The suggestion that the task should be assigned to Solesmes – and thus to Mocquereau – was resisted in some quarters, above all by Dom Pothier. Not even the appointment, in 1904, of a papal commission made up of the best scholars of Gregorian chant was able to break through the entangled rivalries between French and Germans, between Solesmes (Mocquereau) and Dom Pothier, partly because some did not want the official edition to include the rhythmic *ictus* (vertical episemas), which do not appear in the manuscripts but express the rhythmical interpretation of Solesmes. Eventually a compromise worked out by De Santi was accepted: the Holy See was to print an *editio typica* (the so-called *Editio Vaticana*) which every publisher could then use as a model. None the less, Mocquereau finally refused to co-operate, with the result that all the volumes of the *Editio Vaticana* which appeared up to 1912 did so under the supervision of Dom Pothier. They were *Kyriale* (1905), *Graduale* (1908), *Officium pro Defunctis* (1909) and *Antiphonale* (1912). The volumes which followed were chiefly the work of Dom Joseph Gajard, a monk of Solesmes: *Cantus Passionis* (1916), *Officium Majoris Hebdomadae* ... (1922) and *Officium (et Missae) in Nativitate Domini* (1926). For other texts in the liturgical repertory (*Responsoriale* and *Processionale*) there is still no alternative to the old monastic editions from Solesmes (of 1895 and 1893 respectively). Dom Gajard also edited the *Antiphonale Monasticum* (1934), which was a notable advance on the first 'Vatican' editions.

The Solesmes editions themselves conform to the *Editio Vaticana*, but are supplied with rhythmical indications (points to the right of notes, horizontal and vertical episemas). The most practical of them, as well as the most used, is the *Liber Usualis Missae et Officii*, in which are collected the chants for masses and the principal offices of the year.

In its classic form, the 'Solesmes method' (see Dom Gajard's short book *La Méthode de Solesmes*) is still far from gaining the unanimous approval of Gregorian specialists. Although the broad lines of the Solesmes interpretation (free rhythm, etc.) seem to be historically valid and, at any rate, help to obtain, in practice, results of undeniable artistic value, there is still a great deal of discussion about the criteria for identifying 'lesser rhythm' (in other words the use of the vertical episema), which remains linked to Dom Mocquereau's weighty study *Le nombre musical grégorien*. The recent development of a semiology of Gregorian chant makes these criteria even less acceptable. The very definition of Gregorian rhythm as conceived by Mocquereau (free musical rhythm) seems to be losing ground these days in favour of Pothier's earlier formulation (free oratorical rhythm); and the proof seems to lie in the performances of the Solesmes choir itself, which, when subjected to analysis by electronic devices such as oscillographs, have contradicted in practice the theoretical statements about the placing of rhythmic stresses (*ictus*). Furthermore, we have already noted the *souplesse* which today inspires the major figures at Solesmes.

It cannot be denied that the *Editio Vaticana* has turned out to be, from a practical viewpoint, a valuable aid in the purification of the liturgical service. On the other hand, it cannot be accorded the status and validity of a critical edition. The Second Vatican Council itself, in 1963, clearly expressed the wish 'that the *editio typica* of the books of Gregorian chant be completed; and that a more critical edition (*editio magis critica*) of books already edited after the reform of St Pius X be prepared' (Constitution *Sacrosanctum Concilium*, 117).[1] The monks of Solesmes are working on this at present, and have already edited several volumes of methodology and of the sources of the *Graduale*. In addition, under the editorship of the same monks, the *Graduale Romanum* was published in 1974, in a version adapted to the new structure of the *Missale* as it appears after the reforms of Vatican II.

What, then, does the future hold for Gregorian chant? Vatican II stressed that 'the Church recognises Gregorian chant as the chant proper to the Roman liturgy; and therefore, in liturgical use, the principal place should be reserved for it, other things being equal (*ceteris paribus*)' (*Sacrosanctum Concilium*, 116). Today the Council's edict has been overtaken by events, but the history of Gregorian chant shows that it has survived perils far more dangerous than any in the present situation.

IV

LITURGICO-MUSICAL INNOVATIONS OF THE NINTH AND TENTH CENTURIES AND THEIR DEVELOPMENT; SECULAR MONODY IN LATIN

22 Sequences

The encounter and subsequent fusion between the Roman liturgical and musical tradition and that of the countries north of the Alps was not the only development which took place during the Carolingian period. The immediate consequence of Charlemagne's educational reforms was the appearance of an important monastic culture. The great monasteries with their schools, their *scriptoria* and their workshops encouraged intensive artistic activity, which took its basic inspiration from the liturgy which it was to enrich so generously in its turn.

One of the most important innovations of the ninth century, the birth of neumatic musical script, has already been discussed in an earlier chapter. This discussion was brought forward to preserve continuity of argument, and it should not be forgotten that the discovery of notation was taking place at about the same time as the innovations which we are now to consider. The same is true of another significant novelty, the origin and elaboration of early polyphonic forms. The study of these has been assigned to another volume (by F. A. Gallo) in order not to disrupt the unity of the present treatment. But the first traces of polyphonic chant do appear in the Carolingian era; if the invention of notation and the first experiments with polyphony are added, as they should be, to the innovations which are the subject of this chapter, the 'Carolingian Renaissance' will be seen, at least from a musical viewpoint, to be an historically justifiable reality.

The liturgical situation which had arisen throughout those parts of

Europe subject to Frankish rule needs to be taken into account if the nature of these new phenomena is to be fully understood. Although the policy of encouraging liturgical uniformity, based on Roman models, had not achieved its desired aim, it had helped not only to create new conditions, but gradually to promote the prayers and chants of the Gregorian repertory to a position of unchallenged superiority. Furthermore, the belief – by now an established certainty – that this repertory had been created by the divine inspiration of Gregory the Great gave it a sacral character. The attitude towards it of authorities and singers alike came increasingly to be summed up in the motto *ne varietur* ('no deviation'). This had negative consequences on an artistic level, as the process led to the drying up of creativity and the demise of a living tradition, at least for liturgical chant in the strict sense. No doubt the introduction of new feasts into the liturgical calendar meant that more work was needed to produce appropriate texts and melodies, but increasingly this was done by means of imitation and adaptation of existing material.

It was unthinkable, however, that the monastic communities of the Carolingian and Ottonian era should resign themselves to the simple acceptance and reproduction of the musical heritage which tradition had put into their hands. There was still some room for creativity; and the result was an enormous growth in the output of hymns and the long processional antiphons needed in great abbeys for the majestic unfolding of their ritual. Other opportunities were sought and invented anew, as in the case of sequences and tropes.

The term *sequentia* appears for the first time in a passage from the *Liber Officialis*, written before 830 by the liturgist Amalar. After declaring that the verse of the alleluia touches the singer in his inmost soul, he adds that 'haec jubilatio, quam cantores sequentiam vocant' ('this joyous melody, which singers call *sequentia*') puts him in a frame of mind where the spoken word comes to seem superfluous[1] (compare Augustine's definition of the *jubilus*). In Amalar's time, then, there existed a type of melody which could be used, after the singing of the gradual, to replace the *jubilus* on the alleluia which followed the versicle; and this melody was called *sequentia*. In short, *sequentia* was the replacement melody for an alleluiatic *jubilus*. Further evidence is provided by the Mont-Blandin Antiphoner compiled between the eighth and ninth centuries (now in the Bibliothèque Royale in Brussels, 10127–10144). It contains, at the end, a list of alleluias for the mass, six of which are accompanied by the rubric *cum sequentia*.[2] This hint is confirmed by the appearance in later sources of six sequences together with the alleluias marked with this rubric. This leads to several probable – though not yet certain – conclusions. The sequence was originally a melody with a text used to replace a *jubilus*; it was essentially a melisma to which the text was only added later on; the melismas which replaced the *jubilus*, those which Amalar called *sequentia*, had already long been in existence, and the particular contribution of the ninth century was no more than the addition of a text to these melismas.

These simple deductions are further illuminated by the celebrated letter of Notker Balbulus (a monk of St Gall who died in 912), addressed to the Imperial Chancellor Liutward, Bishop of Vercelli, which appeared as a preface to Notker's *Liber Hymnorum*.[3] Writing between 880 and 884, Notker relates that in his youth it was very difficult to memorise the 'longissimae melodiae' of liturgical chant, and he looked round for some solution to the problem. Help came unexpectedly from a monk who had fled from Jumièges, in the western part of the Frankish empire, a region much exposed to the depredations of the Northmen, who laid it waste in 851 and 862. This monk had brought an antiphoner with him, in which Notker found 'certain verses' applied 'for sequences' ('aliqui versus . . . ad sequentias'). It was a clumsy attempt, but the device was the answer to Notker's problem. Encouraged by the support of his superiors, he began to compose similar texts to be sung to the melismas of the alleluia. Thus were born the first of the compositions (*Laudes Deo concinat* and *Psallat ecclesia*) which, together with some others, came to form the volume to which the author gave the name *Liber Hymnorum*. In spite of its title, these were not hymns in the traditional sense, since the forty new compositions neither obeyed metrical rules nor resembled the elegant iambic strophes of 'Ambrosian' hymnody. The structure of these texts, which, according to Notker's candid account, had had their beginnings in France, was wholly new, consisting of a series of phrases freely arranged around sonorous cadences in a classical style or more exuberant, strongly assonanced locutions. In any case this was prose, or more accurately rhythmic prose, and *prosa* was the name given to this kind of text. The periods were constructed according to melodic phrases; a fresh example of the primacy, in Christian chant, of music over words. In the majority of cases, though not invariably, two consecutive lines of text were set to one and the same musical phrase, so that the text was organised in couplets (*copulae*). Taken as a whole, then, the *prosa* consisted of a series of textual couplets, with lines of differing lengths, occasionally separated by phrases with no coupling line. The novelty of this textual structure gave the melody an unaccustomed energy which, along with a clear and accentuated lyricism of expression, became a characteristic trait of this new musical genre.

The texts in Notker's *Liber* can be divided into three groups as follows. Eight of them are short, lack the couplet parallelism and are associated with an alleluia for the mass; the remainder all have the couplet structure, but only nine of them have a corresponding alleluia, while sixteen lack this solid foundation. Although this detail confirms the link between the primitive sequence and the alleluia, it is of little help in working out how that link was formed. It has long been universally accepted that its existence can be taken for granted, but some aspects of the process by which it came about remain a mystery.

More mysterious still is the problem of melody, since there are no musical intonations in the *Liber Hymnorum*, which either confines itself to mentioning an alleluia with its versicle or refers to a melody, presumably of popular origin, which was familiar to the compiler and his ninth-century readers (*Occidentana*, *Graeca*, *Puella turbata*, *Cignea*, etc.) but which has proved very difficult for scholars to identify. Only painstaking researches, recently concluded, have enabled us to identify the most likely melodies for Notker's sequences in western Frankish (especially Aquitanian) sources dating from about 1000.[4] The methods used here have made it possible to distinguish, among the many settings preserved in the sources, a group of melodies which were already known between 880 and 900. Each of them still appears to have such a markedly individual character that the received view, of a genre absolutely uniform even in its early stages, can safely be rejected. Two general observations will suffice: individual lines alternate, apparently at random, with coupled lines, and the syllabic structure of the verses (as distinct from the number of verses itself) can be strikingly different in each line. This does not mean that no common characteristics appear. Most notable of all is the prevalence of the paired-line structure; but this needs to be seen as normal practice rather than as an absolute rule, since – as we have seen – single lines are far from uncommon. It would seem from this that the pattern of paired lines was the result of an aesthetic choice, not a rigid requirement deriving from unknown and pre-ordained motives. This pattern will be better understood if it is recalled that the principle of paired lines is basic to the construction of other lyrical and musical genres in the Middle Ages, such as the *lai*, the *estampie*, the *conductus*, the *cantio* and so on.

An example of Notker's work is reproduced below, in the form of strophes selected from his well-known sequence for Pentecost, *a* and *b* indicating the two sections of the strophic couplet. In other editions the text is subdivided into *quasi-versus*, but the selection made here seems more suitable for demonstrating the nature of the *prosa*.[5]

1. Sancti spiritus assit nobis gratia,
2a. quae corda nostra tibi faciat habitaculum,
  b. expulsis inde cunctis vitiis spiritalibus.
3a. Spiritus alme, illustrator hominum,
  b. horridas nostrae mentis purga tenebras.
4a. Amator sancte sensatorum semper cogitatuum,
  b. infunde unctionem tuam, clemens nostris sensibus.
5a. Tu purificator omnium flagitiorum, spiritus,
  b. purifica nostri oculum interioris hominis,
6a. ut videri supremus genitor possit a nobis,
  b. mundi cordis quem soli cernere possunt oculi.
  . . .
13. Hunc diem gloriosum fecisti.

[The grace of the Holy Spirit be with us (2a) and prepare in our hearts a dwelling-place for you (b) having driven thence all the vices of the soul. (3a) Gracious Spirit, light of men, (b) purify the horrible darkness of our minds. (4a) Holy one, you ever love thoughts of wisdom; (b) pour, in your mercy, your unction on our senses. (5a) You, O Spirit, who cleanse all sin, (b) cleanse the eye of our mind, (6a) so that by us the almighty Father may be contemplated, (b) he whom only the eyes of a pure heart may behold . . . (13) You have made this day glorious.]

Various hypotheses have been put forward to explain the use of paired lines, but it is difficult to accept any of them, either because they are based solely on rhetorical practice (the *bicola*, or repeated segments of rhythmic prose, invoked by some critics, take no account of the musical aspect) or because they are derived from exclusively musical precedent.[6] It is true that, according to this second hypothesis, the discovery of repetitive structures in the melismas of the alleluiatic *jubilus*, in melodies used for the litany and even in Byzantine and Syriac material has considerable significance; but the examples shown in these cases are purely melodic, and have not yet acquired any text. Nor are the sections of which they are made up of equal size within each pair. Other conjectures have involved psalmody, where lines are divided into two hemistichs; parallelism in Hebrew poetry; antiphonal singing of psalms; and the singing of hymns shared between two semi-choruses. None of these, however, offers a definitive solution. What seems to be needed is a more realistic approach to the research, which could be reduced to the following question: what consequences, from a literary and musical standpoint (since the two aspects are inseparable), followed upon the choice of paired-line structure? The first result was to double the length of the composition; however obvious this may seem, it becomes significant in the light of the fact that the sequence is the widest ranging of all the musical forms created for the liturgy in the Frankish period, to the point where it rivals the gradual and the tract, its neighbours in the liturgical structure. This aspiration to vastness of scope seems to be inherent in the sequence as a genre and is realised there in a more sophisticated way than in hymns, where all that happens is the simple repetition of a single melodic pattern which can only be prolonged in accordance with the number of lines. The sequence thus anticipates the procedure of later musical forms in which the function of the *da capo* is evident, repeating melodic material which has already been heard and opening the way to the exposition of new ideas. Repetition is thus a consciously aesthetic device, which permits a progressive articulation of musical thought, by fixing its different stages in the memory and preparing the way for later developments. Even today the immediacy with which the melodic pattern of a repeated sequential line may be conceived and determined remains surprising, even in comparison with other repetitive structures to be found in the liturgical repertory (such as the scheme of responses). The phrasing remains as if sculpted, its architecture and connections laid perfectly bare; in a word, a new art is born with the sequence, an art which was able to exploit the relations of words and music in a wholly fresh way, as if in reaction to the growing melismatic excesses of liturgical pieces which had entered the repertory, and as a vigorous attempt to restrain a tendency to undue subjectivity of expression.

Repetition as a musical principle was powerful enough to involve textual elements as well, and to drag them towards a kind of uniformity. Gradually a kind of reflection, as if in a mirror, took place within the coupled lines, so that their length, accent, final syllables (assonances) and even the broad sense of their ideas became identical. Although the repetition was at first only musical, not verbal, the couplet and not the single line instinctively came to be considered the basic unit of composition.

The use of single lines at the beginning and end of each sequence remained an almost constant element. In the early stages, the initial line was usually very short, consisting sometimes of only one or two words, closely connected by their meaning to the first pair of lines. In striking and deliberate contrast, however, it is precisely at this point that the melody changes, moving from a broadly neumatic opening statement to a rigorous syllabism. As for single lines occurring in the body of the ancient sequence, they sometimes appear as subordinate interpolations, complementary to the preceding pair of lines, but they can also be freely chosen by the composer and used to create an effect of variety. Between the tenth and twelfth centuries these apparent irregularities gradually became standardised, and the sources, especially those from Aquitaine, document the progressive stages by which this normalisation came about.

Analysis of the syllabic consistency of the lines in any given sequence usually reveals a fairly constant increase in the number of syllables, leading to a peak from which their number then begins to decline until the end of the piece. An increase in the length of the lines is usually accompanied by a broadening of the melodic pattern, which precisely at this point moves upwards, often leaving the confines of the original mode, though it will eventually return to the register in which it began. This is, then, a climax on two fronts: that of verbal expression and that of the upward tendency of the melody. A similar parabola, at least as far as the music is concerned, was not unknown in the liturgical pieces of the preceding age; but the sequence, unlike short intonations for hymns, gives the parabola enough room to sketch its unmistakable outline. Given the evident workings of this process and the linear clarity of the melodic movement, which is always the product of a deliberate choice and positioning of its constituent elements, it is difficult to accept that there may have been an early stage in the history of the sequence when it relied on improvisatory techniques. Apart from anything else, the variants for individual melodies preserved in the ancient sources all stem from the routine of graphical practice. Improvisation would have left very different traces.

The question as to whether the sequence should be considered a 'liturgical' piece on the same basis as the other chants of the mass has no more than a purely academic importance today. There can be no doubt that no such question arose in the minds of the Frankish composers, who had witnessed the encounter between Roman and Gallican traditions. They felt themselves to be the creators and propagators of a new liturgy which gave equal status to the old repertory and to the sequences and tropes which it included.

Now that the basic features of the new form have been outlined, it only remains to recount its history in brief. Attempts to venture beyond the ninth century in the hope of finding possible models which lack the paired-line pattern have not so far produced any reliable results. Strange as it may seem, the genre emerges as if from nowhere in the ninth century, possessing almost all the characteristics so far described. It is easier to follow the evolution of the genre in stages as, under the impulse of novelty and its undeniable response to the artistic ideals of the eleventh, twelfth and thirteenth centuries, it rapidly became widespread throughout Europe. Among the early centres, the monasteries of St Gall and St Martial, in the Limousin region of France, stand out, but the flowering of the sequence was soon clearly visible in Italy, Spain and England. From St Gall it passed into Germany and to some monasteries in northern Italy. The schools are distinguished by their different ways of setting out music and text. In the earlier, that of France, the texts are written under the notes, which are shown split up into their individual neumatic elements; while in the area of St Gall's influence the melody is written alongside the text and keeps the usual groupings of neumes. So copious was the production of sequences that it is impossible here to mention the hundreds of sources (sequentiaries or prosers) which have survived, or the dozens of more or less famous versifiers who contributed to the success of the genre. The liturgical calendar provided a pretext for the composition of innumerable texts, for use not only on the main feast-days, but also on those of obscure saints with local connections or belonging to a particular religious order. This information can be of the utmost importance in determining the geographical origin and the dating of sources.

From a formal point of view, as has been mentioned, the tendency to regularity of construction in the couplet and the standardisation of the *copula* became more marked, and this was to give birth to the *cobla* of the troubadours. The technique of versification was perfected by concentrating decisively on the constructive weight of tonic accents, to which the ancient sequence had been indifferent. (The old name *prosa* should not be overlooked; at this time the lines were called *quasi-versus*.) Rhyme became more frequent and varied, in contrast to archaic practice, which had almost exclusively used assonance in -*a*, a remnant of the last vowel of *alleluia*. Popular melodies were more often used, either wholly or in part, in the composition of the required music.

The sequence reached the peak of its development in the polished and composed perfection associated with the name of Adam of St Victor (1110–92), a monk in the celebrated Augustinian monastery at Paris and author of about fifty such works. The following stanzas are from his sequence *De Maria Virgine*[7] (*a* and *b* indicate strophic coupling):

> 1*a*. Salve, mater salvatoris,
> vas electum, vas honoris,
> vas coelestis gratiae;
>
> *b*. ab aeterno vas provisum,
> vas insigne, vas excisum
> manu sapientiae.

Sequences

2a. Salve, verbi sacra parens,
flos de spina, spina carens
flos, spineti gloria;

b. nos spinetum, nos peccati
spina sumus cruentati,
sed tu spinae nescia.

...

10a. In procinctu constituti
te tuente simus tuti;
pervicacis et versuti
tuae cedat vis virtuti,
dolus providentiae.

b. Iesu, verbum summi patris,
serva servos tuae matris,
solve reos, salva gratis
et nos tuae claritatis
configura gloriae.

[(1a) Hail, mother of the Saviour, chosen vessel, honoured vessel, vessel of heavenly grace; (b) vessel ordained from eternity, exalted vessel, vessel formed by the hand of wisdom. (2a) Hail, holy mother of the Word, flower from thorn, flower without thorn, glory of the thornbush; (b) we are the thornbush, we are bloodied by the thorn of sin, but you know no thorn ... (10a) We are in danger, but if you help us we are safe; may the violence of the stubborn, clever enemy yield to your virtue, deceit to wisdom. (b) Jesus, Word of the almighty Father, save your mother's servants, free the guilty, save them with the free gift of your grace and make us worthy of the glory of your splendour.]

Made harmonious by isometric scansion of accents and the countless echoes of internal rhyme, and set out in a broad melodic pattern highly suitable for singing, the Victorine sequence inevitably became the model for the poets and musicians of later centuries. Even composers working in the Dominican and Franciscan traditions of the thirteenth century referred to it, although their works aimed at being more readily comprehensible as texts and more easily learned as pieces of music.

After the Council of Trent Pius V kept just four texts, out of this vast array, for specific liturgical occasions in the missal: *Victimae paschali laudes* (tenth century, possibly by Wipo) for Easter; *Veni Sancte Spiritus* (eleventh century) for Pentecost; *Lauda Sion Salvatorem* (late thirteenth century, Dominican) for Corpus Domini; and *Dies irae* (perhaps by Thomas of Celano) for All Souls. In 1727 Benedict XIII re-introduced the *Stabat mater dolorosa*, attributed to Jacopone da Todi. This drastic restriction on the liturgical use of the sequence cannot be a definitive judgement on its role in musical history. By breaking out of its modal range it speeded up the movement towards modern major/minor tonality; by treating themes especially dear to the mass of the people (it covered many different subjects: lives of saints, miracles, historical events, etc.) it helped to make the liturgical texts more comprehensible and more deeply felt. It restored to the faithful, whom the *schola* had managed to exclude almost entirely, the possibility of at least a partial involvement in the performance of liturgical chant.

23 Tropes

One of the many meanings of the Greek word *tropos* is 'melismatic fragment used to embellish a melody'. Such fragments appeared in the *melodiae* of the Ambrosian and Mozarabic rites, as well as in the Byzantine liturgical repertory. In a process exactly similar to that which gave birth to the sequence, someone had the idea of adding a text to the melismatic parts of liturgical chants. According to tradition, the credit for this invention should go to Tutilo, a monk of the monastery of St Gall who died in 915, but it is all too easy to conclude that this legend is based on Notker's account of the birth of the sequence, and it shows every sign of being historically inaccurate. None the less, the fact remains that from the ninth and tenth centuries onwards the trope became a major new liturgical phenomenon, reaching a peak of importance in the eleventh century and declining gradually until the thirteenth. Although at first texts were added to existing melodies which lacked them, it was not long before new music was being composed for new texts. Eventually nearly all musical forms of the liturgy were introduced, interrupted or commented on by these original compositions. The chants which most often underwent alteration were those of the mass, both of the Proper and the Ordinary, apart from the gradual and – for obvious reasons based on doctrinal caution – the *Credo*. Among the chants of the office, however, only the responsories – the only ornate melodies which appear there – were subjected to expansion by means of tropes.

To understand the nature of this phenomenon it should be remembered that, although the texts of the liturgy had now taken a fixed form which resisted interference, no one had ever forbidden the addition to them of introductions or other extraneous material. It was this practice which gave the greatest scope to the creative impulses of monks and clerics alike. The result was the formation of new liturgical books, the tropers, in which the new compositions were for the most part arranged in the liturgical order used in graduals and antiphoners. Many tropes, however, found their way into the traditional books; so frequently did this happen that it is rare to find examples of such books which have remained completely unaffected. The first wave of tropes became a flood, and came close to overwhelming the official liturgical texts in its luxuriant abundance.

It is not easy to arrive at a single definition which includes all the forms of trope, so disparate are they in appearance and function. For Guillaume Durand (c. 1230–96), liturgist and Bishop of Mende, a trope was simply a kind of versicle, sung on the most important feasts as a prelude and, later, a continuation of the introit.[1] Modern scholars have found this definition too rigid and reductive, and have approached the problem on a more general level. For example, the research group formed at Stockholm to edit the *Corpus Troporum* defined tropes as 'chants (text and melody) which form an introduction, an insertion or an addition, either in a liturgical chant of the Roman mass, or in a chant of the office'.[2] As will be apparent, the definition takes no account of musical technique and excludes both textless tropes and added melismas.

Several attempts at descriptive classification of tropes have been made. That of Jacques Chailley has the advantages of comprehensiveness and reference to the genetic background of the tropes themselves[3] (though not certain, this is at least a genuinely arguable proposition). Further, he does not lose sight of the chronological order of their appearance. The basic pattern is this:

(1) 'adaptation' tropes: this is supposed to be the original form of the trope. A text is adapted to an existing liturgical melody without the latter being altered in any way. This, however, encouraged a fresh development in musical taste; the melismas scattered through many passages of Gregorian melody left room for a stricter (and weightier) syllabic style, similar to that characteristic of hymns and antiphons.

(2) 'development' tropes: not content with adapting words to an existing melodic nucleus, authors took it upon themselves to expand it. The original form thus offered a basic scheme which could be referred to periodically without there being any need to follow it slavishly. This was the original form of the *prosa* or sequence.

(3) 'interpolation' tropes: the basic liturgical text was prolonged by adding commentaries or intercalated sections, thereby creating an entirely new melody. Understandably, the inserted passages were harmonised textually and melodically with the original text, but this

does not mean that they should be considered a 'parasite' form. Some of them took on an independent life of their own, such as the eucharistic chant *Ave verum*, which began as a trope on the *Sanctus*. (4) 'framing' tropes: these marked the transition from interpolation to the forms of prelude and postlude, and required the addition to have a more complete textual and musical meaning. From such additions arose real introductions to the liturgical text, in which the invitation to sing it and to feel it as a living experience becomes more urgent. The effort to actualise the mystery being celebrated becomes more marked, thanks to adverbs such as *hic, nunc, hodie*, etc.[4] The 'liturgical drama' derives to a large extent from one of these prelude-tropes, the famous *Quem quaeritis*, sung before the introit at Easter.

(5) 'completion' tropes: the development of 'framing' tropes ended by their losing all contact with the pieces which they introduced or concluded, and they thus became independent lyrical pieces inserted between two 'official' sections in the unfolding of the liturgy. The result was the birth of the 'conduction' chant (Latin *conductus*), which was to be extensively developed in the polyphonic structures of the thirteenth century. For a long time, however, it remained monodic and was called *versus*, especially in the area around the monastery of St Martial at Limoges. At first *versus* meant 'versicle', but a later shift of meaning led to its denoting a piece in verse. In the eleventh century the autonomy of the *versus* was so complete that it was able to take on an all-purpose role, suitable for a variety of liturgical occasions, and sometimes to acquire passages in the vernacular. It is also significant that at about the same time, and in the same region, the song of the troubadours made its appearance: compositions in this style were at first, and not by chance, called *vers*.

(6) 'substitution' tropes: these form the final phase in the evolution of the genre. It came about when the authors of tropes ceased to restrict themselves to commenting on and embellishing the 'official' liturgical text, and went so far as to replace it altogether, contenting themselves with recalling certain phrases in the course of the composition. Such, for example, were the *versus* which absorbed the liturgical invitation *Benedicamus Domino* with its response *Deo gratias*, and became lengthy compositions with a number of strophes in which the words of invitation were completely smothered and concealed. They were performed as a solemn close (soon also *cum organo*, in two parts) to Lauds or Vespers.

This attempt at classification appears schematic and inflexible when compared with the wealth of evidence available in the sources, partly because it is far from certain that the course of the genre's evolution everywhere followed the lines laid down by Chailley. However, apart from the defences mentioned above, his analysis has the merit of explaining the movement from the trope to some later musical genres. This only underlines its importance as an independent phenomenon, with a right to be judged for what it is.

Tropes were for too long considered to be of secondary importance, a kind of malignant growth on the healthy body of 'official' chant, and therefore of inferior quality as art. This view was certainly encouraged by liturgical theory, which saw tropes as the belated explosion of an unnecessary and often reprehensible yearning for novelty. If such prejudices can be banished, though, it must be admitted that tropes were the most meaningful response made by the musical and liturgical genius of new peoples in a new era. It should be added that, quite apart from their value in history as a transitional phase on the way towards new musical forms, the theological content of tropes remains a buried treasure. For example, the impulse mentioned above, to actualise the liturgical mystery in the *hic et nunc*, may reveal a desire for a more immediate participation in the reality of the celebration, at a time when, for various reasons, the active involvement of the congregation in the liturgical event was becoming less and less important. Consider one of the shortest tropes for the introit at the third mass of Christmas (only the text is printed here; liturgical material is in italics, and phrases not given in full in the source are completed in brackets):[5]

> Predictus a prophetis,
> nunciatus ab angelis, eia hodie
>   *Puer (natus est nobis)*
> Quem virgo Maria genuit,
>   *Et filius (datus est nobis)*
> Nomen eius Emmanuel vocabitur,
>   *Cuius (imperium super humerum eius; et vocabitur)*
> Fabricator mundi, princeps pacis,
>   *Magni consilii angelus*
> [Repeat]
> Omnium votis sanctorum expectatus hac die
>   *Puer . . .*

In this case the added passages do not obey metrical rules, and they are in no way autonomous with regard to the existing text; but the urgent desire to actualise the celebration (*hodie, hac die*) will be evident.

Compare, on the other hand, this trope for the introit to the mass of St Vincent, martyr:[6]

> Cum venerit Verbum summi Patris arbiter orbis
> ut referat cunctis cunctorum gesta bonorum,

Laetabitur justus in domino:
Tunc athleta potens Vincentius alta tonabit
voce loquens cunctis: noster rex ecce coruscat;
et sperabit in eo.
Cunctorum, Christe, sanctorum crimina solve,
ut verum possint te mundi cernere lumen.
et laudabuntur omnes recti corde.

As will be clear, three pairs of hexameters introduce and are inserted into the basic text. It is obvious that words and music alike were composed afresh for the additional material, as indeed was the case with the previous example. We have thus come a long way from the notion of the trope as the straightforward addition of a text to an existing melisma. Here neither music nor text comes from the antiphon itself, but both are added to it from outside; indeed, the hexameters make perfectly good sense on their own. Moreover, although from a melodic point of view no common element can be found in the music of individual phrases, there is no doubt that the section in verse, being the most carefully organised passage, stands out to an extent above the rest. It must therefore be concluded that, at least in some cases, tropes not only do not depend on the antiphon either stylistically or structurally, but (so to speak) leave it behind, seeking and finding a new textual and musical unity on their own account. This forces us to reconsider the customary approach to judging tropes solely as parasitical superstructures erected on the liturgical text, and perhaps allows us to rehabilitate the ancient definition of Bishop Durand. Given that there exists a clear distinction between official (Gregorian) chant and additional material (tropes), especially in the introit or in the parallel antiphons of the Roman mass, the offertory and the communion, the additional material tends to take on the appearance of an autonomous entity, thereby permitting a less fluid and all-embracing definition of the trope.

On the other hand, if the sphere of the trope is to be so severely restricted, space must be made for the related phenomena which certainly exist and demand appropriate definition and classification. The ancient sources themselves, moreover, testify to the shifting ambiguity of the notion and limits of the trope, with their widely varying terminology; though the most common term is *tropus* (*tropi*, *trophi*, etc.), it has been noted that this is most often applied to additions to the Proper of the mass. In other cases other names appear: *laudes* (mostly given to additions to the *Gloria*), *verba*, *carmina, preces*, and so on. In several manuscripts there is no special name for tropes at all, and this confirms the suspicion that the composers or singers of such texts thought of them as an integral part of the liturgical repertory rather than a subordinate one.

The technique which comes closer than any other to that of the trope as traditionally understood is that of the *prosula*, which is conceivable only in terms of its relation to a pre-existing text, which it breaks up by finding its way into the very constituent elements of the basic text so as to form new verbal units. An example taken from the extensive repertory of prosulas for the alleluia and its versicles will be more effective than any description in making its nature clear.[7] (The same technique, however, also appears in the last verse of some offertories.) The basic text – *Dicite in gentibus quia Dominus regnavit a ligno* – re-appears in the prosula as follows:

Dicite chori cuncti et psalli*te in gentibus*, plaudite mani*bus quia* magna *Domin*i clementia suis respiciens ovi*bus regna*t omnia supera et imper*avit a ligno*.

Note how the original text and the added material are so closely interwoven that the final letters of a word are taken up and used again in a new context to echo the continuity of the original phrase. It is clear in this case that the textual additions are governed by the presence of an ornate melody; the new text is used to fill, syllabically, the melismatic gaps. For this reason, the Swedish school defines the prosula, using a crude but functional neologism, as a 'melogene' trope, arising from an existing melody.[8] ('Logogene' is the term applied to a trope formed from a text which existed before its melody.)

The tropes for the Ordinary of the mass are in a category of their own. For while the texts for the *Gloria* and the *Sanctus* may have reached their definitive form by the Carolingian era, the same cannot be said for their melodies, at least for those which have survived in the collections made in liturgical books. These settings date back no further than the ninth and tenth centuries. What characteristics, then, distinguish them from the tropes which were flourishing at the same time? The problem of the *Kyrie* and the *Agnus Dei* is even more delicate, since their position in liturgical practice was, as we know, assured only much later. Perhaps it is not far from the truth to maintain – as some do, relying on the evidence of sources – that these parts of the Ordinary were accompanied by tropes right from the beginning. A reasonably eloquent confirmation of this suggestion, at least in the case of the *Kyrie*, comes from the *Cunctipotens genitor Deus*,[9] one of the most famous of the tropes quoted in official liturgical books. It is written in hexameters. Is it conceivable that a metrical text would be chosen for the syllabic intonation of an existing melody? It seems more likely that this and other so-called tropes for the *Kyrie* are all independent and unitary artistic creations, which ought to be attributed in their entirety to the composers of the Carolingian epoch.

Pius V made no allowance at all for this, and banished every remaining trace of the trope from the Missal and Breviary which he approved after the Council of Trent.

24 Metrical and dramatic offices

Almost nothing survives in post-Tridentine liturgical books of a striking episode which involved the output of musical texts for the offices of saints and their feast-days from the second half of the ninth century onwards: the appearance and development of metrical offices. The Carolingian and post-Carolingian periods were also distinguished by the creative fervour poured into new liturgical formulas, which were used to deal with the increasing number of feasts observed only in local churches or individual religious orders. In general the methods used were those hallowed by tradition: texts were drawn from the Bible (often by way of earlier offices), while melodies were derived by imitating earlier models or adapting and re-arranging old material. However, there were those who set out along new paths, and once again the birthplace of this innovation seems to have been France, especially the north-east of the country. The essence of its novelty lies in the introduction of a narrative element into the antiphons and responsories of the office, in place of the existing lyrical and contemplative elements. From a formal point of view, the custom of providing texts in verse, specifically in hexameters, rather than in prose, became increasingly widespread. The predominance of this narrative aspect explains the name *historiae* which was given to works of this kind. Antiphons and responses, if read in their proper order, constitute a genuine Biblical or biographical *historia*. More detailed research has revealed that the liturgical texts turned into verse are often quotations from ancient *passiones* or from hagiographical sources (*vitae*, etc.).[1]

At first sight the appearance of versified offices may seem no more than a straightforward variant on the familiar process of compiling liturgical formulas, perhaps inspired by the literary pretensions of the versifier. In fact the difference is much more profound than that, as becomes clear when it is recalled that, originally, antiphons were taken from the psalm with which they were linked and that, therefore, it was possible for there to be no logical connection between one antiphon and another. Often, indeed, there was no such connection. The same was true of responsories, whose orderly succession could be changed without any consequent damage to the progress of the office. A more unitary conception, however, is the basis of the versified office, whose constituent parts (antiphons and responsories) obey a logical order imposed by the progression of events in the *historia* itself. The modern reader of a typical metrical office, such as those of St Anthony and St Francis, both composed by the Franciscan Julian of Speyer, has the impression of a complete poetic cycle on a hagiographical theme.[2] These examples are without doubt among the highest points reached by the genre; the first experiments did not reach such a degree of perfection, nor can they be admired for their wealth of rhyme and assonance, the regularity of their accent or the melodious quality of a verse worthy to stand on an equal footing with the most polished hymns and sequences of the same period. The versified offices of the ninth and tenth centuries are for the most part anonymous or of doubtful authorship. In more than one case their dating and geographical origin are uncertain. They sometimes employ fragments of hymns, a fact which, in the early stages, may have provided the necessary encouragement to extend and complete their versified form. The choice of the hexameter can certainly be seen as a product of the classicising ambience which had grown up in cultural circles in the Carolingian period. The office of the Trinity possibly composed by Stephen of Liège stands out among the most significant early examples of the genre.[3] Because of its almost universal diffusion it is used as a touchstone for the morphological definition of the office as a genre. Others in this category include the offices for Sts Medard, Fuscian and companions, Lambert (also by Stephen), and others.[4]

From a musical point of view it is difficult to say whether the authors of the verse were also the composers of the music. Probably some were and some were not. One detail of which we can be certain is the diffusion of some melodic patterns, which re-appear, often in distant parts of Europe, with different texts. This is a clear sign of a loosening of the relationship between words and music. During the early history of the metrical office the progressive method of choosing the modality of the piece also appeared: the first antiphon was in the first mode, the second in the second, and so on. Though this is an indication of the systematic approach of the mediaeval mentality, it may perhaps also be a device for committing pieces to memory.

The themes of metrical offices have their roots in the structure and evolution of the liturgy itself, implicit in which, by its very nature, is a tendency to unfold before the eyes and mind of the faithful as a remembrance and representation of historical events. The dramatic element, made up of story and gesture, cannot be separated from the evocation of the facts of Christ's life, as they are celebrated in the feasts of the liturgical year. The mass itself, which invites us to relive an actualised commemoration of Christ's sacrifice, is a genuine drama. The only difference is that the liturgy has adopted an express-ive code of its own, essentially symbolic in nature, which clearly sets it apart – at least in theory – from theatrical language based on a mimetic or imitative principle. From the beginning, however, there were aspects of the heritage of Christian ritual which embodied denser elements of dramatisation, only to emerge later on, when historical circumstance or cultural movement demanded them and enabled them to come to maturity. The most obvious example of the dramatic potential inherent in Christian worship is provided by the Palestinian liturgical celebrations in which – according to the account of Etheria or Egeria's travels, dating from the end of the fourth century[5] – the rites of Holy Week were celebrated at the very places, and the very times, at which the events of the passion, death and resurrection of Christ had taken place. This was not yet a theatrical 'production' of the events it re-created, but the long processions led by the bishop, and the involvement of the often tearful spectators, who heard these tragic or joyful events described *in situ*, took on the appearance of a dramatic spectacle in which everyone was at once protagonist and spectator.

The Palestinian experience was not without its echoes in the West, especially in Rome, where a vast replica of Jerusalem was built at the beginning of the fifth century. From then on began the process which was to fix in time the various phases of the celebration of the 'three holy days' (*triduum sacrum*) from Maundy Thursday to Easter Sunday: the commemoration of the institution of the eucharist, and of the passion, death and resurrection of Christ.

Between the seventh and tenth centuries the tendency to dramatise took an ever tighter hold on ritual practice, at a variety of levels. Sometimes it was the rite itself which was 'externalised' and took on a visibly concrete character: for example, the rite of the consecration of priests and, above all, of bishops was transformed into a long and complex ceremony in which each effect of the sacrament was rendered visible (anointing with chrism, presentation of the ring and staff, enthronement, and so on). Greater importance was also given to processions, and they unwound in curious ceremonial articulations, such as the procession on Palm Sunday, led by the celebrant astride an ass, like Christ on his entry into Jerusalem. Study of the texts reveals, for instance, that the so-called *Improperia* for Good Friday, with their forcibly expressive dialogue structure (*Popule meus, quid feci tibi* . . .) spontaneously recall the characters who speak the words, and are governed by an obvious dramatic logic. Even the narration of the passion, made compulsory on certain days in Holy Week, soon took on a dramatic form through the different recitation-notes used to set the words spoken by Christ and the other characters. The dramatic effect was heightened when three deacons performed the narration. Later, imitations of the actions of Christ became more common even at the level of gesture; this was the origin of the rite of the washing of feet on Holy Thursday. Many more examples could easily be given to confirm that a sense of the concrete was re-awakening in the Carolingian period. Christian piety itself was centring on Christ 'in the flesh' (*secundum carnem*) – on Christ's humanity. It was in this context that two processions appeared which, though remaining within the ambit of liturgical symbolism, sometimes aspired to make the 'representative' principle their own: they are the processions for the burial of Christ in the form of a crucifix or of a consecrated wafer (*depositio crucis vel hostiae*) on Good Friday, and the subsequent *elevatio* on Easter morning. In these processions the imitative principle did not yet come into play; the 'actors' were still celebrants, and the texts which were sung were taken from the repertory of antiphons and responsories for the office. Furthermore, the rite took place without passages in dialogue being spoken, and the celebrants wore liturgical vestments, without the accessories or costumes which would make them seem to be actors instead of participants.

The custom of embellishing the office in this way spread from the Easter cycle to other feasts in the calendar. The celebrations of the Christmas cycle, the Annunciation, the Ascension, and others, all saw the course of their events brought to life, with parts assigned to various participants in the liturgical action: the *pueri* or *scholares* in the roles of Mary or the angels, the monks or canons playing apostles, shepherds, and so on. This stage has rightly been called that of the 'dramatised liturgy' or 'dramatic offices', though this term was coined in the nineteenth century, whereas the ancients only knew the term *officium* (*officium sepulchri, stellae*, etc.). Along with the many sources which have preserved the traditional repertory of individual churches, the books of rubrics which regulated the performance of these *officia* have also survived: they were called ordinals or consuetudinaries, *Agenda*, and so on, and may be called the first performance-scripts in the modern sense.

A final adornment to the structure of liturgical dramatisation was achieved with the development of the first elements of dialogue. As we have seen, this is connected with the trope *Quem quaeritis in sepulchro, o Christicolae? – Jesum Nazarenum crucifixum, o caelicolae*, the question put by the angel to the Marys who came to Jesus' tomb and their reply, according to the Gospel account. This is not the place to stress the importance of this brief exchange placed as a preface to the introit of the mass of Easter, which has been adjudged the starting-point of modern drama by a host of scholars, who have dedicated a large number of weighty studies to its appearance and development.[6] What concerns us is to record that as far back as the earliest manuscript (a codex from St Martial at Limoges, now in Paris, B.N. lat. 1240, dating from about 920) the dialogue between the angel and the Marys is accompanied by music. The dialogue was always supported by music, even when it forsook the skeletal form of the trope and was transformed into the *Visitatio sepulchri* and the more complex *Ludi paschales*. Modern theatre was thus born as musical theatre. But when did it leave the liturgical context to become theatre proper? The demarcation, when it came about, was neither unexpected, unanimous nor universally accepted. The progressive adoption of the imitative principle, the expansion of thematic treatment to include scenes other than those taken from the Bible, the transformation of the liturgical 'agent' into an actor playing a specific role, the deepening psychological content of the characters, the scenic apparatus used for background, the costumes suitable for the actors' roles, all combined to bring about the movement towards liturgical drama which, let us repeat, was musical drama.

25 Liturgical drama

The oldest surviving copy of the music of *Quem quaeritis* which is known to have formed part of a coherent and self-sufficient drama to be performed at Easter Matins is in one of the famous Winchester Tropers (Bodleian Library, Oxford, Bodl. 775). This text has a complementary collection of performing instructions in the almost contemporary *Regularis Concordia*, a *Liber consuetudinarius* compiled out of Continental monastic traditions for the use of English Benedictines by Ethelwold, Bishop of Winchester, in about 980.[1] The music of the Winchester Troper is very similar to that of sources originating from Limoges, which suggests that the birth of this kind of drama took place on the Continent. It consists of a single scene centred on the dialogue between the angels and the devout women. The initial exchanges of the trope *Quem quaeritis* are followed by antiphons chosen from the official Easter repertory, which extended the dialogue with the angel's invitation to inspect the empty tomb (*Venite et videte* . . .) and to carry the news to the disciples (*Cito euntes* . . .). The antiphon *Surrexit Dominus de sepulchro*, sung by the Marys, is a joyous proclamation of the resurrection, and the singing of the *Te Deum laudamus* ends the short performance. Its chief features are extreme simplicity of technique, a selection of texts and chants already familiar from the office, and an atmosphere which is still semi-liturgical (the *Te Deum* is the hymn sung at the end of Matins, and is present in most liturgical dramas). In this single-scene form the paschal drama, or *Visitatio sepulchri*,[2] as it was called at the time, enjoyed enormous popularity throughout Europe, as is clear from the large number of sources which contain it, in a substantially compact musical form easily explained by its connections with the chants of the official repertory.

The suggestive richness of the Gospel narrative and the imagination of the *clerici* themselves inspired many additions to this basic nucleus of the drama. Taking the additional scenes into account, it is generally accepted that there is a second phase in the development of the genre, characterised by the details of Peter and John running to the tomb (evoked by the antiphon *Currebant duo simul*) and their dialogue with the Marys, taken from the central section of the sequence *Victimae paschali*. Then there is a third phase, marked by the appearance of the risen Christ to Mary Magdalene.[3] But other scenes can also be included: one such is that of the *unguentarius* or perfume-seller, who at first remains silent but in later versions acquires a lively, realistic and even comical character. In the latest examples, from the thirteenth and fourteenth centuries, the order of the scenes is more complex and the number of characters increases. The texts, often in verse, are no longer taken from the Bible or the liturgy, and as a result the melodies are also freshly composed, so that they differ to an extent from source to source or region to region. An outstanding example of this is the fourteenth-century Cividale version (Museo Archeologico Nazionale, MS ci), whose text displays a highly original reworking of traditional material, and whose music, unknown in any other source, achieves an undeniable intensity of effect. The longest example is preserved in a thirteenth-century manuscript at Tours (Bibliothèque de la Ville, MS 927), but it is a weary and incoherent compilation.[4] In contrast, a perfect balance is achieved by the Easter drama which appears in the celebrated MS 201 in the Bibliothèque Municipale at Orléans,[5] written in the thirteenth century at the monastery of Saint Benoît-sur-Loire near Fleury. It contains ten musical dramas arranged in the order of the liturgical calendar.

Little attention seems to have been paid by those involved in mediaeval drama to the theme of the passion, in comparison with the ubiquitous treatments of Easter. It is easy to understand, however, that the mass should have been thought a sufficient celebration of Christ's sacrifice; and from another point of view, there was a widespread preference for seeing the drama of the son reflected in the mother. The result was the appearance of a huge number of *planctus Mariae*[6] which convey Mary's involvement in the sufferings of Christ in a lyric or dramatic form (the other character is nearly always the disciple John). The performance of these *planctus* was the culmination of the ritual veneration of the cross on Good Friday. The dramatic example of the *planctus* preserved in the Cividale manuscript, mentioned above, is justly famous for the wealth of its rubrical directions and the expressive vigour of its musical settings. Apart from the precious twelfth-century text discovered by Inguanez at Montecassino,[7] two dramatic versions of the passion have survived in the codex of the so-called *Carmina Burana* (thirteenth century), but their music, which is not of liturgical origin, cannot be deciphered, as the neumes are written *in campo aperto*.[8]

The *Peregrinus*,[9] a drama depicting the encounter of the two disciples with Christ on the road to Emmaus, is also linked to the Easter cycle; it may have been performed on Easter Monday. It has survived in various versions, some of which – like that in MS 201 at Orléans – include sections in verse as well as music which does not rely on liturgical models.

A similar process of evolution to that of the Easter drama has been identified in its Christmas counterpart. The starting-point was a trope for the introit of the third Christmas mass (*Quem quaeritis in praesepe, pastores?*), clearly based on that of Easter and found most often in French and Italian sources. The formation of the *Officium pastorum* had already been completed by the twelfth century, but its diffusion was restricted in comparison with that of treatments of the theme of Epiphany, which produced the *Officium stellae* (also called *Officium Regum trium*), of which a dozen or so versions are known.[10] It was Herod, one of the most picturesque characters in mediaeval drama, who gradually became the most striking figure as this dramatic form evolved. Musically, lengthy passages of free composition are common. The scene of the massacre of the innocents is sometimes linked to the presentation of the Magi, but in the Fleury manuscript it has a piece to itself. This drama contains one of the greatest works in the whole body of mediaeval dramatic music, Rachel's lament over her dead children, which alternates with the comments of two *consolatrices*.

Among works inspired by characters or episodes from the Old and New Testaments are the large-scale *Ordo prophetarum*[11] (a dramatisation of a sermon wrongly attributed to Augustine), and the 'Resurrection of Lazarus' and the 'Conversion of St Paul', which both appear in the Fleury manuscript. In this manuscript the series of dramas opens with four scenes portraying the miracles of St Nicholas, among them 'The Son of Getron' and 'The Three Daughters'.[12]

The musical value of these dramas varies widely. Some are comparatively poor in a musical sense, using a single melody (two at the most) for all the strophes and all the characters. In other examples, however, the unknown composers seem to have been notably more skilful. In the *Getronis Filius*, for example, the large number of characters are not only distinguished from one another by their individual attire, but by a *Leitmotiv*, a 'personal' tune. This device, which was to be revived by the composers of nineteenth-century music-dramas, has its foundations laid in this mediaeval form. In fact, the results obtained here cannot be said to be flawless, since the various themes of the *Getronis Filius* are too dissimilar and have no close mutual relationship. But it was important to establish a unifying principle, which could also bear fruit in other subjects. Its success can be seen in the *Sponsus*,[13] the famous drama preserved in MS lat. 1139 at the Bibliothèque Nationale in Paris, which originates from St Martial at Limoges (twelfth or thirteenth century). The course of events is based on the Biblical parable of the wise and foolish virgins. Here the allegorical content lent itself far better to a symmetrical construction than did the legendary material of the *Getronis Filius*.

In the *Sponsus* four melodies are used, shared among four or five actors or groups of actors. This conclusion can best be reached by adding a few sensible corrections and conjectures to the source, in which the play has been preserved in an imperfect state. Only metrics and the rhyme-scheme allows us to establish that the same characters come in at the end to conclude the performance as originally appeared to begin it: they are the *Sponsus* (Christ), singing melody A, and the archangel Gabriel, singing melody B. The latter speaks a French which linguists assign to the Angoumois or Périgord (although other *refrains* are also in French). After Gabriel comes the turn of the *fatuae* (melody C), who are followed by the appearance of the *prudentes* (melody D). These two groups have a further exchange (C + D) before the entry of the *mercatores*, who are also given melody C (those who think that the oil of virtue can be sold are no different from the virgins who squandered it so uselessly!). Finally the *fatuae* sing their lament (still to melody C) and are followed by the severe reproof of the *Sponsus* and the words of the archangel. The resulting musical structure thus appears as follows:[14]

$$A, B + \frac{C, D}{C, D} + \frac{C}{C} + A, B$$

This perfect symmetry is achieved not out of a taste for the coldly schematic, but deliberately, out of the need for unity and clarity. It is no coincidence that some are prepared to place this drama among the great sequences, the *lais*, as one of the most mature products of mediaeval poetry.

Although for different reasons, the *Ludus Danielis*[15] may also aspire to the status of a unique phenomenon in mediaeval dramatic art. It is preserved in a manuscript from the first half of the thirteenth century (Egerton 2615 in the British Museum, London), which contains a collection of chant from Beauvais Cathedral, but the likeliest hypothesis dates its composition to about 1140. Most probably it was performed after Matins on the feast of the Circumcision, 1 January, the same day for which Pierre de Corbeil (d. 1222) composed the *Officium stultorum* (*Officium asini*).[16] The text reveals the scholastic origin of the play, with its regular versification and correct Latin style, but it is unmatched in the breadth of its dimensions, the originality and variety of its music and the forceful characterisation of the *dramatis personae*. The 'libretto' seems to have been the first to require crowd scenes (royal courts, armies, and so on). In contrast with the unifying function fulfilled by the music of the *Sponsus*, the *Ludus Danielis* sees the triumph of variety; nearly fifty melodies are used in it. They come from every part of the tradition of Christian chant; there are paraphrases or imitations of Gregorian chant and of tropes, overlaps with melodies which will be taken up by the trouvères, and, most common of all, a plentiful supply of sequences, which were enjoying their golden age in France at the time. These are not, however, literal quotations, but rather reminiscences, which are assimilated and absorbed into a new synthesis of strophic and musical patterns, ranging from the martial, syllabic *conducti* sung by the choir to shorter and more ornate passages. Only a deeper analysis than any we have room for here could hope to offer a faithful impression of this genuine mediaeval 'opera'.

It would not be right, though, to overlook the considerable difficulties which the *Ludus Danielis* and, to a lesser degree, other liturgical dramas, may hold for the modern reader. The aesthetic pleasure afforded by this material should not obscure the problems and uncertainties which stand in the way of a contemporary theatrical revival or recording. (Fernando Liuzzi's essay *L'espressione musicale nel dramma liturgico*,[17] written in 1929, can still be read with profit, though some parts of it are now outdated.) Here I shall restrict myself to mentioning two fundamental aspects of the problem.

One is the difficulty of rhythmic interpretation.[18] This is the most serious question involved, and concerns all sacred and secular mediaeval monody written in the period when mensural notation was either not used fully or not used at all. At first sight it may even seem downright strange that so long a time should have passed before it became possible to express exact proportional values in script. One answer may be that only regular, simplified and rather unsubtle rhythms can be imprisoned within bar-lines. We already know that the bar is not an adequate response to the subtleties of Gregorian chant. In a sense the same could also be said of many musical portions of the liturgical drama. It is important not to assume rigid and preconceived positions, which run the risk of imposing interpretations quite alien to the melodies under consideration. The mental attitude most likely to obtain the desired results is, perhaps, a kind of sensitive pragmatism. This means examining all the hypotheses that the immensely varied nature of the melodies may suggest, from the oldest, based on liturgical melodies, to the most recent, composed for rhythmic and metrical texts. No possible method of enquiry should be left unused, whether metrical analysis of texts or the visual appearance of the notation, which can sometimes provide clues which help towards an objective solution. In practice, and depending on circumstances and an awareness of the often considerable disparity between the probable date of composition of these dramas and their appearance in the sources, it may be necessary to opt for transcription into notes of equal value (as with *cantus planus*) for passages of Gregorian or pseudo-Gregorian origin, tropes, sequences and hymn-tunes, unless there are obvious contradictory indications in the notation. Transcription into mensural values seems not to be in any way justified in the case of the *Sponsus*, for example. This suggestion, as will be apparent, would correspond to the application of the so-called 'rhythmic modes' (see Gallo's companion volume), a system of proportional notation introduced in the second half of the twelfth century and used until about the end of the thirteenth, especially in polyphony. According to some scholars, it can also be used for the melodies of metrical texts of non-liturgical origin composed in this period (the 'modal period'). This would apply, for instance, to many parts of the *Ludus Danielis*. The suggestion that Orléans MS 201 might be seen as exemplifying a 'transitional modal notation', containing traces of a movement from modal to mensural script, does not seem to have found much favour. A more positive contribution may be found in the view, put forward as an alternative to a 'modal' reading, that the syllable may be identified as the basic unit of rhythm (syllabic isochronism). This interpretation, to which we shall return below, obtains its most successful results in the study of syllabic (or almost syllabic) melodies, setting metrical texts like *conducti*. This is because it better respects the free progression of the melody, which is not trapped within modern metres, and manages not to suppress the constituent elements of the verse (such as accents) to the sole advantage of the music. It should not be forgotten, however, that in discussing this suggestion, and indeed others like it, we have entered the domain of scientific hypotheses, which are indispensable for the advancement of interpretation and can only be judged in the light of the results they obtain. But we do not know, given the complex difficulty of the problem, whether a definitive solution will ever be found.

Another question to which it is difficult to find a satisfactory answer is that of the use of instruments.[19] The silence of the sources makes the existence of differing conclusions legitimate, even though it is clear that instruments were used in the later dramas, which included long passages in the vernacular. But it is probable that musical instruments were also employed with older texts as well, to double voices or provide a prelude or interlude. A passage in the *Ludus Danielis* refers explicitly to several instruments, and it would appear unnatural if it were not taken to imply accompaniment by the relevant sound:

> Simul omnes gratulemur,
> resonent et tympana;
> citharistae tangant cordas,
> musicorum organa
> resonent ad ejus praeconia.

Furthermore, pictorial representations and accounts of musical performance in the Middle Ages authenticate the use of instruments in other than strictly liturgical situations. It is more difficult to establish exactly what kinds of instrument were used. To arrive at a reasonably accurate picture it is essential to banish the purely modern preoccupation with instrumental 'colour' and recall that in the Middle Ages certain instruments had functions which were entirely their own. The harp and the lute, for example, were considered more noble than other instruments. The trumpet family had the right to accompany and emphasise the presence of a king or an army, and instruments like the vielle (or *symphonia*) were usually linked with characters from low life, such as beggars. In some sources the use of *cymbala* (tiny bells) is laid down; this we know to have been associated often with the organ, even then the king of instruments. The various kinds of drum had a predominantly rhythmic function.

26 Non-liturgical Latin monody

Although no musical evidence written before the ninth century has survived, it is reasonable and indeed necessary to assume that the tradition of secular song had been unbroken in the preceding centuries. This conjecture is not only permitted but imposed by a large number of references in historical and juridical texts (the edicts of synods and conciliar canons) to the existence of a popular repertory of song and dance, which incurred the frequent but fruitless disapproval of the ecclesiastical authorities. Love songs, drinking songs, *cantiones* of various kinds and dances, even ecclesiastical ones, survived every attempt to abolish them up to the thirteenth century and beyond, displaying an unconquerable vitality which was not unconnected with the existence of related practices which had been introduced even into the structure of ritual itself. Although indirect tradition can make good the lack of documentary evidence for the widespread diffusion of this kind of music, it gives no information about the nature and musical character of such songs. In the past there was much speculation about their role as intermediary between the tradition of classical Latinity and that of the late Middle Ages, but this view had to be abandoned when the analysis of the oldest surviving remnants of popular song, which date from the ninth century, was undertaken. Research has also laid to rest another thesis dear to nineteenth-century scholars, that of the popular origin of poetry and of the liturgical and para-liturgical music which has already been examined. It is thus necessary to relate both to a single source, the same creative fervour which, at this time, was giving birth to tropes, sequences and the liturgical drama. The authors, then, were the same monks or *clerici* (students in the monastic or episcopal schools); as we shall see, it is also from the scholastic milieu of the universities that later collections come, containing the *carmina* of the goliards (*clerici vagantes*), which differ only in theme from the contemporary output associated with the Church. The upshot of all this is only to stress the unitary character of a cultural world, that of Church and schools alike, which produced the heritage of mediaeval Latin lyric, the same world which was also to nurture the earliest forms of Romance lyric.

The oldest treasures of secular music in the Middle Ages may be divided into two groups, the first of which includes the neumatic intonation of poetic texts by Horace, the Virgil of the *Aeneid*, and Boethius. Although readings are not always consistent, thanks to a system of notation which is not yet completely diastematic, these fragments reveal a continuity in the attention paid to the classics, especially in the Carolingian period, and a highly significant musicality of approach.[1] The second group is far richer in suggestion. It is made up of a handful of epic and historical pieces, most common among which are laments (*planctus*[2]) for the deaths of famous men. A dozen of these secular songs are collected in a single manuscript from St Martial (now in Paris, B.N. lat. 1154), compiled in the ninth century and possibly set to music slightly later. The *Planctus de obitu Karoli* (written on the death of Charlemagne), in verse based on a system of accents, alternates the refrain *Heu mihi misero!* with distichs, not lacking a certain crude solemnity, which invite all the regions of the earth to mourn the death of the great emperor (the *incipit* is *A solis ortu usque ad occidua/littora maris* ...). Further evidence of a connection with church music is furnished by the appearance in the notation of the quilisma, a sure sign of the influence of ornate liturgical chant. In *Mecum Timavi saxa, novem flumina* ... Paulinus, Patriarch of Aquileia (d. 802), voices his lament for Henry, Duke of Friuli, killed in battle against the Avars.[3] If this song was composed in 799, its melody is undoubtedly among the very oldest musical treasures we possess, if only because it is preserved in an identical form in a tenth-century codex from Berne, suggesting that even at that time it had already acquired considerable celebrity. Although it describes purely secular events, this piece found a place in the liturgy thanks to the obvious solemn gravity of its prayer. The text of an anonymous celebration (*Aurora cum primo mane*) of the battle fought at Fontenoy between the sons of Louis the Pious, on 25 June 841, is also imbued with liturgical echoes, and its music is derived from ecclesiastical sources. The same features, though dating from slightly later, are found in the *Planctus Hugonis abbatis* (*Hug dulce nomen* ...), possibly for a natural son of Charlemagne who died while making prodigious efforts to settle the dispute among Louis' successors.

Shortage of space prevents us from mentioning other works preserved in a variety of sources, but we cannot ignore the famous farewell of a schoolmaster to his departing pupil (*O admirabile Veneris idolum*),[4] perhaps composed at Verona in the tenth century and sometimes found in other sources with the words of pilgrims marching towards Rome (*O Roma nobilis, orbis et domina*). This is an example of a *contrafactum*, the borrowing of a melody to set different words; the practice is very ancient and includes countless reciprocal exchanges between the sacred and profane spheres of culture.

A reliable witness to eleventh-century secular lyric is found in the so-called *Carmina Cantabrigensia*,[5] a manuscript from the Rhineland (or, more precisely, copied from a Rhenish exemplar), now in Cambridge University Library (MS Gg. v.35). It contains compositions in sequence form, some of which are inspired by a variety of themes: eulogies of emperors, rhythmical jokes, love songs, and so on. The lover's greeting *Iam, dulcis amica, venito*, based on the *Song of Songs*, stands out for its evident qualities as a song; it is in four-line strophes with the musical pattern ABCD. The manuscript Vaticano Regina 1462 belongs to the same period; it contains the famous bilingual *alba Phebi claro nondum orto iubare*, whose refrain has sometimes been thought to be from Provence and sometimes from the Swiss border regions, and sometimes to be influenced by Frankish or Mozarabic precedent.

An especially important place in the history of secular lyric is held by Peter Abelard (1079–1142), whose liturgical hymn *O quanta qualia sunt illa sabbata* has also survived along with its melody. His originality appears most clearly in his six *planctus*, which conceal the vicissitudes of his unfortunate love for Heloise beneath a veil of Biblical imagery.[6] From the point of view of versification the *planctus* form a kind of testing-ground for the technical possibilities open to a twelfth-century poet, and Abelard seems to want to explore them all with stubborn determination. He particularly exploits the sequence and related forms, now free from the yoke of parallelism and restored to the liberty of its earlier history. In a rhythm either perfectly syllabic or determined by the intensive accent, he gives his verses great variety of movement (using ternary rhythm as well as binary) and combines them boldly in new strophic structures permeated by a subtle play of rhyme and assonance. No less original is the musical order of the *planctus*, which are set *in extenso*. We owe the preservation of their melodies to the manuscript Vaticano Regina lat. 288, drawn up, at least in the part with which we are concerned, at the beginning of the thirteenth century. The neumes, written *in campo aperto*, are diastematically imprecise, and the result is a high degree of uncertainty in the definition of the melodic line. Two other sources are known for the sixth piece (*Planctus David super Saul et Jonatha*), and they have helped considerably in establishing a melodic and rhythmic reading.[7] The third lament (*Planctus virginum Israel super filia Jepte Galadite*) has been studied at some length because of its melodic links with the *Lai des pucelles*; according to the prevalent modern opinion the two compositions are both derived from the same prototype. The core of the novelty attributable to Abelard is precisely this connection – however it is to be interpreted – between the Latin *planctus* and the love song. To this may be added, from another direction, the influence of Abelard's *planctus* VI on the *planctus Mariae*, evidenced by the discovery of melodic parallels in the most famous of the latter, Geoffrey of St Victor's *Planctus ante nescia*.[8]

Several scholars have worked in recent years on a modern transcription of Abelard's *planctus*, with results of varying quality, especially in the matter of rhythmic interpretation. They have passed from quadratic Gregorian notation (Laurenzi) to the application of modal theory (Lipphardt) via the 'rhythmic–syllabic' method, which allots the value of a basic unit of tempo to the syllable even when it is covered by more than one note (Machabey and Vecchi). The impossibility of basing any of these readings on convincing and incontrovertible grounds has discouraged other scholars (Lorenz Weinrich, for example) from putting forward suggestions of their own.[9] In such cases modern transcription is reduced to the reproduction of a melody in notes of equal value lacking a precise metrical meaning, with the addition of the most obvious graphical features, such as ligatures and liquescent notes. This should not be interpreted as abdicating responsibility; it is the product of a keener awareness of the difficulties implicit in any choice, and an admission that the problem of rhythm in the monody composed between the eleventh and twelfth centuries cannot today be solved in a dogmatic way. The most obvious proof of this is the fact that we shall have to become accustomed to similarly prudent transcriptions in considering the different musical genres which will be discussed in the next chapter.

The last significant episode in the history of mediaeval Latin music (also involved with the problem of rhythmic interpretation) appears with the songs of the goliards or *scholares*. There are some fifty of these altogether, preserved in a song-book from Benediktbeuern (hence the name *Carmina Burana*) and in other less important sources. Although written towards the end of the thirteenth century, the manuscript from the Abbey of Benediktbeuern (now at Munich, Staatsbibl., Clm. 4660) contains a neumatic notation which is not directly translatable. By great good fortune, some of the songs are found in other manuscripts, which helps in the reconstruction of their melodies. The poetry of the goliards is a true point of arrival which subsumes various poetic experiences (sequences, *lais*, hymnody, rhythmic dance-refrains, and so on) with the now inevitable vernacular passages. Much of this work is anonymous, but the names of some of the poets are known: Abelard, mentioned above, and his pupil Hilarius, who also wrote liturgical plays; Hugh of Orléans, also called the Primate; the Archpoet of Cologne; and Walter of Châtillon, who also set his songs to music.

Music continued to be composed for Latin texts in later centuries, but only in the service of the Church. Henceforth the vernacular languages were to be the mature instrument of poetic and musical expression on secular themes.

V

MONODY IN VERNACULAR LANGUAGES; INSTRUMENTS; THE *ARS MUSICA*

27 Troubadour and trouvère lyric

The vast array of metrical and musical forms in mediaeval Latin lyric was the indispensable basis for the appearance of lyrics in the languages of Provence (*d'oc*) and France (*d'oïl*). This is a simple recognition of undeniable facts, not a statement of position in the dispute over the origins of troubadour and trouvère poetry. The observation becomes even more relevant when it is noted that the new poetry flowered in the very regions which had led the way in the creative ferment which produced tropes, *versus*, sequences and dramas. Furthermore, as mentioned above, it was precisely the name *vers* which was given to the compositions of the first troubadours. Another lexical derivation is also significant, though the evidence for it is not altogether convincing: that of *trovatore* from *trovare*, which in its turn comes from *tropare*, 'to make tropes'. These details are worth bearing in mind before setting out to search abroad for what may be found within easy reach at home. (Consider also the hypothesis of Arab influence mediated through Spain as a result of the Crusades.)

One of the most striking features of troubadour and trouvère poetry is the enormous disproportion between the number of poems known to exist (about five thousand) and the number of surviving melodies (about a third of that number). For the troubadours alone we have 2,542 texts and 264 melodies. Other interesting details also deserve to be recorded. Although the flowering of Provençal poetry begins between the end of the eleventh century and the beginning of the twelfth, none of the manuscripts which contain melodies is earlier than the mid thirteenth century, and some are as late as the fourteenth. Moreover, in general their notation does not belong to the *ars mensurabilis* and, as may be imagined, their transcription involves considerable difficulty in the matter of rhythm. The sources of troubadour melody are more than a dozen in number, but four of the manuscripts are particularly important: Paris, Bibliothèque Nationale, fr. 22543 (containing 160 melodies); Milan, Biblioteca Ambrosiana, R.71 sup. (81 melodies); Paris, B.N., fr. 844 (51 melodies); Paris B.N., fr. 20050 (25 melodies). Among the manuscripts are superb illuminated codices compiled for distinguished individuals, possibly under the direction of an expert musician, as well as more modest copies which might have been used by a jongleur. In general the poetic texts can be assigned to their authors with some certainty, but there are still doubts about the attribution of some of the melodies, partly because the contemporary evidence is contradictory, and partly because we are far from knowing exactly which troubadour–poets wrote the melodies for their own texts. The only sources which provide this kind of information are the *vidas*, whose unreliability has been demonstrated too often for comfort. The problem of determining the authorship of melodies is made the more complex by the existence of widely differing versions of one and the same text; often this is a problem not just of variants, but of genuinely distinct 'editions'.

The first troubadour known to us is William IX, Duke of Aquitaine (1071–1126), for whose work the music of only one fragment has survived. Of the hundred or so troubadours whose *vidas* we have, at least seven are women, and a good fifty belong to noble families; but in any case aristocratic origin was not, even for the authors of the *vidas*, necessary to establish the troubadour's renown. As for performance, according to the *vidas* themselves about a third of the troubadours were also jongleurs, and therefore performers; others, however, are said to have been incapable of composing music or performing. The widespread belief that the troubadours' songs were accompanied on musical instruments is currently being reconsidered; but it must at least be admitted – and several illustrations in the manuscripts would seem to confirm this view – that in certain cases the vielle or some other instrument doubled the singing voice, or played an interlude between one stanza of the poem and the next.

The basic theme of troubadour song was courtly love, a concept at first rather vaguely defined, which, however, came into sharper focus with succeeding generations of poets. The debate as to its origins – Christian devotion to the Virgin, Arabic thought, etc. – is still in progress. One element which should certainly not be undervalued is that of popular culture, to which are indebted, for example, the pastourelles, with their theme of the meeting between an innocent shepherdess (not always as innocent as she seems) and a young nobleman, a theme which appears with innumerable variations in the most disparate popular traditions. The theme of the *alba* (the friend who watches over lovers and warns them when sunrise puts an end to their amorous encounter) also originates outside 'courtly song', and of course the same poetic structures are sometimes used to treat political or satirical subjects and the like. Even religious themes are found in the works of the troubadours, although several songs with religious content are considered to be *contrafacta*. It has been repeated over and over again that, as a whole, or to a large extent, troubadour poetry was intended to accompany dancing, but this view has no historical basis, even if in one song or another there may be rhythmic patterns comparable to those of the dance. (The story is told, moreover, that Raimbaut de Vaqueiras composed his well-known *Kalenda maya* to fit a pre-existing *estampida*.) Probably there is, at the root of this misunderstanding, a different evaluation of the various formulas for the refrain with which the rondeau, the virelai and the ballade were connected; but according to some scholars the troubadours and trouvères wrote neither virelais not ballades in the strict sense of these terms, and only two trouvères composed rondeaux (those of Adam de la Hale being, in any case, polyphonic).

One highly probable explanation of the multiple variants of individual songs attributes them to the fact that for a long time the works of troubadours and trouvères were transmitted orally. Evidence for this kind of transmission may be found in the failure of traditional philology to identify relationships between the surviving sources; no one source appears to be derived from any other known today. The most convincing argument, however, is based on the nature of the differences themselves, as they appear in the manuscripts; they do not appear to conform to the usual classification of copyists' errors. It is clear that major conclusions can be derived from such a premise. The most striking is the possibility that we may not possess any of these songs in its original form; moreover, no one is any longer justified in excluding any part of the material furnished by the sources, since it all has the same claim to be definitive. Nor is it legitimate to put forward any one version as the best or the closest to a model which only we, in the twentieth century, happen to think is perfect according to our own criteria. If such conclusions are valid in the philological sphere, their impact on a musical level is even more disturbing. Where oral transmission prevails, no performer need feel obliged to repeat the same song identically at every performance. According to the criteria of performance in use at that time, the singer might think himself faithful to the original even – I almost wrote 'particularly' – when he introduced his own variations. Is it surprising, then, that when the music was fixed in written form it kept the characteristic traits of the period, the environment and the singer who performed it? Alongside the proliferation of versions caused by oral transmission there are also the usual phenomena of variants attributable to the vicissitudes of the written tradition. Sometimes the analysis of manuscripts even proves that textual affinity itself does not necessarily imply affinity, still less identity, of melody. Such observations have a determining effect on the ends and methodology of research. In a sense, research into this question begins from an even less advantageous position than does research on Gregorian chant. In that case also the earliest phase of transmission was oral, but – unlike the troubadour melodies – Gregorian chant has a tradition which was preserved, for the most part, compact and uniform until the preparation of the earliest written sources. The result is that we can still hope, at least within reasonable limits, to arrive at the original reading. This is not possible with troubadour songs, especially in their brief melismatic sections, which more than ever seem to bear traces of the improvisations of the performer or the preferences of the copyist. With these songs, then, it is necessary to reconstruct text and melody in the most critically valid fashion, as they appear in a given source, a sure witness to the environment and period in which it was written. A critical edition, the result of comparison between the sources, would be misleading were it not impossible.

These difficulties involve only the melodic line, but the problem of metrical value, the length to be assigned to the individual notes of each song, is still more complex. As mentioned above, the songs have come down to us in a notation which is still not capable of expressing the differing lengths of the various notes; with a few exceptions, especially in the trouvère repertory, this is quadratic Gregorian notation. Thus we again encounter the dilemma already confronted in other areas of mediaeval monody.

Once the idea of a metrical translation derived substantially from the form of the notes had been set aside as impossible to maintain, it was thought that it might be possible to apply one of the 'rhythmic modes' to the notation, and this 'modal' theory was the hypothesis which enjoyed the most favour from the beginning of the twentieth century onwards. But, in the end, the drawback of this interpretation could no longer be ignored; no two scholars could be found who achieved similar results from the application of this method. So the imposition of a pre-constituted external pattern on the texts was abandoned, and scholars (such as Hugo Riemann) turned to textual metrics instead. Even here, confronted with the absence of a genuine system of versification with fixed accentuation and regularity in the syllabic construction of the lines, they had to take refuge in subtlety and compromise to save the principle. Other ways out were accordingly sought. Some suggested allotting all the notes an equal value, as in late Gregorian melodies, and rendering them with a modern sign, the quaver; others mingled their modal patterns with the spontaneity of textual rhythm; still others stressed the convergence of textual rhythmics and the nature of melody, in accordance with customary practice in the monodic chant of the time. According to this hypothesis, devised by Raffaello Monterosso, 'every individual note corresponding to a syllable' should be assigned 'a uniform value ... , but even melismatic groupings, considered as a whole, [ought to keep] the same value expressed in length'.[1] This would respect the autonomous rhythmic integrity of each line and would ensure total flexibility of tempo. A broadly similar conclusion was reached by Hendrik van der Werf in 1972, after a lengthy study of all the possible sources of information; his opinion is that all mensuralist or modal interpretations can be abandoned, as most troubadour (and trouvère) songs were performed according to a 'free rhythm' fixed by the flow and meaning of the text. This could better be called 'declamatory rhythm', in the sense that these songs 'were sung, or *recited*, in the rhythm in which one might have *declaimed* the poem without its music'.[2] In practice, then, this scholar offers guidance to performers and editors which might be rendered as 'Take each case on its merits'. Such a pragmatic attitude does not really solve the problem; and indeed van der Werf left his transcriptions in a non-mensural mediaeval notation which he modernised only slightly, thereby provoking adverse comment from certain reactionary supporters of the 'modal' system.

It is time to give some descriptive notes. The conventions of courtly love found direct and immediate expression in the *cansó*, whose structure, in its simplest form, is analogous to that of certain hymnodic compositions. The sub-divisions of the genre are numerous, but the most common is that in which repeated phrases are used. The favourite method is the melodic repetition of the first two phrases, giving the following pattern: AB+AB+CDEF. The organisation of rhyme within the various *coblas* (stanzas) is very complex and varied. The most common scheme appears in the *coblas unissonas*, which not only have the same rhyme-scheme in all stanzas, but also use the very same rhyming syllables in every stanza. For example, in Jaufre

Rudel's *cansó Lanquan li jorn son lonc en may*, the word *lonh* is the rhyme for the second and fourth lines in every stanza:

	melodic pattern
1. Lanquan li jorn son lonc en may	A
M'es belhs dous chans d'auzelhs de lonh,	B
E quan mi suy partitz de lay	A
Remembra·m d'un'amor de lonh:	B
Vau de talan embroncx e clis	C
Se que chans ni flors d'albespis	D
No·m platz plus que l'yverns gelatz.	B
2. Be tenc lo Senhor per veray	A
Per qu'ieu veirai l'amor de lonh;	B
Mas per un ben que m'en eschay	A
N'ai dos mals, quar tan m'es de lonh.	B
Ai! car me fos lai pelegris,	C
Si que mos fustz e mos tapis	D
Fos pels sieus belhs huelhs remiratz!	B

[(1) When the days are long, in May, I love to hear the sweet song of the birds from afar, and when I have gone from there, I remember a love from afar. I go with sad and downcast heart, and neither song nor whitethorn flower can please me any more than does the frozen winter. (2) Certainly I believe the Lord is true, and so I shall see love from afar; but for every blessing I receive from him I have two evils, for so much is far from me. Ah, would I were a pilgrim there, that my staff and habit might be admired by those fair eyes!]

Similarly there are *coblas doblas, alternadas*, etc.; and *coblas cap-caudadas* (identical rhyme between the last line of one stanza and the first of the next) are very numerous. Apart from the *cansó* the most common forms are the *sirventes*, which also treated heroic, moralising and political themes; the *planh*, on a mournful subject and lacking a distinctive musical structure; the *vers*, which avoids repetition of any kind; and so on.

The individuals involved in the history of troubadour culture number about five hundred, some of them known only for a few strophes of a *cansó*. The most famous among the first generation, in the twelfth century, were Jaufre Rudel, Marcabru and Bernard de Ventadorn. In the second half of the century formal experimentation gained the upper hand over inspiration, and developed in two directions: towards the *trobar ric*, a movement which tended to experiment with the possible varieties of versification, represented by Raimbaut d'Orange and Arnaut Daniel; and the *trobar clus*, characterised by a certain subtlety of thought, whose chief exponents were Peire d'Auvergne, Bernard Marti and Guiraut de Borneill. In the thirteenth century troubadour poetry went into decline, especially in the areas which had seen the birth of the genre, while valuable examples of it were being produced elsewhere. In its native land excessive refinement and esotericism led to this decline, further hastened by the tragic course of history.

From a tonal point of view, the troubadour melodies are not reducible to the modalities of church music, since they almost always extend beyond the *ambitus* of the latter. Today, however, we are not so ready as was Pierre Aubry[3] to see clearly foreshadowed in the troubadour scales a tendency towards modern major and minor tonality. Their freedom is such that often it is impossible to state with confidence that the songs belong to any given mode. The shape of these melodies also shows clear traces of a primitive recitative form, which may recall the psalmodic formulas with their *initium* and more or less ornate endings. Equally typical is the restriction or frequent return of the melody to two notes, which may be at intervals of a tone, a third, or, less often, a fourth: for example, G-G-G/B-B-B/G-G-G, and so on. Moreover, the movement of the melody sometimes seems to be organised around only one tonal centre, at other times around two; this practice is similar to those recorded by students of ethnomusicology. In general it will be noted that, in comparison with the complexity of the metrical patterns used, the melodies sound like improvisations, fixed in the memory by very simple and traditional means; and indeed it seems unlikely that notation was used in their composition. With the help of notation the troubadours would have invented new and more complicated forms; without it they 'made up short, simple phrases, smoothly flowing and perhaps charming, but in a traditional and conventional vein' (van der Werf).[4] The term 'composer' does not seem appropriate to this function, while that of troubadour or trouvère (in the sense of 'inventor', 'one who finds') seems very apt. The first real composers and the first genuinely 'composed' music were those of the *ars mensurabilis*, which had already begun to flourish when the collections of troubadour and, still later, trouvère songs were put together. This does not mean that the troubadour repertory does not contain some of the most splendid examples of lyricism ever composed in the monody of any period; some compositions, for the elegance of their poetry and the tunefulness of their settings, stand as an astonishing prelude to Romance literature: they include Bernard de Ventadorn's *Can vei la lauzeta mover*; *Pax in nomine Domini* and the *pastourelle L'autrier just'una sebissa*, both by Marcabru; the *alba Reis glorios, verais lums e clartatz* by Guiraut de Borneill; the anonymous *canzone A l'entrada del tens clar*, and many others.

Many of the above remarks apply equally to the output of the trouvères. The same difficulties bedevil the translation of their melodies into a modern form, but there is also the peculiar detail that some of them were taken over for polyphonic compositions, for which, obviously, the ordinary notation of thirteenth-century polyphony was used. The basic melodic scheme of the trouvères' *chanson* is AB AB CDEF, and so on, where B and B differ only in their final cadence: B is *ouvert* (suspended cadence) and B *clos* (final cadence). Many variations on the basic scheme exist, especially in the position and repetition of the refrains, in the interplay of which it may be possible to identify the earliest examples of the rondeau and the virelai.

A strophic scheme characteristic of the rondeau in its most mature form is to be found in the anonymous *Amereis mi vous*; the text is reproduced below with the melodic pattern indicated at the side:

Amereis mi vous, cuers dous, a cui j'ai m'amour donnée?	AB
Nuit et jours je pens a vous. Amereis mi vous, cuers dous?	AA
Je ne puis durer sans vous, vostre grans biauteis m'agreie.	AB
Amereis mi vous, cuers dous, a cui j'ai m'amour donnée?	AB

[Will you love me, O sweet heart to whom I have given my love? Night and day I think of you. Will you love me, O sweet heart? I cannot endure without you, so much does your great beauty please me. Will you love me, O sweet heart to whom I have given my love?]

Among other forms, that of the *jeu-parti* was fairly widespread – set to a tune given alternately to two interlocutors, with a final *envoi*. Below appear the first two strophes (sections of dialogue) of the *jeu-parti* between an unknown *clers* and King Thibaut of Navarre:

1.	Bons rois Thiebaut, sire, consoilliez moi:	A
	Une dame ai mout à lonctemp amée	B
	De cuer leal, saichiez en bone foi,	A
	Mais ne li os descovrir ma pensée;	B
	Tal paour ai que ne mi soit veée	C
	De li l'amors qui me destroint souvent,	D
	Dites, sire, qu'en font li fin amant?	E
	Souffrent il tuit ausi si grant dolour,	F
	Com il dient dou mal qu'il ont d'amor?	G
2.	Clers, je vos lo et pri que toigniez quoi;	A
	Ne dites pas por quoi ele vos hée,	B
	Mais servez tant et faites le, porqoi	A
	Qu'ele saiche ce que mvostre cuers bée,	B
	Que par servir est mainte amors donée.	C

Par moz coverz et par cointes semblanz	D
Et par signes doit on venir avant,	E
Qu'ele saiche le mal et la dolor	F
Que fins amis trait por li nuit et jor.	G

[(1) King Theobald, Sire, advise me: for a long time I have dearly loved a lady, with a loyal heart and in good faith; but I dare not tell her my secret, because I am so afraid that she will reject the love which so often ravages me. Tell me, Sire, what do true lovers do in such cases? Do they really suffer a pain as intense as they say, on account of the anguish which comes from love? (2) Young man, I beg you sincerely to be calm; do not ask why she hates you, but be her servant and make sure she knows what you need in your heart, for much love is given you to help you to serve. You must proceed by allusion and knowing looks and signs, so that she is aware of the suffering and pain that a true lover feels night and day on her account.]

The *lai* often presents the structure of paired lines characteristic of the sequence, from which it seems to be derived. In the oldest examples, the number and length of the lines and the melody change in each couplet; in general the couplets are twelve in number, but this is not a constant rule. According to their subject, *chansons* may be called *d'histoire* (or *de toile*), *dramatiques, de danse, d'aube, à boire*, and so on.

The first known trouvère is one of the most famous authors of verse-romances, Chrétien de Troyes, author of *Perceval le Gallois*, which provided the inspiration for Wagner's *Parsifal*. Towards the end of the twelfth century, Conon de Béthune and Blondel de Nesle were already able to compete with the poets of the South. In the thirteenth century the musical life of northern France was profoundly transformed, with the renewal of its para-liturgical heritage and the first great examples of polyphony from the Notre Dame school, and monody itself wavered between the old sources of inspiration (the troubadours) and the new models. Between 1219 and 1236 Gautier de Coinci wrote *chansons* to the Virgin, drawing impartially on the melodies of sequence, lais and polyphonic *conducti*, a sign of the coexistence of forms and tastes that at first sight seem irreconcilable. From the beginning of the thirteenth century the influence of fixed musical forms originating in popular culture became more consistent; traces of it are found in the music of Thibaut of Champagne (1201–53) and, above all, in the compositions of the most talented of the trouvères, Adam de la Hale (*c.* 1230–88), author of the famous *Li Geus de Robin et de Marion*, a musical play possibly composed for the court of Naples, for the singing and dancing sections of which he adapted *refrains* and *chansons*. These were the last glimmers of an art which, carried beyond the boundaries of France along with that of the troubadours, had already inspired imitators and successors in almost all the countries of Europe.

28 Monody in the German-speaking countries, the Iberian peninsula and England

Although the existence of a native musical tradition in the German-speaking countries cannot be denied (consider the songs of the goliards), the large amount of evidence which has survived testifies to the birth of a movement inspired by the ideals and fashions of French and Provençal poetry and music. The presence of the trouvère Guiot de Provins in the retinue of Beatrice of Burgundy, who was married to the Emperor Frederick Barbarossa in 1156, is proof that the origins of the closer relationship between French and German culture must date back at least to that period. Such exchanges took place either by the transmission of song-books or through journeys or visits made by French minstrels to German courts. It is even known that in about 1200 Peire Vidal travelled as far as Hungary.

The term used to describe the German poet–musicians is *Minnesinger*. Their movement, *Minnesang* (from *Minne*, courtly love, and *Sang*, song), found its initial impulse, as far as we can tell, in Bavaria and Austria, but a second current, from across the lower Rhine, took it into the Rhineland, Thuringia and Switzerland. The chronological limits of this process can be fixed approximately at 1170 and the mid fourteenth century, and include two or three creative phases, the exact definition of which is, however, not yet agreed upon by scholars. The works of the *Minnesinger* are preserved in sources which appear late in comparison with the period of their activity: the most important are the Jena song-book (fourteenth century, 91 melodies) and that of Colmar (fifteenth century, containing 107 melodies, some of which already belong to the later genre of *Meisterlieder*).

Dependence on French models was almost total until about 1200; the only melodies known to date from this period are also found in Franco-Provençal sources which, very probably, were taken over when the German texts were being composed. Later on as well, the texts composed in Germany show clear signs of the influence of the French repertory on content and form alike, in their poetic imagery, courtly terminology and strophic structure. Very close similarities, moreover, are also to be found in their melodies. Each genre has its corresponding term in French: *Lied* (*cansó*); *Tagelied* (*alba*); *Leich* (*lai*); *Spruch* (*sirventes?*); and so on. The form most often used is that of the *Bar* (*poema, canzone*), whose poetic and musical structure consists of the repetition of two *Stollen* (corresponding to the feet or 'mutations' of the Italian *ballata*) to which is added an *Abgesang* (e.g. AB+AB+CDE...). The *Abgesang* frequently includes, in various ways, the melodic material of the *Stollen*, creating musical echoes (such as AB+AB+CDB); in these cases the song is the type known as *a rotundello*. In the *Lied* love for the 'gentle lady' tends to take on a more idealistic aspect, verging on devotion of a chivalric kind; praise of the natural world and religious themes frequently appear alongside the theme of love.

The best-known among the first generation of *Minnesinger* are Friedrich von Hûsen, Hartmann von der Aue (who also wrote the narrative poem *Der arme Heinrich*), Reinmar von Zweter, and Rudolf von Fenis. The representative authors of the second period have a more personal style; they are Walther von der Vogelweide (author, among much else, of a famous *Palästinalied* which refers to the Crusade of 1228 and bases its melody on that of Jaufre Rudel's *Lanquan li jorn son lonc en may*), Wolfram von Eschenbach (who was to become the Wolfram of Wagner's *Tannhäuser*), and Heinrich von Meissen, called 'Frauenlob', possibly because in poetic debate he defended the term *Frau* (lady) against that of *Wip* (woman). The decline of *Minnesang* began with Heinrich's death in 1318. With each of these singer–poets it is possible to point to the Franco-Provençal model or models from which they took the inspiration for their own work.

As do the corresponding works of Romance lyric, the *Minnelieder* present difficulties of rhythmic interpretation, but with the essential difference that German versification is based on the number of strong accents, and does not require numerical parity among non-accented syllables. This means that 'modal theory' cannot be applied systematically in transcribing them.

The heritage of *Minnesang* was, to an extent, taken over by *Meistergesang* (from *Meister*, master), which, however, was distinguished from its predecessor by originating outside court circles and forming a means of expression for the bourgeois citizenry. It is customary to divide *Meistergesang* into two schools: the first is made up of wandering singers (of whom the typical representative is Behaim), the second of groups of singers settled in one place. The figure who stands at the origins of these latter examples is 'Frauenlob' himself, who was the leader of the school of Mainz, the most important centre of *Meistersinger* until Hans Sachs (1494–1576) raised the Nuremberg school to equal status.

The *Geisslerlieder* (from *Geissler*, flagellant), a repertory of popular religious song which flourished in northern Europe during the fourteenth century, while the Black Death was raging there, are worth mentioning for their similarity to penitential chant (especially that of Italy) and for their anticipation of some aspects of the Lutheran chorale.

The geographical location of Spain and Portugal encouraged a large-scale diffusion of Provençal lyric in both countries. Not only did the courts of Catalonia, Castile and Aragon receive many of the troubadours, but the Catalan lords themselves tried their hands at poetry (the dialect of Limousin was used in Catalonia before Catalan prevailed). The Provençal influence lasted until the fifteenth century in some regions, but the most imposing collection of Iberian monody had already been made, by Alfonso X 'el Sabio' ('the wise'), King of Castile and Leon from 1252 to 1284. This is the book known as *Cantigas de Santa María*. The name *cantigas* was given to compositions, sacred and profane alike, belonging to Galician and Portuguese literature. Seven *canciones de amor* attributed to the *joglar* Martín Codax (early thirteenth century) had already been composed in this language, and six of them have survived, with one melody in nonmensural notation. But this is a tiny foretaste in comparison with the more than four hundred songs which make up Alfonso's collection. In order to understand the nature of the cultural soil from which the *cantigas* flowered, it will be enough to recall that the last of the troubadours, Guiraut Riquier, spent a long time at Alfonso's court.

For the most part, the *cantigas* celebrate the miracles of the Virgin, and take their inspiration from the *Miracles de Notre Dame* of the trouvère–monk Gautier de Coinci. They have survived in several sources, three of which also preserve their melodies; they are anonymous; but the possibility that some of them are the work of King Alfonso himself cannot be excluded. The most common strophic structure is a reworking of that of the French virelai. It opens with a *ritornello* (*estribillo*), followed by the *estrofa*, which ends with a repeat of the *ritornello*; but variations within this pattern are numerous. Another element derived from French tradition is the presence of the suspended and final cadences (*ouvert* and *clos*). According to Higinio Anglès, editor of the melodies of the *cantigas*, several of the Spanish sources were written down by scribes who were highly skilled in musical paleography and perfectly well aware of current musical innovations in Europe, including the polyphonic repertory. In this they differ from the French and Provençal copyists, who were men of letters rather than musicians; and the scribes of the Italian *laudari* seem to have been even less skilful, since they appear to know only quadratic Gregorian notation.

Anglès, distancing himself from the first attempts at transcription made by Aubry (in which 'rhythmic modes' were used) and starting from the presupposition that both ternary and binary rhythm were known everywhere and in every period, puts forward an interpretation based on one or other of these two metres, and accepts as equally legitimate the use of the *modus mixtus*, an alternating combination of the first 'rhythmic mode' (trochaic movement) and the second (iambic movement). He goes on to assert that 'musical rhythm is not always subordinated to the metrics of the text', and that to arrive at the correct rhythm it is necessary to abandon the method of matching it to the number of syllables in the respective lines. Not even the theory which, in troubadour melody, interpreted ligatures or groups of more than three notes as equal to one unit of rhythm can be accepted any longer; to sing these notes as if they were ornaments means 'to spoil the charm and natural tranquillity of these melodies'. Finally, still according to Anglès, the *cantigas* show us how we ought to understand the application of 'rhythmic' modes to monody, frequently using them in combination in one and the same melody. It is, as will be seen, a one-sided method, which gives Spanish monody more importance than other repertories; not to mention the fact that the method of transcription leaves the editor excessive scope for choices which must be subjective and, in the end, arbitrary.

In the study of the origins of the strophic model or models used in the *cantigas*, the hypothesis of an Arabic influence has enjoyed much favour since the early years of the twentieth century. In this view the pattern of the Arabic–Andalusian *zajal* (a three-part structure with *volta* and *ritornello*) is seen as the metrical and strophic forerunner of Romance lyric. There has, however, been no shortage of scholars who maintain that it is illogical to seek in other repertories models which sacred and secular Latin lyric was itself able to offer to poets and musicians. Even the scheme of virelai, for example, occurs in mediaeval Latin compositions, some of them found in Spain itself. The problem is very complex and does not call for dogmatic solutions, least of all in the present work; but the two aspects, literary and musical, must be kept clearly separate. Although the channels of communication and derivation can be identified – or, more accurately, glimpsed – in the metrical and poetic context, the same is not true in the musical sphere. As far as melodies are concerned the theory of Arab influence is, at present, a pure hypothesis.

Provençal lyric spread as far as England, partly thanks to Eleanor of Aquitaine, who was married to Henry of Anjou, head of the Angevin dynasty in England. It appears from one of Bernard de Ventadorn's poems that he lived for some time on the English side of the Channel. But such events did not suffice to produce a coherent and autonomous poetic movement, if only because the literary language used in England until the mid thirteenth century was Franco-Norman. Among the surviving remains, a 'prisoner's song' is worthy of note; it is a French *lai* accompanied by an English translation. Liturgical chant doubtless had a more lasting influence on English musical practice, as may be seen from the songs traditionally attributed to St Godric (d. 1170), a hermit who lived for a long time in a cave somewhere in the north of England. From the thirteenth century, a few examples of secular lyric have survived, shot through with a tone of gloom and pessimism, as well as some instrumental dances.

29 Italian poetry: *laude*

There is no need to look further than certain familiar passages of Dante for evidence of the large-scale penetration of troubadour thought and poetry into Italian culture. Raimbaut de Vaqueiras, Peire Vidal and Gaucelm Faidit, to name only the most famous, all spent some time in Italy. The poets of the 'Sicilian' school came under their influence, as did those Italians (like the Mantuan poet Sordello) who wrote in Provençal. The names given to their poetic forms (*ballata, tenzone, sirventese* and so on) are obviously modelled on their French equivalents. But as far as music is concerned, we only have indirect evidence, the scarcity of which suggests that in Italy 'words were divorced from music', an occurrence which can have been no more than occasional and exceptional in the lands where the art of the troubadours was born. Even the terminology used in Italy, though apparently connected with musical practice (*ballata, canzone, sonetto,* etc.), may be no more than a lexical survival. It is not necessary to assume that it involves direct reference to any kind of performance, even at the earliest stage. If such pieces were performed at the time, it may have been no more than coincidence, attributable not to the authors' wishes but to the demands of minstrels and other improvising musicians. This is confirmed by the legal and judicial character of the education received by most of the 'Sicilian' poets, which was quite unlike the aristocratic, church-based training which included the study of music. It is not by chance that Frederick II of Sicily (1197–1250) who certainly enjoyed this second kind of education, appears so different from the members of the 'Sicilian' school named for his realm. This remains true, indeed, even if the dialogue *Dolze meo drudo*, a setting of which has survived in a polyphonic collection assembled in the fourteenth and fifteenth centuries (the Reina Codex: Paris, Bibl.Nat., nouv. acq. fr. 6771), is not in fact his. The 'Tuscan' school and northerners in general seem to have had even more distant relations with the world of music. In some cases direct evidence exists to show that works by the philosophical poets of the 'stil novo' were given to professional musicians to be set to music; the affectionate portrayal of Casella at the gateway to Purgatory in Dante's poem will suffice as an example.[1]

However, the presence of music becomes much more apparent as soon as we leave the rarefied atmosphere of literary schools for the events of everyday life, whether associated with religious and devotional customs or with occasions of popular celebration. The account in Salimbene de Adam's *Cronica* (mid thirteenth century) could scarcely be more straightforward: who could forget Brother Enrico Pisano? His spontaneous composition of a para-liturgical text based on the *canzonetta E s'tu no cure de me/e' no curarò de te* is a clear indication of the interrelation between music and life and between the religious and secular worlds. Evidence of equal value in another direction is provided by the 'uncommon and beautiful music' ('inusitata . . . et pulcra cantio') which the same Salimbene tells us he heard at Pisa, sung by young men and women accompanied by viols, lyres and other instruments.

Music acted as an expression of the encounter between the sacred and secular dimensions of life. The decisive impulse in this direction was supplied by recent Franciscan visions of earthly reality. Francis' *Laudes Creaturarum* ('Creatures' Hymns of Praise'), like his followers, the *ioculatores Domini* ('fools of God'), speak of an absorption of the worldly sphere in the praise of the Creator. (Unfortunately the musical staves which appear in the source of the *Laudes*, codex 338 at Assisi, carry no notes.) Of course there was no shortage of Biblical and liturgical precedents (such as the *laudes matutinae*); but the Franciscans injected a new vigour into this vein of thought, and Christian spirituality was to feel its effects for centuries, along with the impulse to renewal provided by the other mendicant Orders (Dominicans, Servants of Mary, and so on).

It was in just such a ferment of the worldly life that the *lauda* was born. This was a devotional song for the lay fraternities which had arisen alongside the new kind of testimony to the Gospel offered by the mendicant Orders. Only fragments have survived from the very early phase of the *lauda*'s history (the first half of the thirteenth century). These range from a *Pianto* from Cassino, written in neumes on the pattern of the 'Passion' discovered by Inguanez,[2] to the 'Veronese' *lauda Beneta sia l'ora e 'l çorno*, and the so-called 'Lauda dei Servi di Bologna', *Rayna potentissima*, along with a few other scraps of song. It is a tiny body of work, but very varied from the metrical point of view. Even though their music is lacking, there can be no doubt that such texts were meant to be sung; for example, by the Marian confraternities founded by St Peter Martyr after 1232, which rapidly spread to many towns and cities.[3] However, the crucial moment for the development of this new vernacular form was that of the foundation of fraternities which met with the specific and fundamental purpose of singing *laude*. In a sense these fraternities specialised in the singing of *laude*, and were therefore called *laudesi*. According to recent research, the first fraternity of *laudesi* known to have been active was founded at a Dominican church in Siena in 1267.[4] Material dating from about twenty years later tells us that *pueruli* were trained for the singing of *laude* and that these performances were introduced 'in certain other cities' (*ad quasdas alias civitates*). In the light of these details the great *devotio* organised by Rainerio Fasani at Perugia in 1260, which gave birth to the movement of the *disciplinati*, becomes of secondary importance for the origins of the *lauda*. Certainly the *disciplinati* composed a repertory of *laude*, of which the predominant if not exclusive theme was the Passion; but, as far as we know, it was only in the first decades of the fourteenth century that they encouraged the development of the dramatic *lauda*. (One of the oldest pieces of evidence is a source at Assisi, Bibl. Comunale MS 705, dated 1317 and called 'Illuminati'). The paths taken by *laudesi* and *disciplinati* thus led to different destinations. The *disciplinati* were the forerunners of the Italian vernacular theatre (the manuscripts which mention them have no musical notation, but we know that their *laude* were sung according to melodic formulas, the 'Easter' and the 'Passion'). The *laudesi*, meanwhile, can take the credit for the diffusion of lyrical *laude* (whose subjects vary according to the liturgical calendar) and of the theory of performance based on technical accomplishment. The result of this was a need for adequate materials, such as notated manuscripts, two examples of which have survived intact into modern times.

However, before going on to describe these sources, it is necessary to mention an event of crucial importance in the prehistory of the *lauda*, which took place before the creation of the surviving manuscripts: the adoption of the strophic structure taken from the secular *ballata*. In spite of the vast amount of research done in recent years, it is still not possible to say who was responsible for this highly successful transplant. The candidates most often favoured by critics have been Guido d'Arezzo, Jacopone da Todi and Garzo, the only author's name which appears by self-attribution in the sources themselves, where anonymity is the general rule. It is difficult to judge these hypotheses for chronological reasons, especially when it comes to the dating of the older of the two sources containing melodies – the famous Cortonese 91, compiled, it would appear, before 1297.

It is reasonably credible that Cortona should have been among the towns where this Sienese innovation rapidly took root, and the precious hoard of material preserved in its famous manuscript makes the idea even more plausible. It belonged to the fraternity of Santa Maria delle Laude, formed at the church of San Francesco in Cortona, and consists of two parts, of which only the first contains musical settings.[5] There are forty-four melodies, as well as two more which were added perhaps only a little later. The texts are not arranged at random; the first sixteen are Marian *laude*, while the remainder roughly follow the liturgical calendar, with the insertion or addition of a few saints' days. The manuscript is of modest appearance, lacking miniatures and decorated initials, but as if to make up for this the textual readings are largely accurate, and the value of the melodies is inestimable. It is the oldest *corpus* of Italian texts set to music.

The second *laudario*, now at Florence (Bibl.Naz., B.R.18, formerly Mag. II.I.122), is 'majestic, rich, and splendid in its every page', according to Liuzzi.[6] In the early fourteenth century it was owned by the Florentine Confraternity of Santa Maria, which was based among the Augustinians at Santo Spirito, and later by a group called the 'Umiliati d'Ognissanti'. The *laudario* proper forms the first part of the codex, and is followed by two books of Latin texts (mostly sequences) for use with monodic or polyphonic music. Sometimes much of the page is taken up by sumptuous miniatures whose style, along with the script and the quality of many of the melodies, suggests a date somewhere between 1310 and 1330–40. Some of the settings are obviously several decades older than the manuscript itself. It contains ninety-seven *laude*, of which twenty also appear in Cortonese 91; eighty-eight of the texts have a musical setting, and ten of these melodies are similar (though never completely identical) in the two codices. In the Florentine example there are six cases where the same melody is used for two different texts. There are, then, seventy-two original melodies, to which may be added a final *lauda* with its notation, which comes after the sequences.

For purely textual reasons it seems likely enough that there existed at one time a *proto-laudario* compiled in the Tuscan region, possibly at Siena. To this might also be ascribed the repertory of fourteenth-century manuscripts without music, like the Pisan *laudario* now in Paris (Arsenal, 8251) and others. The recent discovery of notated leaves of a *laudario* from Lucca[7] may serve to confirm this conjecture from a musical point of view, especially when compared with Florence B.R.18. But there may yet be other conclusions to be reached from the restoration, currently in progress, of notated sheets taken from one or more dismembered *laudari* and scattered in various European and American libraries.

In the discussion above of the thirteenth-century *lauda* as being modelled on the secular *ballata*, no mention was made of the hypothesis – already familiar – that it was derived from a Hispano-Arabic model, in the form of the Arabic-Andalusian *zajal*. To leave this unmentioned would be to ignore the opinion of those scholars – philologists, linguists and musicologists alike – who suggest that the common pattern A A A X, B B B X . . . refers directly to the scheme of the *zajal*.[8] However – and the observation has even more weight than it would in the case of the *cantigas* – it was pointed out some twenty years ago that 'at least in the case of the *zajal* pattern . . . its application to the religious sphere took place in a mediaeval Latin context',[9] and the most recent research confirms this view whole-heartedly.[10] Certainly the para-liturgical Latin repertory is not devoid of examples of alternation between soloist and chorus, as the performance of the *lauda* may demand; and so, if anything, the problem becomes that of the origins of the mediaeval Latin forms. In the case of the more complex strophic schemes, it is easier and more probable to admit the possibility of a transfusion between the secular context of the *ballata* and the religious world than to posit, with Fernando Liuzzi, an independent and parallel development in the two sectors.

It may be useful to examine the basic melodic schemes of the *ballate* as collected and defined by Liuzzi himself.[11]

*ballata-*pattern	*ripresa* (refrain)	*piedi* (feet, i.e. mutations)	*volta* (return)	*ripresa*
minor	AB	CC or CD	AB, CD or DE	AB
median	ABC	DEDE or DEF	ABC or DEF	ABC
major	ABAB or ABCD	CDCD or EFGH or EFEF	ABAB, ABCD or GHCD	ABAB or ABCD

As for their relationship with the virelai, there are undeniable points of contact, although it is known that the virelai did not always, in the early stages, possess its initial refrain.

Study of the two surviving *laudari* reveals a visible movement from syllabic or only slightly ornate melody (Cortonese 91) to an evident taste for luxuriant melismatic patterns (B.R.18). This observation does not necessarily imply the loss of a presumed original purity and the onset of decline, as it was once fashionable to maintain. It is simply the sign of an evolution in aesthetic conceptions and perhaps – a conjecture already made by Liuzzi but as yet unverified – the first traceable hint of a tendency which will be fully realised in the output of the *ars nova* composers some years later.

Nothing could be further from the truth than the suggestion that the melodies of thirteenth-century *laude* can all be reduced to a common level of homogeneity or, worse still, monotony. Close analysis reveals in them an unexpected variety: from refined modulations to the flavour of popular song, from simple and austere processional intonations to dance-tunes, from narrative and dramatic chants with insistently repeated notes (such as the stanza *De la crudel morte de Cristo*) to a tone which is sometimes excited, sometimes relaxed, serene, confident. More technical examination uncovers the presence of echoes of litanic structures, with a single formula constantly repeated from verse to verse both in the refrain and in the couplet. There are also forms parallel to the hymnodic couplet, with no repetition of melodic segments (melodic scheme ABCD); some traces of sequential structure in the melodic equivalence of mutations, although the two distinguishing marks of the sequence (identical melody for two lines, forming a pair, and change of melody between one pair of lines and another) find no exact counterpart in any known example of the *lauda*; and occasional remnants of troubadour preciosity, along with a frequent occurrence of the modes of ecclesiastical chant (at least in the oldest examples), though the *deuterus* (the E mode) has almost disappeared. Finally, there are some hints of development towards modern major/minor tonality. Many melodies range from the top F to the lower octave, with a distinct flavour of F major tonality. On the other hand, it could not be otherwise, since we have noted similar tendencies even in para-liturgical Latin chant. In a word, the *laude* show both links with tradition and openness to the future, at least as far as tonal organisation is concerned.

The notation of the two *laudari* is quadratic and non-mensural, usually on a four-line stave. By its very nature it causes the usual problems of rhythmic interpretation in transcription. Apart from sporadic and sketchy attempts carried out using methods unacceptable today, the problem was comprehensively tackled by Fernando Liuzzi[12] in a study which covered the whole repertory. We shall therefore consider here the methods used by Liuzzi, as those which have been followed for decades by all editors and performers.

The starting-point (not only for Liuzzi, but for anyone trying to reconstruct the melody of a text, especially a metrical text) is the fact that the link between word and sound inevitably demands the formation of a rhythmic pattern of sounds. If the words are organised metrically, they condition and determine the melodic line, which in its turn reinforces the metrical arrangement of the text. Here the accented syllable is taken as the basic unit of time, which the values of groups of non-accented syllables must equal. Since, in Liuzzi's opinion, equal (binary) rhythms were most common towards the end of the thirteenth century, and since the most frequent line in the *laude* was the simple eight-syllable line accented on the first, third, fifth and seventh beats, 'the musical rhythm which quite spontaneously matches the verse is the following:

O di	-	vina	virgo,	flore . . .
1		2	3	4

that is, four beats or feet with two elements in each. Therefore to each syllable will correspond a note, or a group of notes whose total will be equal to the single note'. When the line exceeds or falls short of the required length it can be adapted, by elision or by lengthening syllables, to the octosyllabic pattern. In practice this serves to perfect the system used by Riemann (*Vierhebigkeit*)[13] in the transcription of troubadour melodies.

It is undeniable that the methods used by Liuzzi yielded positive results when applied to syllabic or less ornate melodies, but only in the first strophes (indeed Liuzzi took no notice of later strophes). The results of transcribing melismatic melodies were more open to discussion, and were roundly criticised by a number of specialists, since in these cases it is inevitable that there should be groups of notes with tiny values (five or seven demisemiquavers, etc.), not to mention the fact that the prejudicial choice of the four-feet pattern and its inflexibility were generally thought to be unacceptable. Criticisms of this aspect were made in reviews by J. Handschin and Y. Rokseth,[14] although they acknowledged Liuzzi's contribution in offering scholars an invaluable body of material, especially in the facsimile editions of the two manuscripts. Indeed it may be claimed with some justice that the year 1934 saw the beginning of a new phase in the study of the thirteenth-century *lauda*.

Other critical contributions were made by Monterosso and, on several occasions, Anglès.[15] Monterosso reproaches Liuzzi for, among other faults, clinging to the outdated conviction that melody has the function of balancing poetic rhythm and compensating for its anomalies, and puts forward his own interpretative principle for Romance metrics, breaking the line up into accentuated feet differing from one another according to the various positions of the accent (this would solve the problem of the absence of isosyllabism). Anglès, who admires features in the thirteenth-century *laude* which he sees as absolutely original in comparison with the contemporary repertory of European monody, rereads them in the light of his own conclusions about the notation of the *cantigas*,[16] denies their 'modal' character, but affirms the mensural nature of the notation in the two manuscripts and produces in his transcriptions that mixture of binary and ternary measures of which he is known to be so staunch an advocate. The consequent impression is of an empirical formula which sometimes produces successful results, but cannot be completely accepted because it lacks a sound and objective principle of discrimination.

In recent years Clemente Terni (a supporter of the idea of derivation from the *zajal*) and Luigi Lucchi[17] have produced various interpretative essays, but their promised complete critical edition is still awaited.

A final note: the myth of Jacopone da Todi's possession of musical talents matching his gifts as a poet in a mystical and satirical vein has no solid foundation, since no thirteenth-century setting which can be reliably attributed to him has survived.

30 Musical instruments

The function and use of musical instruments have already been discussed in connection with both para-liturgical genres and those completely independent of the liturgy. It is generally accepted that instruments were used in the performance of music for official and public ceremonies, in the castles and palaces of lords and kings, and in the popular festivals which took place in towns and villages. But what role did instruments play in strictly liturgical rites during the Middle Ages? Three kinds of information have generally been used in the search for an answer to this question. They are: the stylistic characteristics of music, which may have implications for instrumental performance; relevant depictions in contemporary works of art; and documentary evidence in chronicles and other literary texts. There is no need to add that here we shall be concerned solely with the monodic period in musical history.

Internal analysis of musical works, though necessary given the scarcity of other clues, produces no decisive results. Scholars are still a long way from reaching unanimous conclusions. Those who suggested that the origin of melismatic tropes was in some way connected with the use of instruments have subsequently been proved wrong. There is not even a commonly accepted opinion about the *conductus*, which appears in the sources with some untexted sections; some think the text is missing because the scribe did not want to copy it out over and over again. Furthermore, it has been pointed out that the *conductus* is on the fringe of ritual music, being a processional chant, linked to the movements of the clergy and intended to fill up the space between one rite and the next. The nature of the *tenor* in motets might require a different interpretation – but that would take us far beyond the boundaries of monody. No conclusive argument, then, can be deduced from the internal analysis of music.

The images found in miniatures and paintings[1] would offer a vast amount of information if we could be sure that they were based on the reality of liturgical practice. Unfortunately we cannot, since the doubt often lingers as to whether this or that painting actually portrays a liturgical scene or simply an idealised composition. It is enough to consider, for example, how the iconography of King David in miniatures is inspired by Biblical texts (*psalterium decem chordarum*, etc.), and how a whole school of portrayals of instruments was influenced by a late (ninth- or tenth-century) letter of pseudo-Jerome to Dardanus (*De diversis generibus Musicorum*).[2] Moreover, a dichotomy had arisen, thanks to certain philosophical preconceptions, between metaphysical reality and the reality perceptible by the senses. When the artist came to depict the celestial spheres, he employed a principle of idealisation which had nothing to do with tangible reality; and even when the subject was a narrative (such as the life of a saint) the two worlds became inseparably fused. Even the enormous number of instruments jumbled together in some pictures (consider, as an example, a Coronation of the Virgin) appears to be based more on the accounts of apocryphal writings and the visions of mystics than on a real scene. Paradise could only be conceived according to a stereotyped model, where the presence of numerous angelic musicians stemmed from that *horror vacui* which Huizinga[3] identifies in the late Middle Ages. Finally, the scenery of the liturgical drama had a definite influence on mediaeval iconography. Paradise raised up on a height among flowers, the eternal Father on a golden throne among clouds of angels – these call to mind a prototype based on dramas and mystery-plays. Even the organ, which plays a prominent part in these depictions, could be linked with Paradise, despite its ecclesiastical background. For the rest, harps, rebecs and lutes, so common in portrayals of Paradise or the Holy Family, accompanied the speeches of Christ on stage in the liturgical drama. To sum up, those who look to iconography for an accurate representation of the situation with regard to instruments are likely to be very disappointed.

As for the participation of instrumentalists in the rites of the Church, it can be illuminating to examine evidence taken from historical or judicial sources. Innumerable edicts were issued by the ecclesiastical authorities, from the time of the Fathers until the early Middle Ages, which forbade the involvement of strolling players and musicians in the liturgy. In fact the condemnation of actors, clowns, singers and instrumentalists which dated from the later Imperial era and had often been invoked by the Fathers was still in force, with all its legal weight behind it. In the Middle Ages the Church's attitude never changed when confronted with the performers of secular music. Although the countless abuses evoked by a series of prohibitions from the eighth century onwards leave us in no doubt about the reality of the situation, these same prohibitions enable us to see what was the ideal which was being aimed at. A capitular decree of 789 forbade bishops and abbots to have any contact with minstrels. Gill da Zamora, a Franciscan active in the second half of the thirteenth century, writes in one of his treatises that because of the abuses of the minstrels, all instruments were forbidden apart from the organ, which was 'used by the Church in various types of chant, in proses, in sequences and in hymns'.[4] Minstrels and strolling players were not allowed to belong to the great schools of chant, such as that of Notre Dame at Paris. The Synod of Chartres in 1358 once again forbade clerics to employ actors and minstrels. These examples, which could be multiplied many times over, may be supplemented by the observation of a practical difficulty: strolling players and minstrels were used to improvising, and it is not easy to see how they could have taken part alongside the cantors in the performance of music, like contemporary church music, which was written down (at least from the ninth century onwards) in manuscripts which required a lengthy educational and professional training on the part of the reader.

Moreover, the Church had valid reasons for its attitude towards instrumental music, which may help to make it more comprehensible from a general point of view. Since Christian chant was, originally, a simple expansion of prayers of praise to God, in accordance with Hebrew tradition, it is understandable that it should have rejected any form of instrumental support. This refusal became even more determined when, after the arrival of the Church in pagan surroundings, instruments inevitably became associated with pagan music and ritual. A significant notion common to many of the Fathers is that instrumental music is the work of the Devil. Even vocal music could contain excessively sensual passages, as Augustine himself gives us to understand in his *Confessions*. Once the musical repertory of the individual rites had substantially been defined, the negative attitude towards the use of instruments could only be reinforced. Amalar, echoing the Roman tradition which had established itself in the Carolingian empire, could write in his *De ecclesiasticis officiis*: 'Our cantors hold in their hands neither cymbals, lyres, nor any other type of instrument.'[5] The subsequent flowering of polyphony made room for the gradual appearance of instrumental performances, but even then they were still considered a kind of *musica vulgaris*, an indication of increasing secularisation, and were officially banned by Councils such as those of Trier (1227), Lyons (1274) and Vienne (1311).

Among the various instruments, only the organ was fully accepted into ritual usage, but this did not come about without its encountering some obstacles. There is evidence for its occasional use from the earliest centuries in the West, at least from the time when the tendency to add ornament and emphasis to liturgical rites first declared itself. At that time the organist was a cleric and could not be treated on a par with the players of other instruments. The organ was certainly used to add pomp to some ceremonies in the great monasteries which grew up during and after the Carolingian age, such as St Gall, but its role in the liturgy is not wholly clear. From the ninth century onwards there is evidence for a notable increase in the practice of playing the organ in southern Germany. In the Italy of the Ottonian period, it is known that a certain Guglielmus gave an organ to the basilica of San Salvatore at Turin, so that the cantors could sing at Easter and the other festivals, in both the mass and the office, 'with both the organ and the boys' (*de organo una cum pueris*). For many years, however, organ-playing and organs themselves must have been a considerable rarity. In his *Roman de Brut* (1155) Wace observes that *Moult oïssies orgues sonner / Et clers chanter et orguener*; and Chrétien de Troyes remarks in his *Lancelot*:[6]

Por oïr les ogres
Vont au mostier a feste annuel
A Pantecoste ou a Noel.

(To hear the organs they went to the Minster on the annual holy days at Whitsuntide or Christmas.)

Only in the thirteenth century is there clear evidence that the organ was being used regularly. This is proved both by the statement of Gill da Zamora quoted above and by the comments of Guillaume Durand in his *Rationale Divinorum Officiorum*.[7] From then on the playing of the organ gradually acquired a more coherent and articulate role in the service, until it replaced, in alternative verses, the singing of liturgical texts (at least from the second half of the fourteenth century).

Among the old and new instruments which entered liturgical use in the fifteenth century, a special role was reserved for the trumpet, either in processions or to announce the beginning of mass (traces of this practice date back to the ninth century). Later on, it was used to mark the moment of consecration and display of the consecrated wafer, a ritual gesture followed with growing and even superstitious devotion by the faithful.

In secular music, instrumental accompaniment normally acted as an accessory throughout the Middle Ages, in the sense that the instrument doubled the voice in unison or on the octave. In the epic romances the minstrel accompanied the singer by playing a melodic formula with some slight ornamentation. As well as this, according to some theoretical texts, he might improvise preludes and postludes to the verses as they were sung (most often using a vielle).

The appearance of the first independent pieces of instrumental music, in sources dating from the second half of the thirteenth century, is of particular interest. They were linked to dances, and were classified by Johannes de Grocheo (late thirteenth and early fourteenth centuries) as *stantipes, ductia* and *nota*.[8] They obeyed a common formal principle and were arranged in different sections (*puncta*), each of which was repeated immediately (AA, BB, CC, and so on, recalling the structure of the sequence). Even some *lais* were solely instrumental, and there are references to *lais de vielle, de rote, de harpe*. The earliest sources containing instrumental compositions, in a curious notation, part modal and part mensural, are of English origin (Oxford, Bodleian Library, Douce 139; London, British Library, Harley 978). The fourteenth century produced the examples of *estampies* and *dances royales* preserved in the *Chansonnier du Roi* (Paris, B.N., fr. 844), and the series of fifteen compositions (*stampita, saltarello, rotta*) contained in a famous codex of Italian *ars nova* now in the British Library, Add. 29987.

31 The *ars musica* in the Middle Ages

If the history of words is the history of culture or ideas, it would be wrong to leave a gap here by omitting even a short note comparing the modern meaning of the term 'music' with what was meant by the same word (*musica*) in the Middle Ages, in the light of its classical heritage. More precisely, we ought to use the term *ars musica*, where the adjective *musica* is applied to the substantive *ars*, taken in the classical sense of 'body of technical ideas; theory; science'. The semantic evolution initiated by the ancient phrase will be apparent. From 'body of knowledge about sounds' it has come to mean, predominantly, works produced with sounds, concrete creations, thereby stressing and even making exclusive that practical aspect which was certainly implicit in the phrase *ars musica* but did not constitute its primary and habitual meaning.

Now that it is restored to its original semantic area, it will readily be understood that music was able to stand in its own right among the liberal arts taught in the Quadrivium. It was second there only to arithmetic, which is the science of the *multitudo per se*, numbers themselves, as opposed to the other sciences of the *multitudo ad aliquid*, applied numbers. Music was thus a material discipline; indeed, since the scope of the *aliquid* to which musical numbers can be applied is enormous, it can claim pre-eminence over all the other arts, as a source of universal knowledge and a key to the explanation of the cosmos.

This conception of the *ars musica* had come down to the Middle Ages from the Greco-Roman tradition, via the mediation of Boethius, Cassiodorus and Isidore of Seville (see chapter 19 above). It is understandable that only a tiny group of privileged individuals should have had access to so complex and abstract a branch of learning, but it is only they who have the right to be called *musici*. The others, those who were involved in the daily practice of music, were *cantores*. There is no need to stress the aristocratic, almost corporatist concept underpinning this distinction, which became a *topos* of mediaeval treatises and was expressed in epigrammatic form in the well-known lines

> Musicorum et cantorum magna est distantia:
> Isti dicunt, illi sciunt quae componit Musica.
> Nam qui facit quod non sapit diffinitur bestia.[1]

('Twixt the students of *musica* and the practising singers there lies a great gulf: the latter sing, the former know what *Musica* consists of. For he who does what he doesn't understand is no more or less than an animal.)

In fact there was always an unbridgeable gulf between *musici* and *cantores* in the Middle Ages. The curriculum of the *cantores*' training is already familiar: a long apprenticeship in a monastic or cathedral school in order to memorise the liturgical repertory, before neumatic notation began to appear; later, careful practice in reading musical script in order to come to a performance in a state of complete technical readiness. Certainly the mediaeval *cantor* must have known some aspects of theory, those which would have been necessary to read his melodies properly (such as the theory of hexachords), but his training was directed towards exclusively practical ends.

What, then, was the stock of knowledge which distinguished the *musicus*? In his chapter *Quid sit musicus* Boethius had already defined three kinds of knowledge relative to the *ars musica*.[2] The first is concerned with instruments and covers the art of performance; the second is that of composers, who bind words and music together; and the third, the only one both characteristic and worthy of the *musicus*, allows him to judge chant and the playing of instruments according to speculative and rational principles.

The first category includes *cantores* and instrumentalists. The long series of treatises on musical theory written by specialists from the monastic and cathedral schools was conceived with the needs of composers in mind, and thus had an obvious professional purpose; Guido d'Arezzo was aware that such treatises went far beyond Boethius' teaching, which he said 'is useful only to philosophers but not to singers' ('non cantoribus, sed solis philosophis utilis est').[3] From another point of view it seems that theorists did not have a very important role in the academic circles where the Quadrivium was studied.

Fortunately we can gain some relevant information from the collections of writings used in university teaching by four *magistri artium*:[4] Bartholomaeus Anglicus (thirteenth century), Roger Bacon (d. 1294), Vincent of Beauvais (d. 1264) and Michael Scot (d. 1234?). Their works differ in many respects from those of the theorists of the eleventh to thirteenth centuries, and reveal the broad lines of the *ars musica* as it was taught in university courses.

Their common starting-point is the definition of the discipline, taken from Isidore, Cassiodorus, Odo of Cluny, Al-Fārābi and others; Scot assembles as many as nine different definitions. These are followed by brief allusions to the effects of music. More space is given to a discussion of the origins and history of the art. Bartholomaeus briefly describes intervals and the proportions of the Pythagorean system; the chapter on the same subject in Vincent's work is more detailed, and digresses into the philosophy of dissonance and consonance, with references to Plato and others (taken from Boethius). Scot devotes almost half of his book to a discussion of proportion and intervals. Unlike the theorists, none of these writers pays any attention to scales (modes), and only Scot mentions the names of the various notes of the scale. Naturally enough, the theorists treat this subject at some length. The flowering of polyphony at St Martial (Limoges) and Notre Dame in Paris is completely ignored by all four.

The wholly philosophical division of music into three categories (*mundana, humana* and *instrumentalis*), proposed by Boethius and sometimes abandoned by the theorists, seems to be a basic theme in the discussion of the *magistri*. For Vincent, who quotes Boethius verbatim, *musica mundana* is that produced by the movement of the celestial spheres, the combination of the elements and the passage of the seasons. Bacon, however, following pseudo-Aristotle, maintains that *musica mundana*, produced 'not by the sound of heavenly bodies, but by the sound generated by the rays of those bodies', is not perceptible to the human ear and for that reason cannot be considered a category of music. (This position is also found in St Thomas Aquinas and was probably shared by Dante.)

As for *musica humana*, it is enough to say that, in Boethius' system, it arises from a *coaptatio*, an organised mutual relationship between the physical and spiritual components of human nature. It is by no means clear whether Boethius – and with him all those who followed him in this speculative and abstract approach to the problem – intended to include vocal music under *musica humana* or *musica instrumentalis*.

To follow the exposition of the four *magistri* as fully as possible it will be useful at this point to recall the doctrine of Cassiodorus as well. This contains no reference to *musica mundana*, but, concentrating on what would in the language of Boethius be called *musica humana*, Cassiodorus divides it into three sub-groups: *harmonica, rhythmica* and *metrica*, basing this division on St Augustine. This triple distinction (which Isidore later does no more than quote) was ideally suited to be expanded on by the mediaeval mind; Scot and Bartholomaeus, for instance, indulge in lengthy discussions of the various aspects which Cassiodorus had simply defined. Bacon, meanwhile, interested like Augustine in metre and accent, explores *musica metrica* in some depth.

As might have been expected, the theme of human vocal capabilities remains outside the interests of the *magistri*, even of those, like Vincent, who accept Boethius' division between *musica humana* and *instrumentalis*. The whole subject of chant is left to theorists concerned with the education of choirs.

Boethius and Cassiodorus had proposed absolutely parallel distinctions for *musica instrumentalis*, since they are both agreed – though they use different terms – on the three classes of instruments, those of percussion, tension and blowing (*genera . . . tria: percussionale, tensibile, inflatile*). Even today, moreover, we still speak of 'percussion', 'stringed' and 'wind' instruments. In his turn, Isidore (chap. v) divided music into three categories, which might be called sub-divisions of *musica instrumentalis*, since the first is 'harmonic, for it corresponds to vocal sounds' ('harmonica, quae ex vocum cantibus constat'); the second is 'organic, for it depends upon breath' ('organica, quae ex flatu consistit'); and the third is 'rhythmic, for it is given measure by the action of the fingers' ('rhythmica, quae impulsu digitorum numeros recipit'). Isidore himself comments on the division in subsequent chapters, where – as we have already seen – he discusses the qualities of the different tones of voice and describes some instruments. All this material from Isidore is quoted verbatim by Vincent, with a few trifling omissions, and reworked in his own terms by Bartholomaeus, who even presents the instruments he discusses in the same order in which they appear in Isidore.

The word-for-word reliance of these two *magistri* on a source which predates them by several centuries leads one seriously to doubt the genuineness of their interest in instruments, and above all the correspondence between their descriptions and the reality of their times. However, the fact that they mention instruments at all is significant in itself, compared with the absolute silence on the subject maintained by the theorists of the monastic schools. This is a clear and unequivocal indication that the musical interests cultivated in such schools were almost exclusively vocal. The only exception is the well-known short essay *De mensura fistularum*,[5] whose diffusion as early as the tenth century suggests that the attention of churchmen was concentrated on the building of organs.

If a comparison is drawn between the information given in theorterical treatises and the material discussed by the *magistri* in their courses for the Quadrivium, up to the end of the thirteenth century, the following observations may be made:

(1) Theorists and academics alike discuss the basic subjects at much

the same length, and these are all taken from antiquity: definition and effects of music, origins and history, proportions and intervals.

(2) The academics show no great interest in the problems of current practice, which, in contrast, are much studied by the theorists: modes, nomenclature (the *gamut*), polyphony.

(3) The academics, unlike the theorists, give a lot of space to the divisions of music and to instruments (and only exceptionally does any theorist discuss instruments).

From the end of the thirteenth century onwards a convergence of interests seems to have taken place between academics and theorists. The most obvious sign of this may be the treatise of Johannes de Grocheo (*c.* 1300), who belonged to the academic community in Paris.[6] Not only is he very well informed on the topics discussed by his predecessors, but he shows a lively interest in contemporary musical life in both religious and secular spheres, from polyphony to instrumental forms, from the songs of the trouvères to the semiotics of notation. But with Johannes a new epoch announces its arrival, even at the level of academic instruction: an epoch whose characteristic feature was to be the philosophy of musical practice.

READINGS

1 The *jubilus* in St Augustine

Born at Tagaste in Numidia in 354, Aurelius Augustinus came to Milan
in 384 to teach rhetoric. His eager search for truth had earlier led him to
study philosophy and Manichaean doctrines, but at Milan he came
under the influence of St Ambrose, who baptised him in 387. Augustine returned to Africa and became Bishop of Hippo, in present-day
Algeria, where he died in 430 during the siege of the city by the
Vandals. The penetration of his thought, the wide range of his interests
and his many writings make him one of the greatest of the Church
Fathers; the development of Christian doctrine in the West was
profoundly affected by his genius.

There are many references to music in his writings, most of which are
of great interest. They include the autobiographical details of the
Confessions, as well as valuable remarks in his masterpiece, the *De
civitate Dei*. The treatise *De musica* considers the problems of metrics
and versification. The *Enarrationes in Psalmos* and other collections of
sermons contain a number of references to the liturgical and musical
practices of Augustine's day, especially in the commentaries on Biblical
passages, where the author sees in music the perfect instrument of the
praise of God and of the elevation of the soul to the sphere of the infinite
and ineffable. It is from such a context that the passage below is taken.
In it Augustine sketches the aesthetics and mystical meaning of the
jubilus, one of the earliest forms of Christian chant. The passage, from
the Vulgate Psalm 32 (i.e. the Hebrew/Reformed Psalm 33), appears as
a liturgical reading in the office of St Cecilia (22 November).

Commentary on Psalm 32

*Praise the Lord on the cithara; sing to him with the psaltery of ten strings.
Sing to the Lord a new song* (Ps. 32, 2-3). Divest yourselves of what is
old; you have learnt a new song. A new man, a new testament, a new
song. The new song does not belong to old men. It is only new men
that learn it, made new through grace from that which is old, and now
belonging to the new testament, which is the kingdom of heaven. All

our love sighs for it and sings a new song. Sing, then, this new song not with your tongue but in your life.

Sing to him a new song, sing to him well. Every man asks how he should sing to God. Sing to him, but do not sing badly. He does not want his ears to be offended. Sing well, brothers. When you are told, 'Sing in order to please him', if [it refers] to any skilled hearer of music, you are afraid to sing without training in the art of music, lest you displease the artist, because the artist finds fault with that which the layman does not perceive in you; who would dare offer to sing well to God, who is such a judge of a singer, such an examiner of everything, such a listener? When will you be able to apply such an elegant technique in singing that you do not in any way displease such perfect ears?

This is how he gives you a way of singing: do not seek for words, as though you could explain what God delights in. Sing in jubilation. For this is singing well to God, singing in jubilation. What is singing in jubilation? Understanding, but being unable to explain in words, what is sung in the heart. Indeed, those who sing, whether at the harvest or in the vineyard or in any ardent work, when they have begun to exult with happiness in the words of the songs, turn from the syllables of the words, as though filled with such joy that they cannot express it in words, and pass into a sound of jubilation.

A *jubilus* [shout] is a kind of sound indicating that the heart is giving birth to what cannot be spoken. And for whom is that jubilation fitting if not for the ineffable God? For the ineffable is he of whom you cannot speak. And if you cannot speak of him, and ought not to keep silent, what remains but that you utter a *jubilus* [that you shout for joy]? That the heart should rejoice without words, and that the limitless expanse of joy should not bear the constraint of syllables. *Sing well to him in jubilation.*

2 From the *De institutione musica* of Severinus Boethius

The celebrated politician, philosopher and mathematician Severinus Boethius was born in Rome in about 480. He became consul in 510, and was subsequently adviser to Theodoric, King of the Ostrogoths, who had him imprisoned and executed for treason in 524.

The *De institutione musica* is the only musical treatise which has survived from this stage of Roman civilisation. It was frequently read in later centuries, and became the starting-point for the whole body of mediaeval theory. The two famous chapters translated here, from the first book, became an indisputable *auctoritas* whose content helped to shape conceptions of music at least until the age of the Renaissance.

CHAPTER II

That there are three kinds of music, in which the power of music is described

In the first place, therefore, as I am discussing music, it seems that for the moment I should say how many kinds of music I know to be recognised by students of it. There are three. And the first is of the world; the second is human; the third is that which is made within certain instruments, such as the cithara or the pipes, and others from which song can come.

And first, that [music] which is of the world can be perceived especially in those things which are seen in the sky itself, or in the combination of elements, or in the variation of the seasons. For how can it be that the mechanism of the sky, which is so swift, should move on a silent and noiseless course? And if that sound does not reach our ears, as must for many reasons be the case, still it is impossible that such very swift motion of such large bodies should produce no sound at all, especially since the courses of the stars are joined in such harmony that nothing so compacted or so intermingled can be imagined. For some are carried at a higher level, others at a lower, and all revolve with equal momentum, so that the settled order of their courses is brought about through different inequalities. Thus a settled order of modulation cannot be absent from this celestial spinning.

Again, if the four varieties of elements and their contrasting properties were not joined by some harmony, how could it be that they should come together in one body and mechanism? But all this variety produces the variety of the seasons and crops, though in such a way as to make a single body of the year. Thus if you should destroy, in mind and thought, any of these, which bestow so much variety on things, they would all perish, and would not preserve, so to speak, anything consonant. And just as in low-pitched strings there is a limit to the pitch, namely that the lowness should not descend to silence, and in high-pitched ones a limit is set to the highness, namely that the strings should not become too tense and be broken when the sound becomes thin, but that everything should be agreeable and in conformity with itself; so in the music of the world we perceive that nothing can be so excessive as to destroy another thing by its own excess. But whatever it is, it either brings its own rewards or helps others to bring them. For that which is frozen by winter is melted by spring, parched by summer and ripened by autumn, and the seasons in turn either bring their own rewards or assist others in bringing them. These matters shall be discussed more fully hereafter.

Human music is understood by anyone who penetrates into himself. For what is it that mingles with the body that bodiless life-force of reason, if not a certain harmony and blending like that of low- and high-pitched sounds, making, as it were, one consonance? What else is it that connects together the parts of the soul itself, which (according to Aristotle) is a combination of rational and irrational? But I shall speak of this also hereafter.

The third is the music which is said to reside in certain instruments. This is managed either through tension, as in strings, or through breath, as in pipes, or those which are worked by water, or through some percussion, as in those which are struck with a bronze rod on some hollow parts; and thus different sounds are created. It seems that this instrumental music should be discussed first in this work. But that is enough by way of preface. Now we must discuss the actual elements of music.

CHAPTER XXXIII
What a musician is

It must now be observed that every art, and also every discipline, naturally holds reason in higher esteem than the craft which is exercised by the hand and work of the craftsman. For it is a much greater and higher thing to know the thing that each man does than to perform that which he knows. Indeed, physical skill ministers like a servant, while reason commands like a mistress; and unless the hand performs in accordance with that which reason ordains, it is in vain. How much more distinguished, therefore, is the science of music in the knowledge of reason than in the work of performance and the act alone! – as much, that is, as the mind is superior to the body. The body lives in servitude, devoid of reason, while the mind commands, and leads it towards the right; and unless it obeys the mind's commands, the work, being also devoid of reason, will be unstable. It follows that the speculation of reason does not need the act of performance, while there are no works of the hands that are not guided by reason. Again, we can understand how great are the glory and merit of reason from the fact that the other bodily artists, so to speak, have taken their names not from a discipline, but rather from the actual instruments: for the citharode is called after the cithara, the flautist after the flute, and the rest by the names of their own instruments. But the musician is he who, with considered reason, adopts the science of music not in the servitude of work but in the rule [*imperio*] of contemplation. We see this in works of architecture and of war, in the fact that they are named in a contrary fashion. For buildings are inscribed with, and triumphs are held in, the names of those by whose command and design they were instituted, not of those by whose work and service they were completed.

There are therefore three classes which deal with the art of music: one class is that which is concerned with instruments, another composes songs, the third is that which judges the work of the instruments and the song. But those who devote themselves to instruments and whose whole occupation is taken up with them, like citharodes and those who show their skill on the organ and the other musical instruments, are cut off from understanding the science of music, since they minister, as has been said, and apply no reason, but are devoid of all speculation. The second class of those who practise music is that of the poets, who are brought to song not so much by speculation and reason as by some natural instinct, and for that reason this class too must be set apart from music. The third is that which acquires the skill of making judgements, so that it can assess rhythms and tunes and the whole of song. When all this is set in reason and speculation, it will properly be regarded as music. And the musician is he who has the ability to make judgements in accordance with speculation and reason, set forth and adapted to music, concerning modes and rhythms, and classes of tunes, and combinations, and all the things which must be explained hereafter, and the songs of poets.

3   From the *Institutiones* of Cassiodorus

F. Magnus Aurelius Cassiodorus was born in Lucania in about 485, into a family with an honourable record of public service. He became questor, consul and prefect of the Praetorian, as well as private secretary to King Theodoric. Shortly after 540 he retired to Squillace in Calabria, where he had founded a monastery at Vivarium. Unlike the more theoretical Boethius, he was an eminently practical man, and his writings also aim at collecting and popularising an encyclopaedic mass of material. The *Institutiones divinarum et humanarum lectionum* were compiled in order to give his monks a thorough programme of cultural education; they include a section on music, written between 550 and 562.

Along with Boethius, though on a more immediately practical level, he found a place as intermediary between the music of the classical world and the ideas of the Middle Ages.

FIFTH CHAPTER
On music

A certain Gaudentius, writing about music, says that Pythagoras discovered the first principles of this subject from the sound of hammers and the striking of tautened strings. Our friend Mutianus, a most learned man, has translated this into Latin, so that his [Gaudentius'] talent should be shown by the quality of the work he undertook. Clement of Alexandria, a presbyter, in a book which he published against the pagans, says that [the word] 'music' is derived from the Muses; and he carefully explains the reason why the Muses themselves had been invented. These Muses themselves are so called ἀπὸ τοῦ μῶσδαι, that is, 'from seeking', because through them, so the ancients believed, were sought the power of songs and the modulation of the voice. We have also discovered Censorinus, who, writing to Quintus Cerellius concerning the latter's birthday, gave a discussion of the discipline of music or of the second branch of mathematics, which should not be neglected; for it is not useless to read it, so that the things themselves may be stored more deeply in the mind by frequent meditation.

The discipline of music, then, is diffused in this manner through all the actions of our life – above all, if we observe the commandments of the Creator, and with pure minds conform to the rules laid down by him. For then whatever we utter and whatever internal movement we make by the pulsing of our veins is shown through its musical rhythms to be associated with the virtues of harmony. Now music is the science of modulating well; but if we lead a virtuous life, we are shown to be always associated with such a discipline; when we commit sins, we have no music. Also the sky and the earth, and all that is accomplished in them by divine dispensation, are not without the disciplines of music, since Pythagoras attests that this world was established, and can be governed, through music.

It is also very much involved in religion itself, for instance the decachord of the Decalogue, the ringing of the cithara, the tympana, the melody of the organ, the sound of the cymbals. There is also no doubt that the Psalter itself is named after a musical instrument, on the ground that a most sweet and pleasant modulation of celestial virtues is contained in it.

Now let us discuss the parts of music, in the version handed down by our ancestors. Music is a discipline or science which talks about numbers, in relationships, [the proportions] that are found between sounds; such as the double, triple, quadruple and the like of these, which are said to be in proportion.

The parts of music are three; it may be harmonic, rhythmic or metric.

Harmonics is the musical science which distinguishes high and low in sounds.

Rhythmics is that which asks whether the sound coheres well or badly with the order of the words.

Metrics is that which knows by probable reason the measures of the various metres, as for example the heroic, the iambic, the elegiac and the rest.

The classes of musical instruments are three, those of percussion, tension and blowing.

Percussion instruments, such as vessels [*acitabula*] of bronze and silver or other materials, which, with their metallic hardness, sweetly give out a ringing sound when struck.

Tension instruments are strings of gut, skilfully tied, which, as soon as they are struck with a plectrum, delightfully soothe the sense of hearing; among them are various types of cithara.

Blowing instruments are those which, when filled with exhaled breath, are stimulated to the sound of a voice, as are trumpets, reed pipes, organs, panduria, and others of this kind.

It now remains that we should speak of *symphoniae* [concords or fusions]. A *symphonia* is the combining [*temperamentum*] of a low sound with a high one, or a high with a low, creating harmony, whether in the voice or in percussion or in breath.

There are six *symphoniae*: first, diatesseron; second, diapente; third, diapason; fourth, diapason together with diatesseron; fifth, diapason together with diapente; sixth disdiapason.

[An explanation of the six intervals follows.]

A tone [*tonus*] is a difference or quantity in the whole harmonic system, and this consists in the accent or tenor of the voice.

There are fifteen tones: Hypodorian, Hypoiastian, Hypophrygian, Hypoaeolian, Hypolydian, Doric, Iastian, Phrygian, Aeolian, Lydian, Hyperdorian, Hyperiastian, Hyperphrygian, Hyperaeolian, Hyperlydian.

[Each is described in turn.]

In these, as Varro mentions, was displayed a power of such effectiveness that it calmed excited minds and also attracted the very beasts, and even serpents, birds and dophins, to the sound of its melody.

To pass over as mythical the lyre of Orpheus and the songs of the sirens, what do we say of David, who snatched Saul from an unclean spirit by the discipline of most healthful melody, and in a novel way bestowed on the king, through hearing, the health which the physicians could not produce by the power of herbs (I Kings 16, 23)? It is related also that the physician Asclepiades, a very learned one according to our forefathers' testimony, restored a madman to his true self by means of *symphonia*. But there have been many miracles achieved in sick men through this discipline. The sky itself, as we mentioned above, is said to revolve through the sweetness of harmony. And, to summarise the whole matter briefly, nothing that is carried on in the celestial or the terrestrial field in a way that conforms to the plan of its Creator is said to be excluded from this discipline.

It is therefore a most welcome and useful type of knowledge, which both directs our sense to things on high and pleases our ears with melody. Among the Greeks it was taught on an acceptable system by Alypius, Euclid, Ptolemy and others. Among the Latins the distinguished Albinus wrote a book on this subject with economical brevity; I remember that I had it in a library at Rome and read it studiously. If it happens to have been removed in the heathen invasion, you have here the Latin Gaudentius of Mutianus; if you reread this with close attention, it opens up for you the entrance-hall of this science. It is said that Apuleius of Madaura has also established the principles of this work in the Latin language.

Father Augustine also wrote six books about music, in which he showed that the human voice naturally has rhythmical sounds and melodious harmony in long and short syllables. Censorinus also subtly discussed the accents necessary to our voice, saying that they belong to the discipline of music; a copy of this I have left for you among the rest.

4   From the *Etymologiae* of Isidore of Seville

St Isidore of Seville has frequently been called the last Father of the Western Church. Born in about 560, he succeeded his brother Leander as Archbishop of Seville in 600 or 601, and died in 636. He was an immensely prolific writer, whose works had a strong influence on the cultural evolution of later centuries; with Boethius and Cassiodorus, he belongs among the greatest intellectual masters of the Middle Ages. The *Etymologiarum sive originum libri XX* enjoyed widespread popularity thanks to their clarity of expression and the encyclopaedic range of their contents. The title was suggested by the fact that the ideas and scientific theses discussed in the book are approached mainly through the etymology of the relevant vocabulary, a technique familiar to ancient grammarians and teachers of rhetoric. In book III, *De quatuor disciplinis mathematicis*, arithmetic, geometry, music and astronomy are discussed; chapters XV–XXIII are concerned with music, but XV–XVIII are omitted below, since they are largely derived from Cassiodorus and cover etymology, the origins of music and its division into three parts.

CHAPTER XIX
Concerning the tripartite division of music

1. But it is agreed that all sound, which is the material of songs, is by nature of three kinds. The first is harmonic, for it corresponds to vocal sounds. The second is organic, for it depends upon breath. The third is rhythmic, for it is given measure by the action of the fingers.

2. For sound is produced by the voice, as through the throat; or by the breath, as through the trumpet or the flute; or by beating, as through the cithara, or through anything else that is made tuneful by percussion.

CHAPTER XX
Concerning the first division of music, which is called harmonic

1. The first division of music, which is called harmonic, that is the modulation of the voice, belongs to comedians, tragedians, choruses, and all who sing with their own voice. This produces movement from the mind and the body, and from movement sound, from which is produced music, which in man is called the voice.

2. The voice is air beaten [*verberatus*] by the breath, after which words [*verba*] are called. The voice properly belongs to men or to irrational animals. For in other things sound is called voice not properly but figuratively, as 'The voice of the trumpet rang out . . . and broken voices to the shore', for the proper expression is that the rocks of the shore resound; or as 'But the trumpet [rang out] a terrible sound from afar with its melodious bronze' [Virgil, *Aeneid*]. Harmony is the modulation of the voice and the concordance or conformity of very many sounds.

3. *Symphonia* (concord or fusion] is a blending of melody from low and high with concordant sounds, whether in the voice or in blowing or in beating. It is through this that higher and lower voices are in concord, so that anyone who departs from it offends the sense of hearing. The opposite of this is discord [*diaphonia*], that of discrepant or dissonant voices.

4. Euphony is pleasantness of voice. This is also called *melos* from its pleasantness and sweetness [*mel*].

5. Diastema is an interval of the voice formed from two or more sounds.

6. Diesis is certain intervals and diminutions of melody and of movement from one sound to another.

7. A tone [*tonus*] is a more or less high utterance of the voice; for it is a difference or quantity of harmony which resides in the accent or tenor of the voice. Musicians have divided its kinds into fifteen parts, of which the hyperlydian is the last and highest, the hypodorian the lowest of all.

8. Song is an inflexion of the voice, for sound is direct, and sound precedes song.

9. Arsis is a raising of the voice, that is a beginning. Thesis is a lowering of the voice, that is an end.

10. Sweet voices are thin and compressed, clear and acute. Distinct voices are those which are carried a greater distance, so that they fill every place entirely, such as the noise of trumpets.

11. Thin voices are those which do not have breath, like those of infants, women or invalids, as in strings. For the strings that are thinnest give out thin and slight sounds.

12. Voices are fat when much breath comes out at once, as in those of men. An acute voice is thin and high, as we see in strings. A hard voice is one which emits sounds violently, like the sound of thunder or an anvil, when a hammer is struck against hard iron.

13. A harsh voice is one that is raucous and is dispersed through minute and dissimilar beats. A blind voice is one that falls silent as soon as it has been emitted, and, being stifled, cannot possibly be prolonged further, as occurs in clay vessels. A delightful [*vinnolus*] voice is gentle and flexible. And it is called *vinnolus* from *vinnus*, that is a gently curled lock of hair.

14. But a perfect voice is high, sweet and clear. High, so that it is capable of high notes; clear, so that it fills the ears; sweet, so that it soothes the minds of listeners. If any of these things is lacking, the voice will not be perfect.

CHAPTER XXI
Concerning the second division, which is called organic

1. The second, organic, division exists in those things which, when filled with exhaled breath, are stimulated to the sound of a voice, as are trumpets, *calami*, *fistulae* [both terms mean 'reed pipes'], organs, the pandura, and instruments similar to these.

2. 'Organ' is a general word for all musical devices. The one to which bellows are applied is given another name by the Greeks; but the common custom is rather to call it an organ.

3. The trumpet was first invented by the Etruscans, of whom Vergil writes, 'And the Etruscan noise of a trumpet blared through the air'. It was employed not only in battles but on all feast-days, for praise and for the expression of joy. Hence it is said in the Psalter, 'Play on the trumpet at the beginning of the month, on the appointed day of your festival'. For the Jews had been commanded to sound a trumpet at the beginning of a new month, as they still do today.

4. They say that flutes were devised in Phrygia, and that for a long time they were used only for funerals, but later also for the rites of pagans. They think that they were called *tibiae* because they were first made from the shin-bones [*tibiae*] of stags and the legs of fawns, then by extension even those which were not made from legs and bones began to be so called; hence also *tibicen* [flautist] as if it were *tibiarum cantor* [flute player].

5. *Calamus* [reed (pipe)] is properly the name of a tree, named from *calere*, that is to pour out sounds.

6. Some think that the *fistula* [reed pipe] was invented by Mercury; others by Faunus, whom the Greeks call Pan; some by Idis, an Agrigentine shepherd from Sicily. It is called a *fistula* because it sends out sounds: for in Greek 'sound' is φώς and 'sent' στόλια.

7. A sambuca among musicians is a kind of *symphonia*, for it is a sort of brittle wood, of which flutes are also made.

8. The pandura is called after its inventor. Vergil says about it, 'Pan was the first to begin joining several reeds with wax; Pan looks after sheep and the masters of sheep.' For among the pagans he was a pastoral god, who was the first to arrange unequal reeds for music and to fit them together with conscious skill.

CHAPTER XXII
Concerning the third division, which is called rhythmic

1. The third is the rhythmic division relating to strings and beating, to which are assigned the various kinds of cithara, the tympanum and cymbalum, the sistrum, vessels [*acitabula*] of bronze and silver or other materials, which, with their metallic hardness, sweetly give out a ringing sound when struck, and the other things of this kind.

2. As has been said before, Jubal is regarded as the inventor of the cithara and the psaltery. But according to the opinion of the Greeks the use of the cithara is believed to have been discovered by Apollo. The form of the cithara is said to have been initially like a human chest, because music issued from it as the voice does from the chest; and it was given its name for the same reason, for in the Doric language the chest is called κιϑάρα.

3. Gradually more kinds of it came into existence, such as psalteries, lyres, barbitons, phoenixes, pectides, and those which are called Indian and are struck by two players at once; and various others, both rectangular and triangular in shape.

4. Also the number of strings was increased, and their kind altered. The ancients called the cithara *fidicala* or *fides*, because its strings are in concord just as men between whom there is trust [*fides*] agree well together. The ancient cithara was of seven strings; hence Vergil says 'differences of seven voices'.

5. Differences because no string makes a sound like that of a neighbouring string, but seven strings either because they fill the whole voice or because the sky sounds with seven motions.

6. Strings [*chordae*] were called after the heart [*cor*], because just as there is a beating of the heart in the chest so there is a beating of the string in the cithara. Mercury was the first to devise these; and he too was the first to tighten strings to make sound.

7. The psaltery, which is commonly called a *canticum*, derives its name from *psallere* [to play, or sing to, the lyre], because the chorus responds in consonance to its sound. There is a resemblance to the barbarian cithara in the shape of a letter Δ. But there is this difference between the psaltery and the cithara, that the psaltery has at the top the hollow wood from which the sound is produced, and the strings are held underneath and make their sound from above, but the cithara has the hollowness of wood at the bottom.

The Hebrews used a ten-stringed psaltery on account of the number of the Decalogue of the law.

8. The lyre is named ἀπὸ τοῦ ληρεῖν, 'from variety of voices', because it produces diverse sounds. They say that the lyre was first invented by Mercury, in this way. When the Nile, retreating to its bed, had left various animals behind on the plain, a tortoise was also left behind. When it had rotted, and its sinews were left extended inside the shell, on being struck by Mercury it made a sound. Mercury made the lyre to its pattern, and passed it to Orpheus, who was particularly devoted to this subject.

9. Hence it is even thought that by the same art he attracted not only wild beasts but also rocks and trees with the melody of his song. Musicians have even imagined in their fabulous tales that the lyre was placed among the stars for love of the art and for the glory of poetry.

10. The tympanum is a skin or hide extended from one side with wood. It is the middle part of a *symphonia* in the likeness of a sieve. It is called a tympanum because it is a half, as half of a pearl is also called a tympanum; and it is, like a *symphonia*, struck with a short stick.

11. Cymbala are certain *acitabula* which touch each other when struck, and make a sound. They are called cymbala because they are struck during dancing. For so the Greeks call things for dancing συμβαλεῖν.

12. The sistrum is called after its inventor, for Isis queen of Egypt is believed to have invented that type: Juvenal says, 'Isis, and she strikes my eyes with an angry sistrum'. Thus also it is struck by women, because the inventor of this type was a woman. Hence also among the Amazons the army of women was called to war by a sistrum.

13. The bell [*tintinnabulum*] gets its name from the sound it makes, as with the clapping of hands and the squeaking of doors.

14. *Symphonia* is the common name for hollow wood with skin stretched on both sides, which musicians strike here and there with short sticks. And very sweet music is created in it from the concord of low and high.

CHAPTER XXIII
Concerning musical numbers

1. You seek numbers in accordance with music as follows. Given the extremes, as for instance 6 and 12, you see by how many units 12 exceeds 6, and it is by 6 units; you square this: six sixes make 36. You add those first extremes 6 and 12: together they make 18. You divide 36 by 18, making two. You join these with the smaller amount, namely 6, to make 8, and it will be a mean between 6 and 12, because 8

exceeds 6 by two units, that is a third of six, and 12 exceeds 8 by 4 units, a third part. Therefore it is exceeded by the same proportion as it exceeds.

2. Just as this order exists in the world from the revolution of circles, so also in the microcosm it has such inexpressible power that without its perfection even a man lacking *symphoniae* does not exist. Even metres by the perfection of the same music consist in arsis and thesis, that is raising and lowering.

N.B. The method which Isidore suggests for finding the harmonic mean between two numbers works only if the larger number is twice the smaller. The method which works with any pair of numbers is not to square the difference of the two given numbers, but to multiply that difference by the smaller number. This is the correct form of the rule as given by Boethius (*De institutione musica*, book II, chap. XVII).

5 From the *Epistola de ignoto cantu* of Guido d'Arezzo

No reliable information has come down to us about Guido's birth or education. He was a monk in the Benedictine abbey at Pomposa, where he incurred the hostility of his brethren on account of his radical new ideas about musical theory and notation. In about 1023 he moved to Arezzo, where he taught in the cathedral's choir-school. After 1029 he retired to the Camaldolese monastery at Fonte Avellana, where he died in about 1050. His experiments and innovations in the teaching of chant made him one of the most famous scholars of the Middle Ages. Apart from the *Prologus in Antiphonarium*, the *Micrologus* and other minor works, he left an *Epistola de ignoto cantu*, written between 1030 and 1032 and addressed to Michael, a fellow-monk in the abbey at Pomposa. This short text is not only a valuable autobiographical document, but explains, in a limpid and concise style, the author's teaching methods and theoretical concepts, which earned him the gratitude and approval of Pope John XIX (1024–33).

The letter of Guido addressed to the monk Michael concerning unknown song

Guido, cast down and raised up by many vicissitudes, to the most blessed and sweet Brother Michael. Either the times are hard or the distinctions of divine providence are obscure, for truth is often trampled on by deceit and charity by envy, which hardly deserts the company of our order; thus the assembly of the Philistines may punish the wickedness of the Israelites, so that, if everything should soon happen as we wish, the mind which is confident in itself may not sink down to die. For it is when we ascribe all we can to our Maker that what we do is truly good . . .

Therefore I, inspired with charity by God, have, with the greatest haste and care, conferred not only on you but on as many others as I could the favour given by God to me, all unworthy as I am; so that the ecclesiastical songs which I and all those before me learnt with the greatest difficulty may be learnt with the greatest ease by men to come, and that they may wish eternal health to me and you and my other helpers and may ask God's mercy to grant a remission of our sins, or at least that a small prayer may come from the gratitude of so many. For if those men, who have up to now been barely able in ten years to gain an imperfect knowledge of singing from their teachers, intercede for those teachers most faithfully with God, what do you think will be done for us and our helpers, who produce a perfect singer in the space of a year, or two years at most? Or if the customary wretchedness of men should prove ungrateful for such great benefits, will the just God not reward our toil? Or, because God does all of this and we can do nothing without him, shall we have nothing? Far from it. For even the apostle, although he is what he is by the grace of God, still sings, 'I have fought a good fight, I have finished my course, I have kept the faith: Henceforth there is laid up for me a crown of righteousness'.

Secure, therefore, in our hope of repayment, let us press on with such useful work; and because after many storms the long-desired calm has returned, we must sail happily.

But because your captivity is mistrustful of liberty, I shall set out the order of the business. John of the highest apostolic seat, who now governs the Roman church, hearing the reputation of our school, and how by our Antiphonary boys were learning songs they had not heard, was much astonished, and invited me to him by three messengers. I therefore went to Rome with Master Grunvaldus, a most reverend abbot, and Master Peter, who is in charge of the canons of the church of Arezzo, a very knowledgeable man by the standards of our age. And so the Pontiff rejoiced greatly at my arrival, making much conversation and asking various questions; and, often turning over our Antiphonary as if it were some prodigy, and pondering the rules forming the preface, he did not cease or move from the place where he was sitting until he had satisfied his desire by learning one versicle that he had not heard, so that he suddenly recognised in himself what he scarcely believed in others. What need of more words? Through pressure of ill health I was unable to stay even a short time at Rome, as the heat of summer in the marshy region by the sea was threatening us with death. At length we agreed that I must soon go back there when winter returned, seeing that I ought to reveal this work to the Pontiff (who had had a foretaste of it) and to his clergy.

A few days later, wanting to see your Father and mine Master Guido, abbot of Pomposa, a man most dear to God and men for the merit of his virtue and wisdom, and a part of my own soul, I paid him a visit. He too, a man of keen intelligence, when he saw our Antiphonary, immediately approved and believed it, and regretted that he had once agreed with our rivals, and asked me to come to Pomposa, urging me that as a monk I should prefer monasteries to bishoprics, and should especially prefer Pomposa, on account of the study which has recently been discovered for the first time in Italy through the grace of God and the industry of the most reverend Guido.

Swayed, therefore, by the speeches of so great a Father, and obeying his commands, I wish first with the help of God to add to the fame of this great and good monastery through this work, and wish as a monk to excel other monks; especially since, when almost all the bishops have just been condemned for the heresy of simony, I am afraid to have anything to do with them.

But because I cannot come at present, I am sending you in the mean time a very good method, which was recently given to us by God and has proved most useful, for the finding of an unknown song . . .

To find an unknown song, then, most blessed Brother, the first and popular rule is this: you sound on a monochord the letters which any neume has, and by listening you will be able to learn from it just as from a human teacher. But that is a childish rule, good for beginners but very bad for those who continue their studies. For I have seen many very acute philosophers, who have sought teachers for the study of this art not only from Italy but also from France and Germany and even Greece itself; but because they relied on this rule alone they were never able to become even singers, let alone musicians, or to imitate our small boy psalmists. For an unknown song, then, we should not always seek the voice of a man or of some instrument, so as to seem like blind men never advancing without a guide; but we should commit deeply to memory the varieties and properties of single sounds and of all descents and ascents. You will then have a very easy and well-tried method for finding an unheard song, if there is anyone who knows how to teach another person not only in writing but preferably aloud, face to face in conversation according to our custom.

For after I had begun to pass on this method to boys, some of them were able in less than three days to sing unknown songs easily, a thing that could not have happened after many weeks by other methods.

If, then, you wish to commit to memory any note or neume in such a way that it can quickly come to your mind wherever you wish, in whatever song, whether you know it or not, so that you may quickly be able to utter it without hesitation, you must observe that note or neume at the beginning of some very well-known *symphonia*, a *symphonia* of this kind, which starts from the same note; in fact let it be this *symphonia*, which I use from first to last for teaching boys.

C	D	F	DE D		D	D	C	D	E	E
Ut	que -	ant	la - xis		re -	so -	na -	re	fi -	bris

EFG	E	D	EC D		F	G	a	G	FED	D
Mi -	ra	ge -	sto - rum		fa -	mu - li	tu - o			- rum,

GaG	FE	F	G	D		a	G	a	F	Ga	a
Sol - ve		pol -	lu -	ti		la -	bi - i	re -	a		- tum,

GF	ED	C	E	D
San -	cte	Jo -	an -	nes.

(That your servants may be able to sing the marvels of your deeds with supple voices, pardon the offence of unclean lips, Saint John.)

Do you see then how this symphonia starts its phrases on six different notes? If, therefore, anyone knows the beginning of every phrase, being so trained that he may immediately begin whichever phrase he wishes without hesitation, he will easily be able to utter the same six notes, according to their properties, wherever he sees them. Also, hearing some neume without seeing it written out, consider which of these phrases is best fitted to its end, in such a way that the last note of the neume and the first of the phrase have the same sound. And be sure that the neume has ended on that note on which the phrase corresponding with it begins. If you have begun to sing some unknown *symphonia* that has been written out, you must take great care to finish every neume correctly, so that in the same way the end of the neume is well connected with the beginning of that phrase which starts from the same note on which the neume has ended. This rule, then, will be a very great help to you, so that you may sing unheard songs competently as soon as you have seen them, or, on hearing unwritten ones that must be quickly written out, you may be well able to distinguish them.

Next I have set out below, note by note, some very short *symphoniae*; and when you look closely at their phrases, you will rejoice to find all the lowerings and raisings of every note in order in the beginnings of those phrases. But if you can attempt this, so that you may modulate any phrases you wish of one *symphonia* and the other, you have learnt by a very brief and easy rule the very difficult and multiple varieties of all neumes. Since we hardly express all these things in any way in writing, we can lay them bare easily only in conversation.

Just as we have twenty-four letters in every piece of writing, so we have only seven notes in every song. For just as there are seven days in a week, so there are seven notes in music. The others, which are added above the seven, are the same, and sing similarly throughout, differing in no respect except that they double the sound higher up. And for that reason we say that seven are grave and we call seven acute. But the seven letters are not written twice over but differently, in this way:

$$\Gamma \quad A \quad B \quad C \quad D \quad E \quad F \quad a \quad \natural \quad c \quad d \quad e \quad f \quad g \quad \begin{matrix} a & b & c & d \\ a & b & c & d \end{matrix}$$

Anyone who wants to make a monochord and distinguish the qualities and quantities, similarities and differences of sounds and tones should study most earnestly to understand the very few rules which we have set out below.

[Advice on the construction of the pattern follows, along with a guide to the intervals of tones and semitones, to modes and their melodic formulas, and so on.]

These few things, said in verse and prose by way of prologue to an Antiphoner concerning the formula of modes and neumes, open the door of the art of music briefly, and perhaps sufficiently. But anyone who is curious should seek our booklet entitled *Micrologus*; he should also read through the book *Enchiridion*, which the most reverend abbot Odo has most excellently composed. I have rejected his example only in the shapes of sounds, because I have descended to the level of children, not following Boethius in this, whose book is not useful for singers but only for philosophers.

End of letter.

6   An example of dramatised liturgy

Two processional books, dating from about 1300, are kept in the Biblioteca Capitolare at Padua (codd. c 55 and c 56), containing dramatic offices for the various feasts of the liturgical year according to the tradition of Padua Cathedral. Although they possess elements which recall the *rappresentazione*, they are not genuine liturgical dramas. Their framework remains strictly liturgical, and the various characters are played by ministers of the liturgy (i.e. the several orders of clergy). Furthermore, the texts used are all taken from liturgical books. These details all apply perfectly to the dramatised liturgy which played so important a part in the customs of local churches during the Middle Ages.

The *Uffici drammatici padovani* have been edited in facsimile and translated by Giuseppe Vecchi (Olschki, Florence, 1954). The melodies are not reproduced here.

On the day of the Annunciation

After dinner at the accustomed hour the great bell is struck, and meanwhile the CLERGY gather at the church, and in the larger sacristy some of the CLERGY prepare themselves with copes and other requirements, and in the said sacristy stand MARY, ELIZABETH, JOSEPH and JOACHIM, prepared with the DEACON and SUBDEACON, carrying silver books in their hands; and at the proper hour they go out of the sacristy in procession and pass on to the places prepared for them. When these have gone, the rest pass on in procession to the baptistery, and there stands a BOY prepared *in the likeness of Gabriel* above a *throne*, and he is lifted out of the baptistery and borne in the church from the side of the square and carried above the staircase towards the choir, and the CLERGY stand through the middle of the church *in the likeness of a choir*, and meanwhile the SUBDEACON begins a prophecy, namely *The LORD spake unto Ahaz, saying*. When the prophecy is over, the DEACON begins the gospel, namely *The angel Gabriel was sent*, up to the words *And the angel came out unto her, and said*.

After this comes GABRIEL, and on bended knees, raising two fingers of his right hand, he begins in a high voice the antiphon written below.

Hail, Mary, full of grace, the Lord is with thee, blessed art thou among women.

When the antiphon is over, the DEACON proceeds further in the gospel, up to *And the angel said unto her*. When this is over, the ANGEL again, with his right hand raised and fully open, begins the antiphon written below.

Fear not, Mary: for thou hast found favour with God. And, behold, thou shalt conceive and shalt bring forth a son.

When the antiphon is over, the DEACON proceeds further up to

Then said Mary unto the angel. When this is over, MARY replies in a level [*plana*] voice with the antiphon written below.

How shall this be, angel of God, seeing that I have not known a man in conceiving?

When the antiphon is over, the DEACON proceeds further: *And the angel answered and said unto her*; and the angel begins the verse written below.

Listen, Mary, virgin of Christ, the Holy Ghost shall come upon thee, and the power of the Highest shall overshadow thee.

But when he has reached the words *The Holy Ghost shall come upon*, then a *dove* is revealed slightly. When the verse is over, the DEACON again proceeds up to *Then said Mary unto the angel.* When this is over, MARY raises herself, and standing with arms open begins in a high voice, *Behold the handmaid*; before the end of the said antiphon the dove is released and MARY receives it under her cloak.

Antiphon: *Behold the handmaid of the Lord; be it unto me according to thy word.*

When these things are over, the DEACON proceeds further in another gospel, namely *Then Mary arose, and went into the hill country*, up to *And she spake out with a loud voice, and said.*

Meanwhile MARY descends from her place and goes to the place of ELIZABETH and JOACHIM, and they both receive MARY, as is written in the gospel. When this has been done, ELIZABETH, on bended knees, touching MARY's body with both hands, begins in a humble voice the antiphon written below.

Blessed art thou among women, and blessed is the fruit of thy womb.

When the antiphon is over, ELIZABETH raises herself, and standing she again begins the antiphon written below.

And whence is this to me, that the mother of my Lord should come to me? For, lo, as soon as the voice of thy salutation sounded in mine ears, the babe leaped in my womb for joy. And blessed art thou, Mary, that believed: there shall be a performance in thee of those things which were told thee from the Lord.

When these things are over, the DEACON again proceeds: *And Mary said.* And MARY turns towards the PEOPLE and sings with a high voice in the eighth tone the three verses written below.

My soul doth magnify the Lord. And my spirit hath rejoiced in God my Saviour. For he hath regarded the low estate of his handmaiden: for, behold, from henceforth all generations shall call me blessed.

When these things are over, there is a response of one verse with the organ and another from the CHOIR, thus proceeding further up to the end; and when these things are over, they all return to the sacristy.

7 Evidence for musical customs in Italy

(A) Two passages from the *Cronica* of Salimbene de Adam

Salimbene de Adam, a Franciscan from Parma (1221 – after 1288) depicts with vivid amazement the worldly refinement in musical life which he came across at Pisa. (The reference to leopards and other foreign creatures probably implies that the episode was linked with a visit to the city by the Emperor Frederick II.) The second passage translated here concerns the so-called 'Alleluia movement', which began in northern Italy in 1233 and spread rapidly to various parts of the country. After a wide-ranging general description Salimbene, characteristically, goes on to observe the details with calm lucidity. Among the figures mentioned the most notable is that of Fra Benedetto, the remarkable trumpet-playing ascetic who encouraged boys to repeat his impassioned prayers (they cannot really be called *laude*) and to sing *alleluia*.

From the *Cronica*

While I was with that companion at Pisa, going out with our bags in search of bread, we happened to come across a courtyard, into which we both entered. A leafy trellis covered it completely, and its green shade was a delight to the eye and an invitation to rest. There were leopards there, and many other beasts from across the sea at which we gazed happily for a long time, for it is always pleasant to behold what is beautiful and unusual. There were also young men and women in the flower of their youth, and the beauty of their clothes and their good looks made them fair and pleasing to look upon. In their hands both women and men held vielles and lyres and other kinds of musical instrument, on which they played most delightful tunes, making the proper gestures as they did so. Otherwise there was not a sound in that place: no one spoke; everyone listened in silence. And the words of the song they sang, the mingling of their voices and the manner of their playing were unfamiliar and beautiful, so beautiful that our hearts were carried away in boundless joy. They said nothing to us, and we too were silent. As long as we remained they interrupted neither their song nor the playing of their instruments. And yet we stayed there a long time and only left with great reluctance. I do not know, though God does, whence a spectacle of such intense delight was offered to us, because we had never seen anything like it before and never have since.

First of all there came to Parma Fra Benedetto, called Fra Cornetta, a simple and unlettered man, but one who led a life of great honesty and virtue. I saw him and came to know him both at Parma and later at Pisa. He did not belong to any religious order, but lived in seclusion, seeking to please God alone; and he was a good friend to the Friars Minor. He seemed like another John the Baptist, come to proclaim the Lord and prepare a perfect people for Him.

On his head he wore an Armenian cap, and he had a long black beard and a small trumpet [*parvula tuba*] of bronze or brass, which he used to blow; it made a noise at once terrifying and sweet to the ear. He was girt with a strip of some animal's skin, and wore a black habit like a rough sack which hung down to his feet. His tunic was worn with a long cloak, like a cleric's, and on front and back was marked a large, long, red cross, which reached from his neck to his feet, like those used on a priest's chasuble. Dressed like this, he went about with his trumpet and preached in churches and squares and praised God, followed by an enormous gang of little boys who often carried branches and lighted candles. I myself, standing on a wall of the bishop's palace, which was then being built, many times saw him preaching and praising God. He began his praises [*lodi*: i.e. *laude*?] by saying in the vernacular: 'Laudato et benedhetto et glorificato sia lo patre!' And the boys repeated what he had said. Then he repeated the same words and added, 'sia lo fijo!' And the boys joined in again, chanting the same words. Finally he repeated the words for the third time, adding, 'sia lo spiritu sancto!' And then, 'Alleluia, alleluia, alleluia!' Then he blew his trumpet and began to preach again and to praise God.

(B) The singing of *laude*: documents concerning the oldest company of *laudesi*

Gilles-Gerard Meersseman's studies on the earliest phase of the singing of *laude* have made a notable contribution to the clarification of the issue. His most valuable discoveries enable us to distinguish, among the confraternities which arose in the thirteenth century, some 'compagnie' who ordained the singing of *laude* in their statutes and were consequently called 'compagnie dei laudesi'. As far as we know, the oldest of these was that founded at Siena in 1267 by Bishop Tommaso Fusconi; we have a letter from the bishop to the people of his diocese, which also contains the statutes of the fraternity. (See G.-G. Meersseman O.P., 'Nota sull'origine delle compagnie di laudesi (Siena 1267)', in *Rivista di storia della Chiesa in Italia*, XVII (1963), pp. 402–5.)

Readings

Fra Tommaso, by the grace of God humble Bishop of Siena, greets and blesses all who believe in Christ, clerics and lay people of the city and diocese of Siena, to whom this letter may come . . .

Since, in the house of Dominican brothers at Siena, at Campo Regio, by our will and with our consent a fraternity has been founded in honour of blessed Mary ever virgin and of blessed Dominic our father, because of the devotion of its members and the usefulness and many benefits which we believe may arise from it, with God's help, we decree that this fraternity shall bear the names of blessed Mary and blessed Dominic, and with our authority we confirm its existence, as also we confirm its statutes, authenticating them with our seal . . . [Lists of indulgences follow, along with statutory decrees concerning the fraternity's responsibilities.]

Decree IV: meetings of the fraternity

We ordain that every day, in the evening, at the hour of Compline or a little before, according to the season, a meeting shall take place in the house of the Dominicans at Campo Regio, *for the singing and hearing of laude*, and that there may be a brief sermon on such occasions, if the prior of the Dominicans thinks it appropriate, especially in Lent . . .

We further ordain that on the second Sunday of the month, early in the morning, the members of the fraternity shall meet at Campo Regio *to listen to laude*, and to hear mass and a sermon. For the same purpose and at the same time the members shall meet in the same place every Monday following [the second Sunday] and shall sing a requiem for the souls of dead members of the fraternity and their relatives . . .

Given at Siena, September 1267.

> The aims of the fraternity of St Mary and St Dominic were confirmed in the letter of indulgence given to its members on 2nd September 1273 by another Bishop of Siena, Bernardo Gallerani. The relevant passages are quoted below.

Since, then, beloved children, *you continue every day to sing laude* to blessed Mary, mother of Christ and ever virgin, and to blessed Dominic (from whom your fraternal community takes its name), and to the whole company of heaven, and since we too wish to share in such wonderful *laude* . . . , with the aim of increasing devotion among the faithful who sing praises [*laudantes*] to the mother of God . . . , for every day in which, according to statute and your custom, you gather together in peace *to raise up your laude* to God, we allow you one hundred days' indulgence . . .

Further information can be gleaned from the biography of the Blessed Ambrogio Sansedoni, who entered the Dominican Order at Siena in 1237 and died in 1286. It appears from certain passages that this brother played an important part in the institution or re-organisation of the city's confraternities, among which that of the *laudesi* is mentioned by name, with details of enormous interest. They include the existence of a *schola* of boys trained for the singing of *laude*, and the spread of this Sienese custom to other cities. The biography of Sansedoni was written in about 1288 by his fellow-Dominican Fra Ildebrando de' Paparoni. The passage about the *laudesi* is reproduced in translation from Meersseman's article.

In his city of Siena, where he [Sansedoni] usually lived, the fruits of the action of the Holy Spirit are particularly evident, and they have there confraternities of outstanding men, even laymen. Some of them *take as their aim the singing of praises* [*laude*] to God; these are sung every day with remarkable devotion in the religious houses (especially and above all among his fellow-Dominicans), even by boys, whose keep is paid for and who are trained to sing these *laude*. This custom has spread from there [Siena] to several other cities [there follows a list of other fraternities – charitable ones and those of the *Disciplinati*]. These efforts were set in train or redoubled in the time of the aforementioned father [Ambrogio Sansedoni].

8 From the *Ars musica* of Gill da Zamora

Gill da Zamora (Johannes Aegidius de Zamora) was born about 1240, and became a Franciscan friar and a student at the University of Paris while St Bonaventure was teaching there (1273–74). He was a friend of the King of Castile, Alfonso X 'el Sabio', to whom he dedicated his *Liber Mariae*, which had some affinities with the *Cantigas de Santa María* collected by the king. He was Provincial of the Franciscans in Santiago from 1300 to 1318, and lived for several years after that date. The author of many works (*Ars dictandi* and *De praeconiis Hispaniae*, among others), he dedicated a short essay called *Ars musica* to the Minister-General of the Friars Minor, Giovanni Mincio da Murrovalle. Since he held this post from 1296 to 1304, we know the chronological limits within which the *Ars musica* must have been composed.

This little treatise is in two parts, one speculative (chapters 1–4) and the other technical (chapters 5–17). On the whole Gill shows himself to be resolutely conservative, relying heavily on the classical theorists of church music; there is no reference in the work to mensural music or polyphony. The choice of two chapters of the *Ars musica* for translation here is intended to demonstrate how it was still possible at the end of the thirteenth century, on the eve of the appearance of the *ars nova*, to write about music in a way which would not have seemed strange to the great masters of the past, Boethius and Isidore. Chapter 17, the last in the book, is given over to a description of instruments, but it is disappointing, being modelled word for word on the text of Isidore which we already know. The one interesting addition is the naming of three instruments (though they are nőt described) which had 'recently' [*postremo*] been discovered, and were perhaps particularly well-known in Spain: the *can(n)one* (or *mezzo-can(n)one*), the guitar and the *rabé* (rebec). Apart from this, the text of chapter 17 appears almost identically in the musical section of the *De proprietatibus rerum* of Bartholomaeus Anglicus – a fact which poses a delicate problem of attribution which has not yet been solved. In any case, it is suggestive that all this material should still have been taken from Isidore.

Third chapter concerning the definition or description of music and its etymology

According to Boethius, music is a motion of voices consonant with each other in fit proportion. According to Guido, music is knowledge of melodies, consisting in discrete sound and song. For there is a discrete sound, as will be said below, and another indiscrete sound. According to John [Cotton or Afflighem], music is a fit motion of voices. Musicians are those who by speculation and reason distinguish every song and every variety of melody, and the celestial harmony itself.

Music is called after the Muses, who are credited with perfecting this art; or from *moys*, which is water, because they assert that it was discovered in water, as nerves and arteries alone were separated in water from bones and flesh through the flowing of the water. When they were touched, they burst forth in a harmonious sound. Or it is so called because the voice does not exist without the moisture of palate and tongue. Others have said that *musica* is like *mundica*, because it derived its origin from the song of the world [*mundi cantus*].

According to Isidore, in the fourth book and first chapter of the *Etymologies*, speaking of mathematics, he says that music is the discipline of the numbers which they use in sounds. In the fifth book, concerning music, he says in the first chapter that music is knowledge of melody, consisting in sound and song. According to him it is called after the Muses, because according to the ancients the law or power of songs and the melody of voices were sought by them. It consists itself of songs and poems, as the same writer asserts in the first book.

Fourth chapter concerning the distinction or division of music and its constitution

There are many kinds or modes of musical knowledge, inasmuch as one is of the world, another human, another celestial, another instrumental or artistic.

The music of the world is the rational consideration of those things which occur in the heavens, or in the elements, or in the changes and varieties of the seasons. For the world is thought by some to be composed of some sort of harmony of sounds. For the qualities of the elements are connected and consonant with each other as if through some fitting consonances and rational harmonies of strings. Similarly seasons are fitted to seasons, and elements to seasons. Air corresponds with spring, fire with summer, earth with autumn and similarly water with winter. And the eternal God of seasons bestows the seasons to relieve man of boredom and relieve man of toils, as if by some most fitting melodies. And just as elements are consonant with seasons, so these two things are consonant with humours and bodies. For air and spring are consonant with blood, fire and summer with choler, earth and autumn with melancholy, water and winter with phlegm, as has been said elsewhere concerning the aforesaid consonances and dissonances in the booklet *Concerning the abridgement of the sciences and concerning natural history*, and in the book entitled *Archivus*, that is *Armarium*.

Human music is that which is studied in the human constitution, which every man can understand in himself. Thus Boethius says a man does not exist – that is he is not composed – without music, which is so naturally connected with us that if we wished to be without it we could not; inasmuch as there is a great musical proportion of soul to body, and vice versa, by their own mediating spirits, namely the natural spirit whose seat is in the liver, the vital spirit whose seat is in the heart, and the animal spirit whose seat is in the head. There is similarly a proportion of humours to each other and to the body, and similarly of bones, nerves, arteries, cartilages, flesh and skin to each other and to the body. Thus Plato says that the god of the soul is the harmony of music. Similarly Boethius says, 'What', he says, 'mingles with the body that bodiless life-force of reason, if not a certain harmony as if of low- and high-pitched sounds, like a blending making one consonance?' And this kind is imitated by philosophical concordance.

Instrumental imitation, which exists in instruments of art or nature, is subject to our consideration. Guido and John and other investigators of musical knowledge have agreed in making the distinction that the first kind of musical knowledge is that which relates to instruments; the second, that which concerns the instruments of songs; the third kind is that which distinguishes by reason the task of instruments and songs. Guido distinguishes the first two modes as lame, because they move on only one foot, namely the foot of practice or operation. They lack the foot of reason or intellect, which properly concerns itself with music. For it is not so much singers who should be called musicians, since they are ruled only by use and confusedly, not by reason, but those who are ruled by the foot of reason, according to Boethius and Guido.

Celestial music is that by which they describe the sky itself with the circles contained in it revolving with harmonic melody [*harmonica modulatio*], because from the motion of the sky and the stars there arise, according to them, certain *symphoniae* observed with musical melodies. Thereto adds Job, 'Who makes the harmony of the sky to sleep?' [Job 38, 37]. Thus Boethius asks how it can be that such a swift mechanism of the sky, and such a very swift motion of it, and the extent or mass of such large bodies, should move on a silent and noiseless course. To this he replies that if that sound does not reach our ears at all, that must come about for many reasons, and that if it does reach them, it is not perceived. But the Philosopher, discussing this question, says that there should not be sound there, because there is no violence or violent motion.

Some instrumental music is live, which is performed by a live instrument, some dead, which is performed by a dead instrument, as is evident in the vielle, the cithara, the organs and the like, which will be spoken of at the end. Or according to others, the knowledge of music resides in two instruments, namely the natural and the artificial, the natural being the arteries, tongue, palate, lips and lung, by which the human voice is formed. Thus Boethius says, 'The sound of natural instruments in accordance with the formation of the voice is suited to harmonic melody [*harmonica melodia*] through one tension and relaxation'. But we must again make the distinction that the sound of the natural instruments of the voice is double, being discrete and indiscrete. The discrete is that in which discretion and consonance are considered. The indiscrete is that in which discretion or consonance is not considered, as in a laugh, a groan or a gesture. An artificial instrument gives out an artificial sound, as is evident in citharae, organs, vielles, and other musical instruments, which are made by art and not by nature, and which give out, as we perceive with our senses, an artificial and not a natural sound, as we shall explain below at the end in an account of such things. But we must make the distinction that some of the artificial instruments, such as citharae and vielles, give out a discrete artificial sound, and some, such as cymbals, tympana and sistra, give out an indiscrete sound. But music does not properly admit indiscrete sound, whether made by art or by nature.

GLOSSARY

ad libitum. A chant thus designated may be selected as desired for performance, not being associated with any particular liturgical occasion.

Agnus Dei. Invocation sung during the *fractio panis* in the mass, in the form of a litany. The fifth chant in the Ordinary of the Roman mass.

alba. Musical form associated with the troubadours rather than the trouvères, on the theme of the friend or friends watching over lovers and warning them at the break of dawn. Often arranged as a dialogue.

alleluia. Hebrew word of acclamation and joy, meaning 'Praise Yahweh'; used as a conclusion or interpolation in certain psalms (alleluiatic psalms) from the Old Testament. In the Christian liturgy it appears as a moment of lyrical contemplation after the gradual and before the Gospel; it is sung twice, with a versicle in between. Musically it was at first a short melodic phrase, but was later transformed into the most melismatic form in the liturgical repertory, closely linked with the *jubilus.*

alleluiatic. Adjective applied to a psalm or versicle introduced or punctuated by an alleluia.

Ambrosian. (1) Refers to Milanese liturgy or chant, which trace their history back to St Ambrose. (2) Hymn composed on the pattern of those of Ambrose (identical versification and strophic scheme). (3) Name formerly given to any repertory of liturgical chant in Latin other than the Roman.

anaphora. In the liturgical sense, indicates the eucharistic prayer of the mass, also called 'canon'.

anisosyllabism. Absence of regular versification, where some verses are hypometric (i.e. have one or more syllables too few) and others are hypermetric (i.e. have one or more syllables too many).

antiphon. Short chant, originally repeated between the verses of a psalm (this kind of performance was known as 'antiphonal psalmody'). Later, and to this day, the name was given to the short melody which precedes and follows the singing of a psalm.

antiphona ad accedentes. Communion-chant in the Mozarabic mass.

antiphona ad confractorium. Chant of the Gallican mass, performed during the *fractio panis.* In the Mozarabic rite it was called *antiphona ad confractionem.*

antiphona ad pacem. Chant of the Mozarabic mass performed during the exchange of a sign of peace.

antiphona ante Evangelium. Chant of the Gallican mass, performed before the announcement of the Gospel.

Glossary

antiphona post Evangelium. Chant of the Ambrosian mass, performed after the singing of the Gospel.

Antiphonarium (Antiphonal, Antiphonary, Antiphoner). Liturgical book containing antiphons. It can be either *Antiphonale Missarum* (= *Liber Gradualis*), the name given, by extension, to the book containing all the chants for mass; or *Antiphonarium Officii*, which contains the chants for the office (the Liturgy of the Hours).

arsis. Means 'raising'; the moment of forward impulsion in rhythmic scansion.

ballade. Poetic and musical form used, according to some scholars, by the trouvères, and usually made up of three stanzas set to the same music. Not all specialists, however, accept the *ballade* as a fixed form in the trouvère repertory, as it was later to appear among French practitioners of polyphony. The musical pattern of each stanza was usually AAB.

ballata. Italian poetic and musical form made up of a *ritornello* (or refrain) and strophes (or stanzas). The strophe consists of two *piedi* (feet or 'mutations'), set to the same melody, and a *volta*, set to the tune of the refrain. Three kinds of *ballata* have been identified, according to the number of lines in them: minor, median and major. Their melodic scheme is XY, ABABXY, XY, and so on.

Bar. Poetic form in *Minnesang*, made up of two *Stollen* (= feet or 'mutations', as in the Italian *ballata*) and an *Abgesang*: the basic pattern is AAB.

benedictiones. Chant for the introductory rites of the Mozarabic and Old Gallican masses.

beracoth. Prayers of blessing used by the Jews, taken up and adapted by Christians for use in the eucharistic prayer or canon.

bicola. In mediaeval prose-rhyme (i.e. prose whose successive phrases have rhyming terminations), a *colon* is a single phrase, a *bicola* a pair of phrases which rhyme.

canon. (1) In the Roman mass, the eucharistic prayer which begins after the *Sanctus* and ends with the *Pater noster*. (2) In the Greco-Byzantine rite, a chant for the office including a given number of 'odes'.

cansó (chanso). Basic form of the troubadour repertory, with the pattern AB, AB, CDE, but capable of wide variation.

canticle. Poetic form used in the Old and New Testaments, distinct from psalms. The three best-known examples in the New Testament are those recorded in the Gospel of St Luke: the *Magnificat* and the *Benedictus Dominus*, sung at Vespers and Lauds respectively in the liturgy of the Hours, and the *Nunc dimittis*, sung at Compline.

cantigas. Marian chants composed in the thirteenth century in Portuguese, collected by Alfonso X 'el Sabio'.

cantio(nes). Lyrical poem in Latin with a varying structure including a refrain.

cantus. Chant of the Ambrosian liturgy corresponding to the Roman *tractus*.

cantus planus. Name given to liturgical monody, in contrast to *musica mensurata*.

carmina. One of the names given to tropes.

Centonate method. A method of composition used in ecclesiastical monody, which takes pre-existing melodic material (melodic formulas) and joins them together in new combinations. The word derives from the Latin *cento*, a kind of patchwork blanket.

191

Glossary

chanson. Trouvère composition, corresponding to the *cansó* of the troubadours. It can cover various subjects, hence the names *chanson d'histoire, de danse, d'aube, à boire,* etc.

cherubicon. Melismatic chant of the Greco-Byzantine liturgy, performed by a soloist (*psaltista*).

cheironomy. The hand-movements which indicate the movement of a melody in ascending and descending lines. The name is thus given to the art of conducting a choir with hand-gestures.

clamor. Meditative chant after a reading from the Prophets in the Mozarabic mass, a kind of prolongation of the *Psallendum.* It includes acclamations from the congregation, hence the name *clamor* or *clamores.*

cobla. Strophe in a troubadour composition. The term seems to be derived from *copula,* which referred to strophic coupling in the sequence. According to the rhyme-scheme, it may be *unissona, dobla, capcaudada, capfinida,* and so on.

colon. See **bicola.**

comes. Latin name given to the liturgical Lectionary.

communio (communion-chant). A chant peculiar to the Roman mass, performed during the administration of the eucharist. In ancient times a whole psalm was sung, together with its antiphon; later only the antiphon survived.

completorium (Compline). (1) Private prayer at evening in the Roman office (see **Liturgy of the Hours**). (2) Chant peculiar to the Ambrosian office, performed at the end of Vespers.

conductus. Religious composition intended to accompany (to *conduct*) the movements of the clergy; hence, a processional chant. It originated in the trope and quickly became an independent para-liturgical chant, used in liturgical drama, and even acquired a secular form. Examples of *conductus* in polyphonic form are found from the second half of the twelfth century onwards.

confractorium. Chant of the Ambrosian mass performed at the moment of the breaking of bread. See also **antiphona ad confractorium.**

contrafactum. A text composed on the metrical scheme of a previous composition and sung to an existing melody.

copula. Couplet of strophes in a sequence, sung to the same melody.

Credo (Symbolum). Statement of the truth of Christian belief. The third chant of the Ordinary of the Roman mass, performed on Sundays and feast-days after the Gospel and the homily.

custos. Small sign or note used at the end of a line in liturgical books, to indicate the pitch of the first note on the next line.

Diaspora. Dispersal of the Jews beyond the borders of Palestine.

diastema. Vertical distance between two written notes, indicating the greater or lesser extent of the interval which separates them. Diastematic notation is that which conveys such intervals; non-diastematic notation is that which suggests the line of the melody without aspiring to fix the size of intervals in writing.

diatonic. Adjective applied to an interval (or a scale) which proceeds by natural tones and semitones (without sharps or flats). Liturgical monody is constructed on diatonic scales (modes or modality).

differentia. Variable conclusion of a psalmodic tone which helps to make the pitching of the antiphon easier. In the model intonations of psalms the various *differentiae* (also called 'finals') are sung on the vowels *e u o u a e*, taken from *seculorum. Amen.*

doxology. Formula or prayer glorifying God, Christ or the Trinity. The major doxology is the *Gloria in excelsis Deo* (the second chant of the Ordinary of the Roman mass); the minor doxology is the *Gloria Patri*, which ends the psalms in the office and remained in the introit even after the reduction of the psalm to a single verse.

echoi. The eight types of scale on which Greco-Byzantine monody is constructed; not to be confused with the *tonoi*, the scales of classical Greek music.

ecphonetic. Means 'declamatory'; the term applied to an embryonic form of Greek notation, consisting of various signs derived from grammatical accents. It was used to recall a familiar intonation to the mind of the reader of liturgical texts.

episema. (1) Horizontal dash above a note, marking its rhythmic and expressive importance; already appears in neumatic notation. (2) Vertical dash under a note, marking a rhythmic stress (*ictus*). Found in the modern editions of liturgical melodies with rhythmic signs prepared by the school of Solesmes.

Epistolarium (Epistolary). Ancient liturgical book containing the Epistles (letters of the Apostles) to be read at Mass.

eschatology. Christian teaching about the fate of man after death and the end of the world.

estampie (*estampida*). Form of thirteenth- and fourteenth-century instrumental music, made up of sections (*puncta*) repeated twice over.

estribillo. Ritornello or refrain in the *cantigas* and other fixed Iberian forms.

Evangeliarium (Evangeliary). Ancient liturgical book containing the Gospels to be read at mass.

Exultet. Paschal announcement, or proclamation of Easter, sung by a deacon in the rites for the vigil of that feast. The name comes from its beginning with the words *Exultet iam angelica turba coelorum* . . .

figured. The term 'figured music' (*musica figurata*) is used generally to mean polyphonic music, as opposed to plainchant. *Cantus figuratus* is a part elaborated with some form of artifice, superimposed upon its opposite, plain *cantus planus*, to create a polyphonic texture.

fractio panis. Rite of the breaking of bread, which the celebrant performs before communion in the mass. It arose from the practical need to make the bread available for the clergy and faithful to take in communion; now it remains as a commemoration of Christ's actions at the Last Supper, in conformity with the Jewish ritual of the Passover meal. During the *fractio panis* the *Agnus Dei* is sung in the Roman rite.

Gallican. Name given to a kind of liturgy (rites, prayers and chant) distinct from Roman usage, which flourished in northwestern Europe (including northern Italy) until the age of the Franks.

Gamut. System of nomenclature for musical sounds or notes. The word derives from the lowest note in alphabetical notation, *gamma* (the third letter of the Greek alphabet), to which corresponded the first note of the 'hard' hexachord (*Ut*).

Geisslerlieder. Religious chants of the flagellants (*Geissler*), composed in

Glossary

fourteenth-century Germany; equivalent to the *laude* of the Italian *Disciplinati*.

Gloria (in excelsis). Christological doxology (song of praise to Christ) sung at the beginning of mass in Western rites (called *Laus angelorum* in the Ambrosian rite).

Gnosis. Heretical tendency which took various forms based on a rationalistic explanation of Christian revelation. The best-known representatives of Gnosticism were Marcion, Bardesanes and others.

Graduale (Gradual). (1) Responsorial chant of meditation in the Roman mass, performed by a soloist, originally between the reading from the Prophets and the Epistle. From the fifth century it was moved to a position after the Epistle. It was so called, perhaps, because it was sung on the steps (*gradus*). (2) Liturgical book (*Graduale* or *Antiphonale Missarum*) containing the chants for the Proper of the mass and, as an appendix, those of the Ordinary. The latter could also be copied into a separate book called the *Kyriale*.

Hesperinós. Evening prayer in the Greco-Byzantine office, corresponding to Vespers in the Roman rite.

hexachord. Succession of six notes according to the diatonic scale, with four intervals of a tone and one of a semitone, in a fixed position between the third and fourth notes (T T S T T). According to the initial note one could construct the 'natural' hexachord (starting on C), the 'hard' hexachord (G . . .), and the 'soft' hexachord (F . . . , including a flat on B).

Hirmologion. Greco-Byzantine liturgical book containing the 'canons' made up of a given number of 'odes'. The 'odes' were sung according to a model setting called the *hirmós*.

hirmós. Greek term for a melody serving as a model for various texts.

Historia. Name given to versified or metrical offices because of the prevalence in them of narrative material over the original lyrical aspect.

Hours. See **Liturgy of the Hours**.

hymn. Poetic composition of praise addressed to God, originally lacking regular forms of versification and fixed strophes. Later it was made up of lines composed according to the classical system of quantities and gathered in regular strophic structures. Finally, it was written in lines governed by the number of syllables required and the placing of the tonic accent. Musically, a single melodic pattern is used to set all the strophes. Each section of the liturgy of the Hours is introduced by the singing of a hymn.

Hymnarium (Hymnal, Hymnary). Liturgical book containing the hymns for the liturgy of the Hours.

hymnody. Singing of hymns; the body of liturgical hymns.

Improperia. Responsorial chants performed on Good Friday using the text of the reproaches uttered by Christ against the ingratitude of the Jews. Of Gallican origin.

Ingressa. Introductory chant (an antiphon without a psalm) in the Ambrosian rite, corresponding to the Roman introit.

introitus (introit). Entry-chant for the mass in the Roman rite (the first chant of the Proper). Originally it consisted of the singing of a whole psalm, whose verses were interspersed with an antiphon; later only a single verse of the psalm remained, along with the *Gloria Patri*, preceded and followed by the *antiphona ad introitum*.

194

jeu-parti. Trouvère composition, whose strophes are sung alternately by two characters in the form of a dialogue.

jongleur. A mediaeval entertainer in general; in the musical sense, a minstrel.

jubilus. Melodic vocal phrase, with no text; an expression of pure contemplation, most often using the last vowel of *alleluia*.

kérygma. Proclamation of the Gospel message in the preaching of the Apostles, later set down in the four canonical Gospels.

kontakion. Melismatic chant (a kind of poetic homily) of the Greco-Byzantine liturgy, performed by a soloist.

Kyrie eleison. First chant of the Ordinary in the Roman mass, a remnant of the initial litanic prayer and of the original liturgical language, Greek. It is made up of three invocations each repeated three times: *Kyrie eleison* (Lord, have mercy), *Christe eleison* (Christ, have mercy), *Kyrie eleison* (Lord, have mercy). Since the reform required by Vatican II the three invocations are repeated only once.

lai. Poetic and musical form of the twelfth to fourteenth centuries, thought to be the secular equivalent of the sequence, from which it takes the repetitive principle of the strophic couplet. It may be narrative or lyrical in character, with a considerable number of strophes. It was popular with the trouvères and later imitated by the troubadours and the *Minnesinger*.

lauda. Italian devotional chant which flourished from the thirteenth century onwards.

Laudes. (1) Morning prayer, Lauds (*laudes matutinae*): see **Liturgy of the Hours**. (2) Chant preceding the Gospel in the Mozarabic mass. (3) Chant following the Gospel in the Gallican mass. (4) Name given to tropes on the *Gloria in excelsis*.

laudes cum alleluia. Sung in the Gallican mass after the *sonus* (offertory).

lauds. See **Liturgy of the Hours**.

Lectionarium (Lectionary). Ancient liturgical book containing the readings (Epistles, Gospels) for mass. Re-introduced to common use as part of the reform which followed Vatican II.

Leich. A composition of the *Minnesinger* corresponding to the French *lai*.

Lied. Poetic and musical form of *Minnesang* corresponding to the Provençal *cansó*, with the same melody repeated in each strophe.

litany. Chant made up of brief invocatory prayers sung to a single melodic formula, to which the congregation responds with an acclamation such as *Kyrie eleison*. In the Roman mass the *Kyrie eleison* is all that remains of an early litanic prayer.

Little Hours. See **Liturgy of the Hours**.

liturgical year. Liturgical celebration of the mysteries of Christ in the course of a year. The year begins with the Christmas cycle (with four weeks of preparation called Advent) and culminates in the Easter cycle (prepared in Lent and Passiontide), which closes fifty days later at Pentecost (descent of the Holy Spirit). The period between Pentecost and the next Advent, once called 'Sundays after Pentecost', is now called 'ordinary time of the year'. These celebrations form the Temporal cycle; feasts and commemorations of saints, on fixed days, form the so-called Sanctoral cycle (cycle of the saints).

liturgy. (1) The whole body of rites and prayers expressing the dimension of the Church's worship as a community of believers sharing in Christ's priesthood and called to lift perfect praise up to the Father along with Him. It finds expression in two ways: the liturgy of the sacraments (visible signs with which Christ saves), among which the Eucharistic liturgy (the mass, or memorial of Christ's sacrifice, and communion) stands as the most important; and the Liturgy of the Hours, the official prayer of the Church arranged across the hours of each individual day, which together form the cycle of the liturgical year. (2) If qualified by an adjective (Roman, Gallican, etc.) it is synonymous with 'rite'.

Liturgy of the Hours. Expression referring to the office, the prayer of the Roman Church, made up of psalms, Biblical readings and other formulas, and arranged for each day of the liturgical year. It consists of Lauds (morning prayer) and Vespers (evening prayer); of the Little Hours (Prime, now abolished, Terce, Sext and None); of the readings for the office (at one time this was a nocturnal prayer and was called Matins, with one or three Nocturns); and of personal evening prayer (Compline or *Completorium*). The book containing the texts of these prayers was for a long time called the Breviary, because as a consequence of various reforms the prayers in it appeared in abbreviated form.

lucernarium. (1) Chant of the Ambrosian office performed at the beginning of Vespers (taking its name from the lighting of lamps). (2) Responsory, followed by a metrical hymn, in the Gallican rite.

Matins. See **Liturgy of the Hours**.

Meistergesang. Poetic and musical movement based in the bourgeoisie, which followed the development of *Minnesang* in German-speaking countries; the compositions connected with the movement are called *Meisterlieder*.

melisma. Group of several notes sung on a single syllable. The name 'melismatic' is given to melodies in which melismas predominate.

mensural. An adjective used to describe a system of notation whose individual symbols denote precise and unvarying durations. Mensural notation succeeded modal notation, where interpretation of a symbol depended on context: see also **mode** (2).

Minnesang. Poetic and musical movement which arose in German-speaking countries as an imitation of the art of the troubadours. (*Minne* = courtly love; *Sang* = song). The singer–poets were called *Minnesinger*.

Minor Hours. See **Liturgy of the Hours**.

Missale Plenarium. Liturgical book appearing from the tenth and eleventh centuries onwards, containing prayers, chants and readings for mass. Called *plenarium* because the various repertories of prayers, chants, etc. are collected in a single book.

modal. (1) Concerning the orderly arrangement of sounds; applied to the series of notes which follow one another in the scale of one of the eight modes of church music. (2) Concerning rhythmic organisation; used of the theory or interpretation which applies one of the six 'rhythmic modes' to musical notation.

modality. See **mode**.

mode. (1) One of the eight diatonic scales of liturgical music defined by their basic sound (tonic) and by the varying positions of tones and semitones. (2) Rhythmic mode: a ternary rhythmic pattern applied in polyphony and, by extension, monody in the thirteenth century. There are six rhythmic modes, and they result from combinations of the values of Greco-Latin metrics based on long and short syllables (for example, mode I = trochaic metre ($-\smile$) = ♩♪; mode II = iambic metre ($\smile-$) = ♪♩; etc.). As a result every note takes on a specific meaning within the scheme as it is applied, independently of its graphic form. In the past this interpretative system was occasionally misused by being applied indiscriminately to Middle Latin music, the songs of the troubadours, and so on.

monochord. Scientific and musical instrument with a single string, used to define the laws of musical acoustics and the mathematical proportions of the pitches produced by reducing the length of the vibrating string.

monody. Music for a single voice, as opposed to diaphony and polyphony, music for two or more voices. Ancient liturgical chant in the Christian Church was monodic.

Mozarabic. Adjective (meaning 'among the Arabs') applied to Spanish Christians living under the Moorish empire. Hence the name of their 'Mozarabic' liturgy, rites and chant, which some would prefer to call 'ancient Hispanic' or 'Hispano-Visigothic'.

mutation. Passage from one hexachord (natural, hard or soft) to another, allowing a melody to be extended beyond the range of a single hexachord. The movement was brought about in such a way that the semitone should always correspond to the notes *Mi-Fa*.

neumatic. Adjective applied to notation based on neumes, or to a melody in which groups of two or three notes for each syllable predominate (as opposed to 'syllabic' or 'melismatic' melody).

neumatic pause. Interruption in the line sketched by a neume of several notes, to indicate the rhythmic importance of the note on which the scribe paused, which is that preceding the interruption.

neume. (1) Sign used in musical notation to indicate one or more notes to be sung on the same syllable. (2) Melodic interpolation.

Nocturns. See **Liturgy of the Hours**.

offertorium (offertory). Chant of the Roman and Ambrosian rites performed during the procession in which bread, wine and the offerings of the faithful are brought to the altar.

office. See **Liturgy of the Hours**.

oktoechos. The eight scales characteristic of the corresponding 'modes', to which liturgical melodies were forced to conform towards the end of the eighth century.

Ordinary of the mass. Made up, in the Roman rite, of the five chants whose text remains unchanged from one mass to another: *Kyrie eleison*, *Gloria*, *Credo*, *Sanctus* (and *Benedictus*) and *Agnus Dei*.

Ordines Romani. Mediaeval texts describing and laying down the rules for certain liturgical rites, especially in the papal liturgy.

orthrós. Morning prayer in the Greco-Byzantine office, corresponding to Lauds in the Roman rite.

para-liturgical. Adjective applied to a rite or chant which, not being an integral part of a ceremony or of the liturgical repertory, remains on the margins of the liturgy and acts as a kind of extension of it. Sometimes equivalent to 'devotional'.

Glossary

parousia. Presence or Second Coming of Christ at the end of time.

passio, passiones. A *passio* (plural *passiones*) is a chronicle of the death (often through martyrdom) of a saint.

pastorela. Provençal song (*pastourelle* in *langue d'oïl*) on the theme of a meeting between a girl and the young man who seeks her love.

planctus. Middle Latin poetic and musical form expressing deep sorrow. The epic and historical *planctus* of the Carolingian era (for the deaths of Charlemagne, Duke Eric, and others) are famous, as are the autobiographical ones composed on Biblical models by Peter Abelard.

planctus Mariae. Lyric or dramatic composition set in the form of the Virgin's lament for the death of Christ.

planh. Poetic and musical form from the troubadour repertory, expressing anguish and sorrow.

praelegendum (*antiphona ad praelegendum*). Introductory chant for the mass in the Gallican and Mozarabic rites.

preces. (1) Chants which precede the Epistle in the Mozarabic mass; considered by some to be the prototype of the sequence. (2) Chants which follow the Gospel in the Gallican mass. (3) One of the names given to tropes.

preface. Chant for the celebrant ending with the *Sanctus*, which introduces the eucharistic prayer or canon.

Processionale (Processional). As a noun, refers to the liturgical book containing the chants for processions.

Proper of the mass. Made up, in the Roman rite, of the chants which vary from one mass to another; introit, gradual, alleluia (sometimes replaced by a tract), offertory, communion-chant (*communio*).

prosa. Used in some parts of mediaeval Europe (especially southern France) to denote the text of a sequence, or both text and melody as a whole. (Correspondingly, *sequentia* may then be restricted to denoting the melody of the sequence.) Also used to denote the texted melismas of alleluias, offertories, responsories, etc., although the diminutive *prosula* is now more widely used to refer to these.

prosula. Form of trope applied to existing melismatic passages. The text is integrated by inserting new syllables into the preceding words and thus creating new verbal units. Such are the tropes for the alleluia verse and the verses of the offertory.

psallenda. Chant with psalmodic versicles and doxology performed during processions in the Ambrosian rite.

psallendum. See **clamor.**

Psalm. (1) Biblical poem collected in the book of Psalms in the Old Testament. (2) Poem from the early centuries of the Christian era, composed in the style of the Biblical psalms (with no fixed criteria of versification).

psalmellus. Meditative chant in the Ambrosian mass, performed after a reading from the Prophets.

Psalmodic hymnody. Early form of Christian hymn, lacking fixed metrical or strophic structure and therefore resembling the psalms of Hebrew poetry.

psalmody. Singing or recitation of psalms; the body of psalms.

Psalterium (1–2 = Psalter, 3 = psaltery). (1) Book of the Bible containing the

Glossary

psalms. (2) Liturgical book containing the psalms to be sung in the liturgy of the Hours. (3) Musical instrument.

Responsory. Form of liturgical chant which originally alternated a solo chant with an invariable response from the congregation, on the pattern AA, BA, CA, and so on. Usually the responsories follow the readings at Matins (*responsorium prolixum*) or the short readings at Lauds or Vespers (*responsorium breve*).

Responsoriale (Responsorial). As a noun: the liturgical book containing the responsories for the liturgy of the Hours. As an adjective: applied to a chant (like psalmody) which follows a responsorial pattern.

rite. (1) Sacred activity characteristic of a particular form of worship. (2) Body of ceremonies, prayers and chants which differs from other similar bodies within the context of the same religious tradition: for example, Roman rite, Greco-Byzantine rite, etc.

rondeau. Trouvère composition following the musical pattern AB, AA, AB, AB.

Sacramentarium (Sacramentary, *Liber sacramentorum*). The oldest book of Roman liturgy, it contains prayer-formulas for use by the celebrant. Historically, three types have been identified: Veronese (pseudo-Leonine), Gelasian and Gregorian.

sacrificium. Chant of the Mozarabic mass corresponding to the Roman offertory.

Sanctoral. Liturgical cycle of saints' days (as opposed to Temporal).

Sanctus. First word of a chant derived from Jewish prayers and performed, in the Roman liturgy, after the preface, at the beginning of the eucharistic prayer (see also **trisagion**).

Sequentiarium (Sequentiary). Mediaeval liturgical book containing sequences.

sirventes. Troubadour poetic composition with political, heroic, moral, satirical and even religious content. Musically it took no particular form.

solmisation. System for indicating the notes of the musical scale using syllables; especially the system attributed to Guido d'Arezzo, which identifies the musical notes with the syllables of the hexachord. In later practice it applied to education in reading music and the study of melodies based on hexachords and mutations. The term derives from the fact that, in the passage from one hexachord to another, the movement is from *Sol* to *Mi*.

sonus. Chant of the Gallican mass corresponding to the Roman offertory.

Spruch. Composition in *Minnesang*, possibly corresponding to the *sirventes* of the troubadours.

Sticherarion. Greco-Byzantine liturgical book, containing single-strophe compositions and tropes (*stichos* = verse, versicle).

syllabic. Adjective applied to a melody in which one syllable of text corresponds to each note.

Symbolum. Name given to the *Credo* in the Ambrosian rite.

Tagelied. Composition in *Minnesang*, corresponding to the Provençal *alba*.

Te Deum laudamus. Hymn of thanksgiving, with a psalmodic structure, wrongly attributed to St Ambrose.

Temporal. Liturgical cycle of the feasts of the Lord and Sundays distributed throughout the year (as opposed to Sanctoral).

Glossary

thesis. Means 'deposition' (lowering); the moment of repose in rhythmic scansion.

threnos. Also called *versus* and *lamentationes*; the chant which precedes the Epistle in the Mozarabic mass, and is performed on certain days of penitence. The term derives from the Greek *thrênos*, 'lament'.

Tonarium (Tonary). Mediaeval liturgical book (or section of a book) in which chants (antiphons, graduals etc.) are arranged in musical (rather than liturgical) order, according to key-note. The *incipit* of the piece's text is shown, along with the intonation formulas, expressed in several syllables (*Noeagis*, for instance) intended to serve as a mnemonic.

Torah. Jewish Law, entrusted by God to Moses.

tractus (tract). Chant of the Roman mass, originally performed by a soloist, sung instead of the alleluia on the occasions when the latter may not be sung (in Lent, for example). The term is probably derived from *cantus tractus*, i.e. continuous chant, without repetitions.

transitorium. Communion-chant in the Ambrosian mass, corresponding to the Roman *communio*.

trecanum. Communion-chant in the Gallican mass, corresponding to the Roman *communio*, possibly made up of three psalmodic verses.

trisagion. Chant of the introductory rites in the Mozarabic and Old Gallican masses. Etymologically it means 'thrice holy' and recalls the *Sanctus* of the Roman rite.

Troparium (Troper). Liturgical book containing tropes.

trope. (1) Melismatic fragment used to embellish a melody. (2) Text added to an existing melisma. (3) New melody with new text used as a prelude or interpolation in an existing piece of music.

Verba. One of the names given to the trope.

vers. Poetic and musical form in the troubadour repertory. It derives its name from *versus*, a musical composition in Latin which is associated particularly with the abbey of St Martial at Limoges.

verse (versicle). (1) Rhythmic unit in poetry; a succession of versicles constitutes a psalm, generally characterised by the conceptual parallelism of the two hemistichs (half-verses). (2) In responsorial chants the verse (*versiculus*) is the part of the text which changes, as opposed to the *responsum*, the repeated part which remains unaltered. (3) Poetic form which was developed especially in the monastery of St Gall towards the end of the ninth century. (4) Chants in the repertory of St Martial at Limoges, also called *conductus*.

Vespers. see **Liturgy of the Hours**.

virelai. French musical form with the melodic pattern AB, CCAB, AB, to which the musical pattern of the *ballata* has often been related. Its appearance takes place after the trouvère and troubadour period.

Visitatio sepulchri. Office of the Easter vigil or Easter morning, whose central scene is that of the visit of the three Marys to the empty tomb of Christ.

Vulgate. Latin translation of the Bible, mostly the work of St Jerome.

zajal. Arabic–Andalusian composition with a strophic pattern aaax, bbbx, and so on; thought by some scholars to be the model for certain forms of Romance lyric.

NOTES

Part I. The origins of Christian worship; liturgy and chant

Chapter 1. The evidence of the early Christian sources

1 For a transcription of the Oxyrhynchus fragment see E. Wellesz: *A History of Byzantine Music and Hymnography*, pp. 125–9.
2 As in E. Cattaneo: *Il culto cristiano in Occidente*, p. 21.
3 E. Cattaneo: *Il culto*, p. 40; M. E. Boismard: *Quatre hymnes baptismales dans la première épître de Pierre*, p. 13.
4 E. Cattaneo: *Il culto*, p. 23.

Chapter 2. The Jewish roots of Christian worship

1 M. McNamara: 'The liturgical assemblies and religious worship of the early Christians', *Concilium*, VII/5 (Hilversum, 1969), p. 15.
2 E. Cattaneo: *Il culto*, p. 37.
3 Such as E. Werner: 'The music of post-biblical Judaism', *Ancient and Oriental Music*, ed. E. Wellesz, NOHM I (London, 1957), pp. 317–21; G. Reese: *Music in the Middle Ages* (New York, 1940), p. 114.
4 For a general account of Jewish liturgy that includes references to music see A. Z. Idelsohn: *Jewish Liturgy and its Development* (New York, 1932).
5 Especially A. Z. Idelsohn: *Hebräisch–orientalischer Melodienschatz*.
6 Such as H. Avenary: *Studies in the Hebrew, Syrian and Greek Liturgical Recitative*, and A. Herzog: *The Intonation of the Pentateuch in the Heder of Tunis*.

Chapter 3. The early forms of Christian chant

1 Section 'La lecture biblique (cantillation)' in 'Musique (dans la Bible)', *Dictionnaire de la Bible: supplément* vol. 5 (Paris, 1957), col. 1449–64.
2 'Formal structure of psalms and canticles in early Jewish and Christian chant', pp. 3–6.
3 H. Hucke: 'Die Entwicklung des christlichen Kultgesangs zum gregorianischen Gesang'; summary in 'Das Responsorium' (see bibliography to ch. 20), p. 146.
4 For further details see P. G. Cobb: 'The liturgy of the Word in the early Church', in C. Jones *et al.* (eds.): *The Study of Liturgy*, pp. 186–7.
5 Such as J. Dyer: 'The offertory chant of the Roman liturgy and its musical form' (see bibliography to ch. 20).

6 For an extended account see E. T. Moneta Caglio: *Lo jubilus e le origini della salmodia responsoriale*, Jucunda Laudatio XV (Milan, 1977).
7 E.g. *PL*, vol. XXXVI, col. 283.
8 For further details see F. Hawkins: 'The Didache', in C. Jones *et al.* (eds.): *The Study of Liturgy*, pp. 55–7.
9 See for instance R. M. Grant: *Gnosticism and Early Christianity* (New York, 1966).
10 'Le Christ dans les psaumes', *La Maison-Dieu*, XXVII (1951), 86–113.
11 *The Mass of the Roman Rite*, vol. I, pp. 377–8.

Chapter 4. Liturgy and chant after the Edict of Milan

1 For the early stages of mass chants see J. Jungmann: *The Mass*, vol. I, *passim*.
2 The arrangement and early history of liturgical books is described in detail by A. Hughes: *Medieval Manuscripts for Mass and Office*.
3 *Registrum epistularum* II, ed. L. Hartmann, MGH Epistolae II (Berlin, 1899), p. 344. See G. G. Willis: *Further Essays in Early Roman Liturgy*. Alcuin Club Collections I (London, 1968), pp. 191–8.

Chapter 5. Hymnody

1 *Enarrationes in Psalmos*, *PL*, vol. XXXVII, col. 1947.
2 *PL*, vol. XLIII, cols. 23–32.
3 Compare for instance G. M. Dreves: *Aurelius Ambrosius: 'Der Vater des Kirchengesanges'*, Stimmen aus Maria-Laach, Supplement LVIII (Freiburg, 1893), and V. Ermoni: 'Ambrose (Saint) hymnographe', *Dictionnaire d'archéologie chrétienne et de liturgie* I/1, ed. F. Cabrol and J. Leclerq (Paris, 1924), cols. 1347–52.
4 *Sermo contra Auxentium*, *PL*, vol. XVI, col. 1017
5 *Libellus de exordiis et incrementis quarundam in observationibus ecclesiasticibus rerum*, ed. A. Boreticus and H. Krause, MGH Legum II: Capitularia regum francorum II/2 (Hannover, 1897), p. 506.

Part II. Christian chant at Byzantium and in the Western churches

Chapter 6. Greco-Byzantine chant

1 For a general survey of the Byzantine liturgies see H.-J. Schulz: *Die byzantinische Liturgie*.
2 *Dionysiaca: Recueil donnant l'ensemble des traductions latines des ouvrages attribués au Denys de l'Aréopage* (Bruges, 1950), vol. 2, pp. 943–79 etc.
3 See T. Bailey: 'Modes and myth' (bibliography to ch. 19).
4 Transcription ed. E. Wellesz: *The Akathistos Hymn*, MMB Transcripta IX (Copenhagen, 1952).

Chapter 7. Old Roman (paleo-Roman) chant

1 'Préface', *PM* I/2 (Solesmes, 1891), pp. 6–9.
2 'Le chant romain antégrégorien', *Revue du chant grégorien*, XX (1911/2),

61–75 and 107–14; German trans. in *Gregorius-Blatt*, XXXVII (1912), 73–7 and 96–9.
3 'Zur Frühgeschichte des römischen Chorals'.
4 'Choral', *MGG*, vol. 2 (1952), cols. 1271–5; 'Kann der gregorianische Choral im Frankreich entstanden sein?', *AfMw*, XXIV (1967), 153–69, etc.
5 No. XIX in M. Andrieu (ed.): *Les Ordines Romani du haut Moyen Age*, vol. 3, pp. 223.14–224.20.
6 Introduction to M. Landwehr-Melnicki (ed.): *Die Gesänge des altrömischen Graduale*, pp. 3*–164*; *Schriftbild der einstimmigen Musik*, pp. 21–5.
7 'Neues über die Schola Cantorum zu Rom'.
8 E. Jammers: *Musik in Byzanz, im päpstlichen Rom und im Frankenreich*, pp. 107–26; S. J. P. Van Dijk: 'The urban and papal rites in 7th and 8th century Rome'; further bibliography in A. Hughes: *Medieval Music*, pp. 89–93.
9 'Le chant "vieux-romain"'.
10 'Die Einführung des gregorianischen Gesanges im Frankenreich'; 'Gregorianischer Gesang in altrömischer und fränkischer Überlieferung'; 'Toward a new historical view of Gregorian chant'; further bibliography in A. Hughes: *Medieval Music*, pp. 89–93.
11 W. Apel: 'The central problem of Gregorian chant'; R. J. Snow: 'The Old-Roman chant'.
12 'Neue Forschungen zur Gregorianik'.
13 Such as T. H. Connolly: 'Introits and archetypes'; P. F. Cutter: 'The Old Roman chant tradition', and H. Hucke: 'Toward a new historical view'.
14 'The northern and southern idioms of early European music', 41.
15 For instance John the Deacon: *Sancti Gregorii Vita*, PL, vol. LXXV, col. 90; Adhémar of Chabannes: *Chronicon*, ed. J. Chavanon, Collection des textes pour servir à l'étude et à l'enseignement de l'histoire XX (Paris, 1886), p. 81.

Chapter 8. Ambrosian (Milanese) chant

1 See T. Bailey: 'Ambrosian psalmody: an introduction' for further discussion of the music.
2 K. Levy: 'A hymn for Thursday in Holy Week' adduces Byzantine models for the hymn *Coenae tuae*.
3 B. Baroffio: 'Die mailandische Überlieferung des Offertoriums Sanctificavit', especially the examples at the end.
4 H. Hucke: 'Die gregorianische Gradualeweise des 2. Tons und ihre ambrosianische Parallelen'.
5 R. Jesson: 'Ambrosian chant', p. 465, n. 1.
6 G. Morin: 'Un système inédit de lectures liturgiques en usage au VIIe/VIIIe siècle dans une église inconnue de la haute Italie', *Revue Bénédictine*, XX (1903), 375–88; P. Borella: *Il rito ambrosiano*, pp. 84–92.
7 Ed. P. Cagin, *PM* I/5 and 6. For further sources see M. Huglo *et al.* (eds.): *Fonti e paleografia del canto ambrosiano*.
8 G. M. Sunyol: 'Contributo del canto ambrosiano allo studio della modalità', *Ambrosius*, XXII (Milan, 1946), 6–9.

9 T. Bailey: *The Ambrosian Alleluias* (Englefield Green, 1983).
10 E. Cattaneo: *Note storiche sul canto Ambrosiano*, Archivio Ambrosiano III (Milan, 1950).

Chapter 9. The ancient chant of Aquileia and Benevento

1 Ambrose: *De Sacramentis*, III, 6; English edn in E. J. Yarnold: *The Awe-Inspiring Rites of Initiation* (St Paul Publications, 1972).
2 *PL*, vol. xx, col. 551f.
3 *PL*, vol. xxvII, col. 507.
4 *PM* I/14 (1936), p. 452.

Chapter 10. Ancient Hispanic (Mozarabic) and Gallican chant

1 Two possible Irish chants are discussed in B. Stäblein: 'Zwei Melodien der altirischen Liturgie'. For early references to liturgical music in Ireland see A. Fleischmann and R. Gleeson: 'Music in ancient Munster and monastic Cork'. *The Bangor Antiphonary* was edited by F. E. Warren, Henry Bradshaw Society Publications IV and X (London, 1893–5), and *The Stowe Missal* by G. F. Warner, Henry Bradshaw Society Publications XXXI and XXXII (London, 1906–15).
2 Proceedings ed. J. D. Mansi: *Sacrorum conciliorum nova et amplissima collectio x* (Florence, 1764).
3 Facsimile ed. L. Brou and J. Vives: *Antifonario visigótico mozárabe*.
4 General discussions of Mozarabic chant in C. Rojo and G. Prado: *El canto mozárabe*, and in G. Prado: 'Mozarabic melodies'. B. Stäblein: 'Altspanische Liturgie', in *Schriftbild der einstimmigen Musik*, pp. 9–13 is based on more recent research.
5 Madrid, Archivo Histórico Nacional (Real Academia de la Historia), Aemil. 56 (12th-century additions to a 10th-century *Liber ordinum* of San Millán de la Cogoila). Twenty-one decipherable melodies are transcribed in C. Rojo and G. Prado: *El canto*, pp. 66–82.
6 For a detailed list of sources and a brilliant study of Gallican chant see M. Huglo: 'Gallican rite, music of the'.
7 M. Huglo: 'Gallican rite', pp. 115–19.
8 *Libellus de exordiis et incrementis*, ed. A. Boreticus and H. Krause, p. 508.
9 M. Huglo: 'Gallican rite', p. 117.
10 One example, *Rogamus te rex saeculorum*, is transcribed in B. Stäblein: 'Gallikanische Liturgie', *MGG*, vol. 4 (1955), col. 1313. More in J. Pothier (ed.): *Variae preces de mysteriis et festis* (Solesmes, 5th edn 1901).

Part III. Gregorian chant

Chapter 11. Gregory the Great

1 Goussainville, 'Notae in dialogos et epistolas', *Sancti Gregorii Papae Primi . . . Opera* (3 Vols., Paris, 1675).
2 For biography and social background see F. H. Dudden: *Gregory the Great*, and J. Richards: *Consul of God*.

3 J. Deshusses: *Le sacramentaire grégorien: ses principales formes d'après les plus anciens manuscrits*, Spicilegium friburgense xvi (Fribourg, 2nd edn 1979). For the *Hadrianum* see H. Lietzmann: *Das Sacramentarium Gregorianum nach dem Aachener Urexemplar*, Liturgiegeschichtliche Quellen III (Münster, 1921; repr. 1967).

4 Exemplified by the controversy between A. Burda and H. Hucke – see chapter bibliography.

5 John the Deacon: *Vita Gregorii Magni, PL,* vol. LXXV, cols. 60–242.

6 B. Colgrave (ed.): *The Whitby Life of Gregory the Great* (Lawrence, Kansas, 1968); L. Duchesne and C. Vogel (eds.): *Le Liber Pontificalis: texte, introduction et commentaire* (3 vols., Paris, 1955–7); the Venerable Bede: *Historia ecclesiastica, PL,* vol. XCV, cols. 175 and 275

7 B. Stäblein: '"Gregorius praesul"'; R. J.-J. Hesbert: *Antiphonale missarum sextuplex* (see bibliography to ch. 20), pp. 2–3.

8 ed. M. Andrieu: *Les Ordines Romani,* vol. 3, p. 224; Paul the Deacon: *Vita Gregorii Magni, PL,* vol. LXXV, col. 41–59.

9 J. Smits van Waesberghe: 'Neues über die Schola Cantorum'; S. J. P. Van Dijk: 'Gregory the Great, founder of the urban *Schola Cantorum*'.

10 J. Smits van Waesberghe: 'Neues'.

11 See J. Dyer: 'The offertory chant of the Roman liturgy'.

12 Pope Paul I: *Epistolae, PL,* vol. LXXXIX, col. 1187.

13 ed. Andrieu: *Les Ordines Romani,* vol. 5, p. 195.

14 See n. 7.

Chapter 12. The liturgy of the Western churches in the Carolingian period: Franco-Roman chant

1 *PL,* vol. LXXXIX, col. 496: Gregory wished Boniface to adhere strictly to Roman forms of baptism.

2 *Epistola generalis,* ed. A. Boreticus: MGH Legum II: Capitularia regum Francorum I (Hanover, 1883), p. 80.

3 *PL,* vol. XCV, col. 720.

4 *Capitularia regum Francorum,* ed. A. Boreticus, p. 61.

5 Further details of the exchanges between Rome and the Frankish kingdom in T. Klauser: 'Die liturgische Austauschbeziehungen zwischen der römischen und der fränkisch–deutschen Kirche', and C. Vogel: 'Les échanges liturgiques entre Rome et les pays francs'.

6 Lists of sources containing neumes from the early ninth century are given in S. Corbin: *Die Neumen* (see bibliography to ch. 13), pp. 30–41.

7 On the musical significance of the Franco-Roman liturgy see M. Huglo: 'Römisch–fränkische Liturgie'.

8 Bernhard of Lucca: *Bernhardi cardinalis et Lateranensis ecclesiae ordo officiorum ecclesiae Lateranensis,* ed. L. Fischer (Munich and Freising, 1916), p. 140. It is not fully certain that Bernhard was the author.

9 P. F. Cutter: 'The Old Roman chant tradition'; H. Wagenaar-Noltenius: 'Ein münchener Mixtum'; etc.

10 H. Hucke: 'Karolingische Renaissance und gregorianischer Gesang', *Mf,* XXVIII (1975), 4–18.

11 M. Huglo: 'Le chant "vieux-romain"'.

Chapter 13. From oral tradition to neumatic notation

1 *Estetica gregoriana*, parts 1 and 2. W. Apel has made similar conjectures in *Gregorian Chant*, 201–464 *passim*, but with different methods of analysis. On oral transmission see the three articles by L. Treitler listed in the chapter bibliography.

2 Various theories of the origins of neumes are summarised in S. Corbin: *Die Neumen*, pp. 11–21. For the cheironomic theory explained here see J. Pothier and A. Mocquereau: 'Origine et classement des différentes écritures neumatiques', *PM* I/I (Solesmes, 1889), pp. 96–160. On the evidence for cheironomy in western Europe see H. Hucke: 'Die Cheironomie und die Entstehung der Neumenschrift', *Mf*, XXXII (1979), 1–16.

3 A.-M. Bautier-Regnier: 'A propos des sens de *neuma* et de *nota* en latin médiévale', *Revue Belge de Musicologie*, XVIII (1964), 1–9.

4 *De harmonica institutione*, pp. 114–21; trans. W. Babb: *Hucbald, Guido, and John on Music*, pp. 32–44 (for this and following references, see bibliography to ch. 19).

5 I.e. Guido's system of staff notation. See *Guidonis prologus in antiphonarium*, ed. J. Smits van Waesberghe, pp. 66–81; trans. O. Strunk (ed.): *Source Readings in Music History*, pp. 118–20.

6 Ed. M. Gerbert, p. 45; trans. O. Strunk (ed.): *Source Readings*, p. 124.

7 Guido did not, of course, invent the theory of the hexachords; that was left to his expositors. See G. G. Allaire: *The Theory of Hexachords, Solmization and the Modal System*.

Chapter 14. Notation: problems of derivation and regional variation

1 *Schriftbild der einstimmigen Musik*, p. 27.

2 See ch. 10, n. 1.

3 J. Hourlier (ed.): *La notation musicale des chants liturgiques latins*, p. 1.

4 S. Corbin: *Die Neumen*, pp. 141–71.

Chapter 15. Neumes and their classification

1 Editions of the earliest neume tables in M. Huglo: 'Les noms des neumes et leur origine'.

2 Such as the *Graduale Romanum* and *Liber usualis*; for further books of chant in square notation see chapter bibliography.

3 L. Agustoni: *Le chant grégorien*, pp. 50–2.

4 E. Cardine: *Semiologia gregoriana*, p. 7, 'Sémiologie grégorienne', p. 4.

5 J. Froger: 'L'épître de Notker sur les "lettres significatives"'; J. Smits van Waesberghe: *Verklaring der letterteekens (litterae significativae)*. For the system used at Metz see M.-C. Billecocq: 'Lettres ajoutées à la notation du codex 239 de Laon'.

6 Most of these manuscripts are available in complete facsimile editions: see chapter bibiliography for details. For the exceptions single pages are reproduced as follows: Bamberg, Staatliche Bibliothek, lit. 6 in S. Corbin: *Die Neumen*, pl. 6 and *PM* I/3, pl. 125B; Paris, Bibliothèque Nationale, fonds latin 776 in *PM* I/2, pl. 84 and P. Wagner: *Neumenkunde*, p. 276;

Piacenza, Biblioteca Capitolare, 65 in *Early Medieval Music up to 1300*, opposite p. 178.
7 Facsimile edition ed. A. Mocquereau: *PM* I/7–8; complete transcription ed. F. E. Hansen: *H. 159 Montpellier*.

Chapter 16. Neumes and words

1 L. Agustoni: *Le chant grégorien*, p. 241.
2 See W. Apel: *Gregorian Chant*, pp. 268–9, 345 and 399–400.

Chapter 17. Neumes and Gregorian time

1 For Cistercian practice see S. R. Marosszéki: *Les origines du chant cistercien: recherches sur les réformes du plain-chant cistercien au XIIe siècle*, Analecta sacri ordinis cisterciensis VIII (Rome, 1952), pp. 48–79. Dominican reforms were dependent on the Cistercian.
2 J. Jeannin: 'La séquence *Sancti spiritus* dans les manuscrits rhythmiques grégoriens', *EL*, XLV (1931), 128–39, etc.; J. W. A. Vollaerts: *Rhythmic Proportions in Early Medieval Ecclesiastical Chant*; G. Murray: *Gregorian Chant according to the Manuscripts*. E. Cardine fiercely attacked their views in 'Le chant grégorien est-il mesuré?'.
3 Full bibliography in J. Rayburn: *Gregorian Chant: A History of the Controversy Concerning its Rhythm*; more selective bibliography in W. Apel: *Gregorian Chant*, pp. 126–32.
4 Such as E. Cardine: 'Sémiologie grégorienne', 6–16.
5 E. Cardine: 'Sémiologie grégorienne', 12.

Chapter 18. Neumes and Gregorian rhythm

1 Taken from L. Agustoni: *Le chant grégorien*, p. 251.
2 See chapter bibliography for seminal works. The writings of the Solesmes 'school' inspired many derivative works in a wide range of languages for teaching purposes, notably those in English by J. Ward.
3 Such as G. Reese: *Music in the Middle Ages*, pp. 141–8.
4 E. Cardine: 'Neumes et rhythme'; 'Sémiologie grégorienne', pp. 48–55 and *passim*. Bibliography of the 'Cardine school' in N. Albarosa: 'La scuola gregoriana di Eugène Cardine'.
5 E. Cardine: 'Neumes et rhythme', p. 12. See also H. Hucke: 'Die Cheironomie und die Entstehung der Neumenschrift', *Mf*, XXXII (1979), 1–16.

Chapter 19. Modal theory and structure

1 R. L. Crocker: '*Musica Rhythmica* and *Musica Metrica* in antique and medieval music theory', *Journal of Music Theory*, II (1958), 2–23.
2 A. T. M. S. Boethius: *De institutione musica*, ed. G. Friedlein, p. 199.
3 Trans. O. Strunk (ed.): *Source Readings*, p. 93.
4 *Les tonaires*, pp. 23–9.
5 *Einführung in die gregorianischen Melodien*, vol. 3: *Gregorianische Formenlehre: eine choralische Stilkunde* (Leipzig, 1921), pp. 329 and 368.

6 'Les répertoires liturgiques avant l'octoéchos', *passim*.
7 On hexachords see G. G. Allaire: *The Theory of Hexachords*; compare R. L. Crocker: 'Hermann's major sixth', *JAMS*, xxv (1972), 19–37.

Chapter 20. Classical forms of the Gregorian repertory

1 Such as the *Graduale Romanum* or *Liber usualis*.
2 R. H. Hoppin: 'Reflections on the origin of the cyclic mass', *Liber Amicorum Charles van den Borren*, ed. A. Vander Linden (Antwerp, 1964), pp. 85–92.
3 *Gregorianische Formenlehre*, p. 451.
4 *Gregorian Chant*, p. 409.
5 Reproduced in Mother T. More: 'The performance of plainsong in the late Middle Ages and the sixteenth century', *Proceedings of the Royal Musical Association*, xcii (1962), pl. iii opposite p. 135.

Chapter 21. Decline and revival

1 In English as Second Vatican Council: *Constitution on the Sacred Liturgy* (1963).

Part IV. Liturgico-musical innovations of the ninth and tenth centuries and their development; secular monody in Latin

Chapter 22. Sequences

1 Ed. J. M. Hanssens: *Amalarii episcopi opera liturgica omnia*, Studi e testi cxxxix (Vatican City, 1948), p. 304.
2 R.-J. Hesbert: *Antiphonale missarum sextuplex*, p. 198.
3 Ed. W. von der Steinen: *Notker der Dichter und seine geistige Welt*, vol. 2, pp. 8–10 and 160; trans. R.L. Crocker: *The Early Medieval Sequence*, pp. 1–2.
4 R. L. Crocker: *The Early Medieval Sequence*.
5 Full text and melody in R. L. Crocker: *The Early Medieval Sequence*, pp. 200–1.
6 See for instance R. L. Crocker: 'The repertory of proses at Saint Martial de Limoges in the 10th century', *JAMS*, xi (1958), 149–64.
7 Ed. E. Misset and P. Aubry: *Les proses d'Adam de Saint-Victor*, pp. 213–14 (text) and 302–4 (music).

Chapter 23. Tropes

1 Trans. in R. L. Crocker: 'The troping hypothesis', p. 184.
2 R. Jonsson (ed.): *Corpus troporum*, vol. 1, p. 11, n. 3.
3 *L'Ecole musicale de Saint Martial de Limoges jusqu'à la fin du XIe siècle* (Paris, 1960), p. 191.
4 B. Stäblein: 'Zum Verständnis des "klassischen" Tropus'.
5 R. Jonsson (ed.): *Corpus troporum*, vol. 1, p. 315, transcribed from

London, British Library, MS Add. 19768; the melody has not been published in full.
6 Text and melody in G. Weiss (ed.): *Introitus-Tropen*, pp. 344–5.
7 O. Marcusson (ed.): *Corpus troporum*, vol. 2, p. 37.
8 These terms are attributed to I. Milveden in O. Marcusson (ed.): *Corpus troporum*, pp. 7–8.
9 Ed. C. Blume and H. M. Bannister: *Tropen des Missale im Mittelalter*, vol. 1: *Tropen zum Ordinarium Missae*, AH XLVII (Leipzig, 1905; repr. Frankfurt, 1961), p. 50.

Chapter 24. Metrical and dramatic offices

1 See for instance M. J. Epstein: '*Ludovicus decus regnantium*', or R. Jonsson: *Historia*.
2 R. Jonsson: *Historia*, p. 177.
3 R. Jonsson: *Historia*, pp. 164–76, text pp. 221–4.
4 R. Jonsson: *Historia*, pp. 54–63, text pp. 206–10 (Medard); pp. 77–114, text 187–98 (Fuscian and companions); pp. 127–64, text pp. 218–21 (Lambert).
5 Trans. J. Wilkinson: *Egeria's Travels* (London, 1971).
6 The 'genetic' theories of K. Young: *The Drama of the Medieval Church*, vol. 1, pp. 201–38, etc., are possibly the best known. His views have been strongly challenged of recent years by H. De Boor: *Die Textgeschichte der lateinischen Osterfeiern*; O. B. Hardison: *Christian Rite and Christian Drama*; T. J. McGee: 'The liturgical placement of the *Quem quaeritis* dialogue'; and others.

Chapter 25. Liturgical drama

1 Ed. T. Symons: *Regularis concordia Angliae nationis monachorum sanctimonialiumque: The Monastic Agreement of the Monks and Nuns of the English Nation*, Medieval Classics X (London, 1953).
2 Useful synoptic transcriptions by N. Sevestre in R. Jonsson (ed.): *Corpus troporum*, vol. 1, pp. 297–9 and 299–304.
3 Various aspects of these dramas discussed in S. K. Rankin: 'The Mary Magdalene scene in the *Visitatio sepulchri* ceremonies', especially the re-use of earlier material.
4 Ed. H. Krieg: *Das lateinische Osterspiel von Tours*, Literarhistorisch–musikwissenschaftliche Abhandlungen XIII (Würzburg, 1956).
5 Ed. G. Tintori: *Sacre rappresentazioni nel manoscritto 201 della Bibliothèque Municipale di Orléans*.
6 Ed. W. L. Smoldon (Oxford, s.d.).
7 M. Inguanez: 'Un dramma della passione del secolo XII', *Miscellanea Cassinese*, XII (1936), 7–38; repr. *Latomus*, XX (1961), 568–74.
8 Facsimile of the manuscript ed. B. Bischoff; see next chapter.
9 Ed. W. L. Smoldon (Oxford, s.d.).
10 W. L. Smoldon: *Officium Pastorum* (Oxford, s.d.); M. Bernard: 'L'Officium stellae nivernalis', *RdM*, LI (1965), 52–65.
11 Ed. F. Collins, Jr.: *Medieval Church Music Dramas*, pp. 167–88.

12 Ed. F. Collins, Jr.: *Medieval Church Music Dramas*, pp. 365–95 (*The Son of Getron*) and 283–311 (*The Three Daughters*).
13 Ed. W. L. Smoldon: *Sponsus (The Bridegroom)* (Oxford, s.d.).
14 H. Wagenaar-Nolthenius: 'Sur la construction musicale du drame liturgique', 452.
15 Ed. W. L. Smoldon, rev. D. Wulstan (London, 1976).
16 Ed. W. Arlt: *Ein Festoffizium aus Beauvais, Editionsband.*
17 *Studi medievali*, New Series III (1930), 82–109.
18 See R. Weakland: 'The rhythmic modes and medieval Latin drama'.
19 See E. A. Bowles: 'The role of musical instruments in medieval sacred drama'.

Chapter 26. Non-liturgical Latin monody

1 S. Corbin: 'Notations musicales dans les classiques latins', *Revue des études Latines*, XXXII (1954), 97–9.
2 There is no study of the *planctus* that takes full account of the music. P. Dronke: *Poetic Individuality in the Middle Ages*, pp. 26–31, is a useful introduction to the texts and contains an appendix of melodies transcribed by I. Bent (pp. 202–31).
3 C. Cohen: 'Les éléments constitutifs de quelques *planctus* des Xe et XIe siècles', *CCM*, I (1958), 83–6.
4 J. Westrup: 'Medieval song', *Early Medieval Music up to 1300*, p. 221.
5 Facsimile ed. K. Breul: *The Cambridge Songs: A Goliard's Song Book of the XIth Century* (Cambridge, 1915).
6 See P. Dronke: *Poetic Individuality*, pp. 114–19; complete edition of the *planctus* ed. G. Vecchi: *I 'Planctus'.*
7 For sources and a list of transcriptions of *planctus* by Abelard see M. Huglo: 'Abélard, poète et musicien'.
8 L. Weinrich: 'Peter Abelard as musician', 483–6.
9 F. Laurenzi: *Le poesie ritmiche di Pietro Abelardo* (Rome, 1911); W. Lipphardt: 'Unbekannte Weisen zu den Carmina Burana', 129; A. Machabey: 'Les planctus d'Abélard'; G. Vecchi (ed.): *I 'Planctus'.*

Part V. Monody in vernacular languages; instruments; the *ars musica*

Chapter 27. Troubadour and trouvère lyric

1 R. Monterosso: *Musica e ritmica dei trovatori* (Milan, 1956), pp. 107–9.
2 H. van der Werf: *The Chansons of the Troubadours and Trouvères*, p. 44.
3 Aubry: *Trouvères*, pp. 180–7.
4 H. van der Werf: *The Chansons of the Troubadours and Trouvères*, p. 70.

Chapter 29. Italian poetry: *laude*

1 J. E. Stevens: 'Dante and music', *Italian Studies*, XXIII (1968), 1–18, *passim.*
2 See ch. 25, n. 7.
3 See B. J. Blackburn: *'Te matrem dei laudamus*: a study in the musical veneration of Mary'.

210

4 D. Fusi: 'La Compagnia della Vergine Maria e di "Madonna" Sant'Agata di Bibbiena', *Università di Siena: Annali della Facoltà di Lettere e Filosofia*, II (Florence, 1981), pp. 21–34.
5 Ed. in F. Liuzzi: *La lauda e i primordi della melodia italiana.*
6 Also ed. in F. Liuzzi: *La lauda.*
7 A. Ziino: 'Frammenti di laude nell'Archivio di Stato di Lucca'.
8 Such as C. Terni: 'Per una edizione critica del "Laudario di Cortona"'.
9 A. Roncaglia: 'La lirica arabo-ispanica e il sorgere della lirica romanza fuori della penisola iberica', *'Oriente e Occidente' nel Medioevo* (Rome, 1957), p. 334.
10 A. Ziino: 'Testi religiosi medioevali in notazione mensurale'.
11 *La lauda*, vol. I, p. 233.
12 *La lauda.*
13 *Handbuch der Musikgeschichte* I/2: *Die Musik des Mittelalters* (Leipzig, 1920), pp. 224–31.
14 J. Handschin: 'Über die Laude: à propos d'un livre récent', *AcM*, x (1938), 14–31; Y. Rokseth in *Romania*, LXV (1939), 383–94.
15 R. Monterosso: 'Il linguaggio musicale della lauda dugentesca'; H. Anglès: 'The musical notation and rhythm of the Italian *laude*'.
16 For the *cantigas* see H. Anglés (ed.): *La música de las Cantigas de Santa María.*
17 L. Lucchi: 'Intorno alle melodie del Laudario di Cortona', *Laude dugentesche*, ed. G. Varanini (Padua, 1972), pp. 94–106.

Chapter 30. Musical instruments

1 As in J. W. McKinnon: 'Representations of the mass in medieval and Renaissance art'; T. Seebass: *Musikdarstellung und Psalterillustration im früheren Mittelalter.*
2 *PL*, vol. xxx, cols. 213–15. See also R. Hammerstein: 'Instrumenta Hieronymi', and C. Page: 'Biblical instruments in medieval manuscripts'.
3 J. Huizinga: *The Waning of the Middle Ages: A Study of the Forms of Life, Thought and Art in France in the XIVth and XVth Centuries*, trans. F. Hopman (London, 1948; reissued Harmondsworth, 1978).
4 Johannes Aegidius of Zamora: *Ars musica*, ed. and trans. H. Robert-Tissot, CSM xx (1974), p. 108.
5 Ed. J. M. Hanssens: *Amalarii episcopi opera liturgica omnia*, Studi e testi, CXXXVIII–CXL (Rome, 1948–50), vol. 2, pp. 267–8.
6 Quoted in E. A. Bowles: 'Were musical instruments used in the liturgical service during the Middle Ages?', 49.
7 Quoted in E. Bowles: 'Musical instruments', 50.
8 *Der Musiktraktat des Johannes de Grocheo*, ed. E. Rohloff, Media Latinitas II (Leipzig, 1943), pp. 52–3.

Chapter 31. The *ars musica* in the Middle Ages

1 Guido of Arezzo: *Regulae musicae rhythmicae*, ed. M. Gerbert: *Scriptores*, vol. 2, p. 25.
2 Trans. O. Strunk (ed.): *Source Readings*, pp. 85–6.

3 *Epistola de ignoto cantu*, ed. M. Gerbert: *Scriptores*, vol. 2, p. 50; trans. O. Strunk (ed.): *Source Readings*, p. 125.
4 For works see chapter bibiliography; for further details see N. C. Carpenter: *Music in the Medieval and Renaissance Universities*.
5 Ed. M. Gerbert: *Scriptores*, vol. 2, pp. 283–7.
6 Ed. E. Rohloff: *Der Musiktraktat des Johannes de Grocheo*.

BIBLIOGRAPHY

A useful annotated bibliography is given in A. Hughes: *Medieval Music: The Sixth Liberal Art* (Toronto and Buffalo, 1974). A companion volume to the present book is A. Gallo: *Il Medioevo II* (Torino, 1979; English translation forthcoming, Cambridge).

Part I. The origins of Christian worship; liturgy and chant

Chapters 1-3. The evidence of the early Christian sources; the Jewish roots of Christian worship; the early forms of Christian chant

The earliest Christian music

General:
H. Hucke: 'Die Entwicklung des christlichen Kultgesangs zum gregorianischen Gesang', *RQ*, XLVIII (1953), 147–94
B. Stäblein: 'Frühchristliche Musik', *MGG*, vol. 4 (1955), cols. 1036–64
E. Wellesz: 'Early Christian music', *Early Medieval Music up to 1300*, ed. A. Hughes, NOHM II (London, 1954), pp. 1–13

Christian music and the Church Fathers:
S. Corbin: *L'Eglise à la conquête de sa musique* (Paris, 1960)
L. Gamberini: *La parola e la musica nell'antichità: confronto fra documenti musici antichi e dei primi secoli del medio evo*, Historiae musicae cultores biblioteca XV (Florence, 1962)
J. Quasten: *Musik und Gesang in den Kulten der heidnischen Antike und christlichen Frühzeit*, Liturgiegeschichtliche Quellen und Forschungen XXV (Münster, 1930)

For liturgical material 'embedded' within the New Testament:
M. E. Boismard: *Quatre hymnes baptismales dans la première épître de Pierre* (Paris, 1961)

Jewish and Christian traditions compared

H. Avenary: 'Formal structure of psalms and canticles in early Jewish and Christian chant', *MD*, VII (1953), 1–13
E. Werner: 'Notes on the attitude of the early Church Fathers towards Hebrew Psalmody', *Review of Religion*, VII (1942/3), 339–52
The Sacred Bridge: The Interdependence of Liturgy and Music in Synagogue

Bibliography

and Church during the First Millennium (New York, 1959). A second volume is in preparation

Ethnological studies of Jewish chant:
H. Avenary: Studies in the Hebrew, Syrian and Greek Liturgical Recitative (Tel Aviv, 1963)
A. Herzog: The Intonation of the Pentateuch in the Heder of Tunis (Tel Aviv, 1963)
A. Z. Idelsohn: Hebräisch–orientalischer Melodienschatz (10 vols., Leipzig, 1914–33; repr. New York, 1970)

Chapter 4. Liturgy and chant after the Edict of Milan

Christian liturgy

General history:
E. Cattaneo: Il culto cristiano in Occidente: note storiche, Bibliotheca Ephemerides Liturgicae: subsidia XIII (Rome, 1978)
C. Jones, G. Wainwright and E. Yarnold (eds.): The Study of Liturgy (London, 1978)
J. A. Jungmann: Missarum solemnia: eine genetische Erklärung der römischen Messe (2 vols., Freiburg, 5th edn 1962); trans. F. A. Brunner: The Mass of the Roman Rite (New York, 2nd edn 1954). The English translation should be used with caution
T. Klauser: A Short History of the Western Liturgy: An Account and Some Reflections, trans. J. Halliburton (London, 2nd edn 1979)

Liturgical books:
M. Andrieu: Les Ordines Romani du haut Moyen Age, Spicilegium Sacrum Lovaniense XI, XXIII, XXIV, XXVIII, XXIX (5 vols., Louvain, 1931–61; repr. 1960–5)
A. Hughes: Medieval Manuscripts for Mass and Office: A Guide to their Organization and Terminology (Toronto, 1982)

Chapter 5. Hymnody

Hymnody

Early history:
J. Kroll: Die christliche Hymnodik bis zu Clemens von Alexandria, Verzeichnis der Vorlesungen an der Akademie zu Braunsberg, Sommer-Semester 1921 und Winter-Semester 1921/2 (Kaliningrad, 1921–2)
J. Szoverffy: Die Annalen der lateinischen Hymnendichtung, vol. 1: Die lateinischen Hymnen bis zum Ende des 11. Jahrhunderts (Berlin, 1964)

Versification etc.:
R. E. Messenger: The Medieval Latin Hymn (Washington, DC, 1953)
U. Sesini: Poesia e musica nella latinità cristiana dal III al X secolo, Nuova biblioteca italiana VI (Turin, 1949)

Bibliography

Place in the liturgy:
H. Darre: 'De l'usage des hymnes dans l'église des origines à saint Grégoire le Grand', *EG*, IX (1968), 25–36

Editions of Latin hymns

W. Bulst (ed.): *Hymni latini antiquissimi* (Heidelberg, 1956)
A. S. Walpole (ed.): *Early Latin Hymns* (Cambridge, 1922)

Part II. Christian chant at Byzantium and in the Western churches

Chapter 6. Greco-Byzantine chant

Byzantine liturgy

F. E. Brightman (ed.): *Liturgies Eastern and Western*, vol. I (Oxford, 1896). A useful selection of texts translated into English
H.-J. Schulz: *Die byzantinische Liturgie* (Freiburg, 1964)

Byzantine music

General:
E. Wellesz: *A History of Byzantine Music and Hymnography* (Oxford, 2nd edn 1961, 3rd edn 1963)
 Eastern Elements in Western Chant, MMB: Subsidia II, American series I (Oxford, 1947)

Notation:
C. Floros: *Universale Neumenkunde*, vol. I: *Entzifferung der ältesten byzantinischen Neumenschriften und der altslavischen sematischen Notation* (Kassel, 1970)
H. J. W. Tillyard: 'The stages of early Byzantine musical notation', *Byzantinische Zeitschrift*, XLV (1952), 29–42
E. Wellesz: 'Early Byzantine neumes', *MQ*, XXXVIII (1952), 68–79

Style and modality:
J. Raasted: *Intonation Formulas and Modal Signatures in Byzantine Musical Manuscripts*, MMB: Subsidia VII (Copenhagen, 1966)
O. Strunk: 'The antiphons of the oktoechos', *JAMS*, XIII (1960), 50–67

Chapter 7. Old Roman (paleo-Roman) chant

Old Roman chant

General:
R. J. Snow: 'The Old-Roman chant', in W. Apel: *Gregorian Chant* (Bloomington, Indiana, 1958), pp. 484–505

Bibliography

Sources:

P. F. Cutter: *Musical Sources of the Old-Roman Mass*, MSD XXXVI (Stuttgart, 1979); important corrections are listed in the review by T. H. Connolly in *EMH*, II (1982), 363–9

M. Huglo: 'Le chant "vieux-romain": liste des manuscrits et témoins indirects', *SE*, VI (1954), 96–124

M. Landwehr-Melnicki (ed.): *Die Gesänge des altrömischen Graduale Vat. Lat. 5319*, MMMA II (Kassel, 1970)

For a Roman origin of Gregorian chant

In the context of Christian chant in general:

E. Jammers: *Musik in Byzanz, im päpstlichen Rom und im Frankenreich: der Choral als Musik der Textaussprache*, Heidelberger Akademie der Wissenschaften, philosophisch–historische Klasse: Jahrgang 1962, Abhandlung 1 (Heidelberg, 1962)

Stages in the development of Stäblein's theories:

B. Stäblein: 'Zur Frühgeschichte des römischen Chorals', *Congresso internazionale di musica sacra, Roma 1950*, ed. I. Anglès (Tournai, 1952), pp. 271–5

Introduction to M. Landwehr-Melnicki: *Die Gesänge*, pp. 3*–164*

Schriftbild der einstimmigen Musik, MgB III/4 (Leipzig, 1975)

An argument based on the *Liber pontificalis*:

J. Smits van Waesberghe: 'Neues über die Schola Cantorum zu Rom', *Zweiter internationaler Kongress für katholische Kirchenmusik, Wien 1954: Bericht* (Vienna, 1955), pp. 111–19

A primarily liturgical argument:

S. J. P. Van Dijk: 'The urban and papal rites in 7th and 8th century Rome', *SE*, XII (1961), 411–87

For a Frankish origin of Gregorian chant

The documentary evidence in Hucke's argument:

H. Hucke: 'Die Einführung des gregorianischen Gesanges im Frankenreich', *RQ*, XLIX (1954), 172–87

Musical aspects of Hucke's argument:

'Gregorianischer Gesang in altrömischer und fränkischer Überlieferung', *AfMw*, XII (1955), 74–87

'Toward a new historical view of Gregorian chant', *JAMS*, XXXIII (1980), 437–67

General assessments of the controversy, partly from Hucke's point of view:

W. Apel: 'The central problem of Gregorian chant', *JAMS*, IX (1956), 118–27

P. F. Cutter: 'The question of the "Old Roman" chant: a reappraisal', *AcM*, XXXIX (1967), 2–20

Bibliography

Other matters

Lipphardt's thesis:
W. Lipphardt: 'Neue Forschungen zur Gregorianik', *Jahrbuch für Liturgik und Hymnologie*, II (1956), 134–41.

Recent research:
T. H. Connolly: 'Introits and archetypes: some archaisms of the Old Roman chant', *JAMS*, XXV (1972), 157–74
P. F. Cutter: 'The Old Roman chant tradition: oral or written?', *JAMS*, XX (1967), 167–81

'Continuous' and 'gapped' scales:
H. Avenary: 'The northern and southern idioms of early European music – a new approach to an old problem', *AcM*, XLIV (1977), 27–49

Chapter 8. Ambrosian (Milanese) chant

Ambrosian liturgy

W. C. Bishop: *The Mozarabic and Ambrosian Rites*, Alcuin Club Tracts XV (London, 1924)
P. Borella: *Il rito ambrosiano* (Brescia, 1964)

Sources and editions of Ambrosian chant

P. Cagin (ed.): *Antiphonarium Ambrosianum du Musée Britannique (XIIe siècle)*, *Codex Additional 34209*, *PM* I/5 and 6 (2 vols., Solesmes, 1896 and 1900)
M. Huglo, L. Agustoni, E. Cardine and E. T. Moneta Caglio (eds.): *Fonti e paleografia del canto ambrosiano*, Archivio Ambrosiano VII (Milan, 1956)
G. M. Sunyol (ed.): *Antiphonale missarum juxta ritum sanctae ecclesiae Mediolanensis* (Rome, 1935)
Liber vesperalis juxta ritum sanctae ecclesiae Mediolanensis (Rome, 1939)

Secondary literature

General:
B. Baroffio: 'Ambrosianische Liturgie', *GkK*, pp. 191–204
R. Jesson: 'Ambrosian chant', in W. Apel: *Gregorian Chant*, pp. 465–83

Ambrosian chant compared with other repertories:
B. Baroffio: 'Die mailandische Überlieferung des Offertoriums Sanctificavit', *Festschrift Bruno Stäblein zum 70. Geburtstag*, ed. M. Ruhnke (Kassel, 1967), pp. 1–8
H. Hucke: 'Die gregorianische Gradualeweise des 2. Tons und ihre ambrosianische Parallelen', *AfMw*, XIII (1956), 285–314
K. Levy: 'A hymn for Thursday in Holy Week', *JAMS*, XVI (1963), 127–75

Bibliography

Psalmody:
T. Bailey: 'Ambrosian psalmody: an introduction', *SMUWO*, II (1977), 65–78
'Ambrosian choral psalmody: the formulae', *SMUWO*, III (1978), 72–96

Performance:
E. T. Moneta Caglio: 'I responsori "cum infantibus" nella liturgia ambrosiana', *Studi in onore di Mons. Carlo Castiglioni, prefetto dell'Ambrosiana*, Fontes Ambrosiani XXXII (Milan, 1957), pp. 481–577
R. G. Weakland: 'The performance of Ambrosian chant in the twelfth century', *Aspects of Medieval and Renaissance Music: A Birthday Offering to Gustave Reese*, ed. J. LaRue (New York, 1967), 856–66

Chapter 9. The ancient chant of Aquileia and Benevento

Aquileian and Beneventan chant

On ancient Western liturgies outside Rome:
A. A. King: *Liturgies of the Past* (London, 1959). Musical references are rather few

Aquileian chant:
EL LXV (1951), 113–14 has a bibliography of the writings of G. Vale on Aquileian chant
G. Folena (ed.): *Storia della cultura veneta*, vol. I: *Dalle origini al Trecento* (Vicenza, 1976) contains important essays by M. Huglo: 'Liturgia e musica sacra aquileiese', and C. G. Mor: 'La cultura aquileiese nei secoli IX-XII'

Beneventan chant:
PM I/14 (Tournai, 1936) contains an important survey by R.-J. Hesbert: 'La tradition bénéventaine dans la tradition manuscrite'
R.-J. Hesbert: 'L'Antiphonale missarum de l'ancien rit bénéventain', *EL* LII (1938), 28–66, 141–58; LIII (1939), 168–90; LIX (1945), 69–95; LX (1946), 103–41; LXI (1947), 153–210
PM I/15 (Tournai, 1937–53) contains a study of Beneventan notation by R.-J. Hesbert
B. Baroffio: 'Liturgie im beneventanischen Raum', *GkK*, pp. 204–8
K. Levy: 'The Italian Neophytes' Chants', *JAMS*, XXIII (1970), 181–227

Exultet rolls:
G. Cavallo: *Rotoli di Exultet dell'Italia meridionale* (Bari, 1973)

Chapter 10. Ancient Hispanic (Mozarabic) and Gallican chant

Mozarabic and Gallican liturgies

W. C. Bishop: *The Mozarabic and Ambrosian Rites*
A. A. King: *Liturgies of the Past*
F. E. Warren: *The Liturgy and Ritual of the Celtic Church* (Oxford, 1881).

218

Bibliography

Mozarabic chant

Sources and editions:
L. Brou and J. Vives (eds.): *Antifonario visigótico mozárabe de la Catedral de León*, Monumenta Hispaniae Sacra, serie litúrgica V/I and 2 (2 vols., Barcelona and Madrid, 1953 and 1959); vol. 2 is a facsimile of the manuscript
G. Prado: 'Mozarabic melodies', *Speculum*, III (1928), 218–39
D. M. Randel: *The Responsorial Psalm Tones for the Mozarabic Office*, PSM III (Princeton, 1969)
C. Rojo and G. Prado: *El canto mozárabe*, Publicaciones del departamento de musica V (Barcelona, 1929)

Secondary literature:
C. W. Brockett: *Antiphons, Responsories and Other Chants of the Mozarabic Rite*, Musicological Studies XV (New York, 1968)
L. Brou: 'Notes de paléographie musicale mozarabe', *Anuario musical*, VII (1952), 51–76; X (1955), 23–44
D. M. Randel: *An Index to the Chant of the Mozarabic Rite*, PSM VI (Princeton, 1973)
'Responsorial psalmody in the Mozarabic rite', *EG*, X (1969), 87–113

Music of the Celtic, Gallican and Irish rites

A. Fleischmann and R. Gleeson: 'Music in ancient Munster and monastic Cork', *Journal of the Cork Historical and Archaeological Society*, 2nd ser., LXX (1965), 79–98
M. Huglo: 'Gallican rite, music of the', *NG*, vol. 7, pp. 113–25
B. Stäblein: 'Zwei melodien der altirischen Liturgie', *Musicae scientiae collectanea: Festschrift Karl Gustav Fellerer zum siebzigsten Geburtstag*, ed. H. Hüschen (Regensburg, 1973), pp. 590–7

Part III. Gregorian chant

Chapter 11. Gregory the Great

Gregory the Great

Biography:
F. H. Dudden: *Gregory the Great: His Place in History and Thought* (2 vols., London, 1905). The standard work in English
J. Richards: *Consul of God: The Life and Times of Gregory the Great* (London, 1980). A more recent study

Gregory's alleged musical activities:
H. Anglès: 'Sakraler Gesang und Musik in den Schriften Gregors der Grossen', *Essays presented to Egon Wellesz*, ed. J. Westrup (Oxford, 1966), pp. 33–42
A. Burda: 'Gregor der Grosse als Musiker', *Mf*, XVII (1964), 388–93

Bibliography

'Nochmals: Gregor der Grosse als Musiker', *Mf*, XX (1967), 154–66. These are contributions to a controversy with H. Hucke

H. Hucke: 'Die Entstehung der Überlieferung von einer musikalischen Tätigkeit Gregors des Grossen', *Mf*, VIII (1955), 259–64. This was the beginning of the controversy with A. Burda

'War Gregor der Grosse doch Musiker?', *Mf*, XVIII (1965), 390–3

S. J. P. Van Dijk: 'Gregory the Great, founder of the urban *Schola Cantorum*', *EL*, LXXVII (1963), 335–56

E. Wellesz: 'Gregory the Great's letter on the alleluia', *AnnM*, II (1954), 7–26

The origins of the Gregory legend:

B. Stäblein: '"Gregorius Praesul": der Prolog zum römischen Antiphonale', *Musik und Verlag: Karl Vötterle zum 65. Geburtstag*, ed. R. Baum and W. Rehm (Kassel, 1968), 537–61

Chapter 12. The liturgy of the Western churches in the Carolingian period: Franco-Roman chant

Franco-Roman liturgy

General:
M. Huglo: 'Römisch–fränkische Liturgie', *GkK*, pp. 233–44

Exchanges between Rome and the Frankish Kingdom:
T. Klauser: 'Die liturgische Austauschbeziehungen zwischen der römischen und der fränkisch–deutschen Kirche vom 8.–11. Jh.', *Historisches Jahrbuch*, LIII (1933), 169–89

C. Vogel: 'Les échanges liturgiques entre Rome et les pays francs jusqu'à l'époque de Charlemagne', *Settimane di studio del centro italiano di studi sull'alto medioevo*, VII/1 (Spoleto, 1960), pp. 185–295

Assimilation of northern elements into the Old Roman tradition

Liturgical:
G. Frénaud: 'Les témoins indirects du chant liturgique en usage à Rome aux IXe et Xe siècles', *EG*, III (1959), 41–74

M. Huglo: 'Le chant "vieux-romain"'

Musical:
J. Claire: 'Les répertoires liturgiques avant l'octoéchos, I: L'office férial romano-franc', *EG*, XV (1975), 5–192

H. Wagenaar-Nolthenius: 'Ein münchener Mixtum: gregorianische Melodien zu altrömischen Texten', *AcM*, XLV (1973), 249–55

Chapter 13. From oral tradition to neumatic notation

Motivic structure of Gregorian chant

W. Apel: *Gregorian Chant*, pp. 201–464

Bibliography

P. M. Ferretti: *Estetica gregoriana: trattato delle forme musicali del canto gregoriano*, part I (Rome, 1934); French trans. A. Agaësse: *Esthétique grégorienne* (Paris, 1938). Part 2, assembled from Ferretti's unpublished notes: *Estetica gregoriana dei recitativi liturgici*, ed. P. M. Ernetti, Quaderni dei Padri Benedettini di San Giorgio Maggiore III (Venice and Rome, 1964)

Oral and literate transmission of chant

L. Treitler: 'Homer and Gregory: the transmission of epic poetry and plainchant', *MQ*, LX (1974), 333-72
'"Centonate" chant: *übles Flickwerk* or *e pluribus unus?*', *JAMS*, XXVIII (1975), 1-23
'Oral, written and literate process in the transmission of medieval music', *Speculum*, LVI (1981), 471-91

Neumes and their origins

S. Corbin: *Die Neumen*, Palaeographie der Musik I/3 (Cologne, 1975)
C. Floros: *Universale Neumenkunde*, vol. 2
L. Treitler: 'The early history of music writing in the West', *JAMS*, XXXV (1982), 237-79

Chapter 14. Notation: problems of derivation and regional variation

Collections of facsimiles

H. M. Bannister (ed.): *Monumenti Vaticani di paleografia musicale latina*, Codices e Vaticanis selecti phototypice expressi XII (2 vols., Leipzig, 1913; repr. London, 1968). Vol. 2 consists of facsimiles; the tables of neumes at the beginning are especially useful
J. Hourlier (ed.): *La notation musicale des chants liturgiques latins*, PM II/3 (Solesmes, 1960)
E. Jammers (ed.): *Tafeln zur Neumenschrift* (Tutzing, 1965)
A. Mocquereau (ed.): *Le répons 'Iustus ut palma' reproduit en fac-similé d'après plus de deux cents antiphonaires manuscrits d'origine diverse du IXe au XVIIe siècle*, PM I/2 and 3 (2 vols., Solesmes, 1891-2)
B. Stäblein: *Schriftbild der einstimmigen Musik*, pp. 106-225

Chapter 15. Neumes and their classification

Classification of neumes

Early neume tables:
M. Huglo: 'Les noms des neumes et leur origine', *EG*, I (1954), 53-67

Classification according to musical signification:
L. Agustoni: *Le chant grégorien: mot et neume*, trans. O. Lagger and ed. E. Mosser (Rome, 1969), pp. 47-57. This French translation is the latest version

Bibliography

E. Cardine: *Semiologia gregoriana* (Rome, 1968); French trans. M.-E. Mosseri: 'Sémiologie grégorienne', *EG*, XI (1970), 1–158, also issued separately
'Neume', *EG*, X (1969), 13–28

Significative letters

M.-C. Billecocq: 'Lettres ajoutées à la notation du codex 239 de Laon', *EG*, XVII (1978), 7–144
J. Froger: 'L'épître de Notker sur les "lettres significatives"': édition critique', *EG*, V (1962), 23–71. An edition and source study making extensive use of stemmatics
J. Smits van Waesberghe: *Muziekgeschiedenis der Middeleeuwen*, vol. 2: *Verklaring der letterteekens (litterae significativae) in het gregoriaansche neumenschrift van Sint Gallen*, Nederlandsche muziekhistorische en muziekpaedogogische studiën, Series A (Tilburg, 1942)

Modern editions of Gregorian chant in square notation

For the modern liturgy:
Antiphonale monasticum pro diurnis horis (Tournai, 1934; repr. Solesmes, 1969)
Graduale Romanum (Solesmes, 1974). Revised from earlier editions according to the directions of the Second Vatican Council
Liber usualis (Tournai, 1895; numerous reprs.). Now useful only for its selection of chants for Matins; its transcriptions and rubrics are out of date

Editions with neumes and square notation in parallel:
M. C. Billecocq and R. Fischer (eds.): *Graduale triplex* (Solesmes, 1979). The *Graduale Romanum* of 1974 with Messine and St Gall neumes above and below the stave
E. Cardine (ed.): *Graduel neumé* (Solesmes, 1972). Contains useful marginal notes on special features of the St Gall neumes
R. Fischer (ed.): *Offertoires neumés avec leurs versets, d'après les manuscrits Laon 239 et Einsiedeln 121* (Solesmes, 1978)

A complete manuscript transcribed into modern square notation:
F. E. Hansen (ed.): *H 159 Montpellier: Tonary of St Benigne of Dijon*, Studier og publikationer fra Musikvidenskabeligt Institut Aarhus universitet II (Copenhagen, 1974)

Facsimiles of complete manuscripts

A. Mocquereau (ed.): *Cantatorium, IXe siècle, No. 359 de la Bibliothèque de St. Gall*, *PM* II/2 (Tournai, 1924)
J. Froger (ed.): *Antiphonaire de l'office monastique, transcrit par Hartker: Mss. Saint-Gall 390–391 (980–1011)*, *PM* II/1 (Berne, 2nd edn 1970)
A. Mocquereau (ed.): *Le Codex 121 de la Bibliothèque d'Einsiedeln (X–XIe siècle)*, *PM* I/4 (Solesmes, 1894)

Bibliography

G. Beyssac (ed.): *Antiphonale Missarum Sancti Gregorii, IX–Xe Siècle, Codex 239 de la Bibliothèque de Laon, PM* I/10 (Tournai, 1909)

A. Ménager (ed.): *Antiphonale Missarum sancti Gregorii, Xe siècle, Codex 47 de la Bibliothèque de Chartres, PM* I/11 (Tournai, 1912)

P. Ferretti (ed.): *Le Codex 903 de la Bibliothèque Nationale de Paris (XIe siècle, Graduel de St. Yrieix), PM* I/13 (Tournai, 1925)

J. Gajard, R. J. Hesbert, J. Hourlier and M. Huglo (eds.): *Le Codex VI. 34 de la Bibliothèque Capitulaire de Bénévent avec Prosaire et Tropaire, PM* I/15 (Tournai, 1937)

J. Froger (ed.): *Le Codex 123 de la Bibliothèque Angelica de Rome (XIe siècle): Graduel et Tropaire de Bologne, PM* I/18 (Berne, 1969)

A. Mocquereau (ed.): *Antiphonarium Tonale Missarum, XIe siècle, Codex H159 de l'Ecole de Médecine de Montpellier, PM* I/7–8 (2 vols., Tournai, 1901–5)

Chapter 16. Neumes and words

Words and music

L. Agustoni: *Le chant grégorien*, pp. 230–47

E. Cardine: 'Paroles et mélodie dans le chant grégorien', *EG*, V (1962), 15–21

M. H. Gavel: 'À propos des erreurs d'accentuation latine dans les livres liturgiques', *EG*, I (1954), 83–148

J. Pothier and A. Mocquereau: 'De l'influence de l'accent tonique latin et du cursus sur la structure mélodique et rhythmique de la phrase grégorienne', *PM* III (1892), pp. 27–86; IV (1894), pp. 25–204

Chapters 17–18. Neumes and Gregorian time; neumes and Gregorian rhythm

Chant rhythm

General:

A. Angie: 'Die Tradition der Notenwerte im gregorianischen Choral', *KmJb*, XXIX (1934), 22–31. Most useful for its numerous quotations of texts on rhythm from mediaeval music theory

J. Rayburn: *Gregorian Chant: A History of the Controversy Concerning its Rhythm* (New York, 1964). Contains a detailed bibliography of the subject

'Mensuralist' theories:

E. Jammers: *Der gregorianische Rhythmus*, Sammlung musikwissenschaftlicher Abhandlungen XXV (Strasbourg, 1925)

G. Murray: *Gregorian Chant according to the Manuscripts* (London, 1963)

J. M. A. Vollaerts: *Rhythmic Proportions in Early Medieval Ecclesiastical Chant* (Leiden, 2nd edn 1960)

P. Wagner: *Einführung in die gregorianischen Melodien*, vol. 2: *Neumenkunde* (Leipzig, 1913; repr. Hildesheim, 1962), pp. 353ff

Bibliography

'Equalist' theories:

J. Gajard: *The Solesmes Method: Its Fundamental Principles and Practical Rules of Interpretation*, trans. R. C. Gabain (Collegeville, Minnesota, 1960)

A. Mocquereau: *Le nombre musical grégorien* (2 vols., Tournai, 1908–27)

J. Pothier: *Les mélodies grégoriennes* (Tournai, 1881; repr. Paris, 1980)

The 'school' of Cardine:

N. Albarosa: 'La scuola gregoriana di Eugène Cardine', *Rivista italiana di musicologia*, IX (1974), 269–97; XII (1977), 136–52. Summaries and bibliography of work completed under Cardine's supervision

E. Cardine: 'Le chant grégorien est-il mesuré?', *EG*, VI (1963), 7–38. Cardine's response to the work of Vollaerts and Murray

'Neumes et rhythme: les coupures neumatiques', *EG*, III (1959), 145–55

'Sémiologie grégorienne' (see bibliography to ch. 15)

Chapter 19. Modal theory and structure

Modal theory

Collections:

W. Babb (trans.) and C. Palisca (ed.): *Hucbald, Guido, and John on Music*, Yale Music Theory Translation Series III (New Haven, Conn., 1978)

E. de Coussemaker (ed.): *Scriptores de musica medii aevi nova series* (4 vols., Paris, 1864–76; numerous reprs.)

M. Gerbert (ed.): *Scriptores ecclesiastici de musica sacra potissimum* (3 vols., St Blasien, 1784; numerous reprs.)

O. Strunk (ed.): *Source Readings in Music History* (New York, 1950; repr. 5 vols., 1965), pp. 1–190 or vol. 1

Single works:

Alia musica, ed. J. Chailley, Publications de l'Institut de Musicologie de l'Université de Paris VI (Paris, 1965)

St Augustine: *Aurelii Augustini: De musica*, ed. G. Marzi, Collana di classici della filosofia cristiana I (Florence, 1969): *St. Augustine on Music*, trans. R. C. Taliaferro (Annapolis, 1939)

Aurelian of Réomé: *Musica disciplina*, ed. L. Gushee, CSM XII (Rome, 1975); *The Discipline of Music*, trans. J. Ponte, CMPT III (Colorado Springs, 1973)

A. T. M. S. Boethius: *De institutione musica*, ed. G. Friedlein (Leipzig, 1897)

Cassiodorus: *Institutiones*, ed. R. B. Mynors (Oxford, 1937); *An Introduction to Divine and Human Readings*, trans. L. Jones, Records of Civilization: Sources and Studies LXXXIV (New York, 1946)

Commemoratio Brevis, ed. and trans. T. Bailey (Toronto, 1979)

Guido of Arezzo: *Micrologus*, ed. J. Smits van Waesberghe, CSM IV (Rome, 1955); trans. W. Babb: *Hucbald, Guido, and John on Music*, pp. 47–83

Tres tractatuli Guidonis Aretini: Guidonis prologus in antiphonarium, ed. J. Smits van Waesberghe, Divitiae musicae artis A/III (Buren, 1975); trans. O. Strunk (ed.): *Source Readings*, pp. 117–20

Bibliography

Epistola de ignoto cantu, ed. M. Gerbert: *Scriptores de musica medii aevi*, vol. 2, pp. 43–55; trans. O. Strunk (ed.): *Source Readings*, pp. 121–5

Hucbald of Saint-Amand: *De harmonica institutione*, ed. M. Gerbert: *Scriptores*, vol. 1, pp. 104–52; trans. W. Babb: *Hucbald, Guido, and John*, pp. 1–46

Isidore of Seville: *Etymologiarum sive originum libri XX*, ed. W. M. Lindsay (2 vols., Oxford, 1911)

De ecclesiasticis officiis, in *PL*, vol. LXXXIII, cols. 737–826

Musica enchiriadis, in H. Schmid: *Musica et Scholica Enchiriadis una cum aliquibus tractatulis adiunctis*, Veröffentlichungen der musikhistorischen Kommission III (Munich, 1891); *Music Handbook (Musica Enchiriadis)*, ed. L. Rosenstiel, CMPT VII (Colorado Springs, 1976)

Regino of Prüm: *Epistola de harmonica institutione*, ed. E. de Coussemaker: *Scriptores*, vol. 1, pp. 230–47

Tonarius, ed. E. de Coussemaker: *Scriptores*, vol. 2, pp. 1–73

Practical applications of modal theory

T. Bailey: *The Intonation Formulas of Western Chant* (Toronto, 1974)

M. Huglo: *Les tonaires: inventaire, analyse, comparaison*, Publications de la Société Française de Musicologie III/2 (Paris, 1971)

Secondary literature

General:

W. Apel: *Gregorian Chant*, pp. 133–78

J. Chailley: *L'Imbroglio des Modes* (Paris, 1960)

M. Marcovits: *Das Tonsystem der abendländischen Musik im frühen Mittelalter*, Publications de la Société Suisse de Musicologie II/30 (Berne, 1977)

H. Potiron: 'Les modes grégoriens selon les premiers théoriciens du moyen âge', *EG*, V (1962), 109–18

On the term 'mode':

H. Hüschen: 'Der Modus-Begriff in der Musiktheorie des Mittelalters und der Renaissance', *Mittellateinisches Jahrbuch*, II (1965), 224–32

More sceptical accounts of modes and modal theory:

T. Bailey: 'Modes and myth', *SMUWO*, I (1976), 43–54

E. Ferrari Barassi: 'I modi ecclesiastici nei trattati musicali dell'età carolingia: nascita e crescita di una teoria', *SM*, IV (1975), 3–56

Studies in the tonality of Gregorian chant:

J. Chailley: 'Essai analytique sur la formation de l'octoéchos latin', *Essays presented to Egon Wellesz*, ed. J. Westrup (Oxford, 1966), pp. 84–93

F. E. Hansen: *The Grammar of Gregorian Tonality* (2 vols., Copenhagen, 1979)

Later developments:

G. G. Allaire: *The Theory of Hexachords, Solmization and the Modal System: A Practical Application*, MSD XXIV (Rome, 1972)

Bibliography

Chapter 20. Classical forms of the Gregorian repertory

Chants in early sources

Mass:
R.-J. Hesbert (ed.): *Antiphonale Missarum Sextuplex* (Brussels, 1935)

Office:
R.-J. Hesbert (ed.): *Corpus antiphonalium officii*, Rerum ecclesiasticarum documenta, Series major VII–X (4 vols., Rome, 1963–70)

Psalmody

General:
L. Agustoni: *Le chant grégorien*, pp. 277–305
W. Apel: *Gregorian Chant*, pp. 201–45

Differentia, etc.:
T. Bailey: 'Accentual and cursive cadences in gregorian psalmody', *JAMS*, XXIX (1976), 463–71
C. W. Brockett: 'Saeculorum Amen and differentia: practical versus theoretical tradition', *MD*, XXX (1976), 13–36
S. J. P. Van Dijk: 'Medieval terminology and methods of psalm singing', *MD*, XI (1952), 7–26

Proper chants

General:
W. Apel: *Gregorian Chant*, pp. 305–404
J. Hourlier: 'Notes sur l'antiphonie', *Gattungen der Musik in Einzeldarstellungen: Gedenkschrift Leo Schrade*, ed. W. Arlt, E. Lichtenhahn, H. Oesch and M. Haas (Berne, 1973), pp. 116–43
H. Hucke: 'Das Responsorium', *Gattungen der Musik in Einzeldarstellungen*, pp. 144–91

Alleluia:
K.-H. Schlager: *Alleluia-Melodien*, vol. 1: *Bis 1100*, MMMA VII (Kassel, 1968). Vol. 2 is in press
Thematischer Katalog der ältesten Alleluia-Melodien aus Mss des 10. und 11. Jh., Erlanger Arbeiten zur Musikwissenschaft II (Munich, 1965)

Offertory:
J. Dyer: 'The offertory chant of the Roman liturgy and its musical form', *SM*, XI (1982), 3–30
R. Steiner: 'Some questions about the Gregorian offertories and their verses', *JAMS*, XIX (1966), 162–81

Ordinary chants

Kyrie:
M. Melnicki: *Das einstimmige Kyrie des lateinischen Mittelalters*, Forschungsbeiträge zur Musikwissenschaft I (Regensburg, 1955)

226

Bibliography

Gloria:
D. Bosse: *Untersuchung einstimmiger mittelalterlicher Melodien zum 'Gloria in excelsis Deo'*, Forschungsbeiträge zur Musikwissenschaft II (Regensburg, 1955)

Credo:
T. Miazga: *Die Melodien des einstimmigen Credo der römisch-katholischen lateinischen Kirche* (Graz, 1976)

Sanctus:
P. J. Thannabaur: *Das einstimmige Sanctus der römischen Messe in der handschriftlichen Überlieferung des 11. bis 16. Jh.*, Erlanger Arbeiten zur Musikwissenschaft I (Munich, 1962)

Agnus dei:
M. Schildbach: *Das einstimmige Agnus Dei und seine handschriftliche Überlieferung vom 10. bis zum 16. Jh.* (Sonneberg, 1967)

Hymns

General:
B. Stäblein: 'Hymnus: B. Der lateinische Hymnus', *MGG*, VI (1957), cols. 993–1018

Melodies:
Stäblein (ed.): *Die mittelalterliche Hymnenmelodien des Abendlandes: Hymnen 1*, MMMA I (Kassel, 1956)

Chapter 21. Decline and revival

Decline

Modal changes:
J. Gajard: 'Les récitations modales des 3ᵉ et 4ᵉ modes et les manuscrits bénéventains et aquitains', *EG* I (1954), 9–45

Cistercian and Dominican modifications:
S. R. Marosszéki: *Les origines du chant cistercien: recherches sur les réformes du plain-chant cistercien au XIIe siècle*, Analecta sacri ordinis cisterciensis, VIII (1952), 1–179
D. Delalande: *Vers la version authentique du graduel grégorien: le graduel des Prêcheurs* (Paris, 1949)

The impact of polyphony:
J. Vos and F. de Meeûs: 'L'introduction de la diaphonie et la rupture de la tradition grégorienne au XIe siècle', *SE* VII (1955), 177–218
G. Fellerer: 'La "Constitutio docta Sanctorum Patrum" di Giovanni XXII e la musica nuova del suo tempo', *L'Ars Nova italiana del trecento I: Certaldo 1959*, 9–17

227

Bibliography

Revival

A. M. Gontier: *Méthode raisonnée de plain-chant: le plain-chant considéré dans son rythme, sa tonalité et ses modes* (Paris, 1859)

J. Pothier: *Les mélodies grégoriennes d'après la tradition* (Tournai, 1880, repr. 1980)

A. Mocquereau: *Le nombre musical grégorien*

R. F. Hayburn: *Papal Legislation on Sacred Music 95 A.D. to 1977 A.D.* (Collegeville, Minnesota, 1979) contains translations of the *Motu proprio* of 1903 and many other important documents

J. Gajard: *La méthode de Solesmes. Les principes constitutifs, ses règles pratiques d'interprétation* (Tournai, 1956); for trans. see bibliography to ch. 17–18

P. Combe: *Histoire de la restauration du chant grégorien d'après des documents inédits: Solesmes et l'édition vaticane* (Solesmes, 1969)

Recent research at the Pontificio Istituto di Musica Sacra, Rome:

N. Albarosa: 'La scuola gregoriana di Eugene Cardine', *Rivista italiana di musicologia* IX (1974), 269–97; XII (1977), 136–52

Towards a new critical edition:

Le graduel romain: édition critique par les moines de Solesmes (Solesmes, 1957–). Two volumes have so far appeared, containing, respectively, a catalogue of sources and an account of the selection of the sources to be used, based on a survey of melodic variants

J. Froger: 'The critical edition of the Roman Gradual by the monks of Solesmes', *Journal of the Plainsong and Mediaeval Music Society*, I (1978), 81–97

Part IV. Liturgico-musical innovations of the ninth and tenth centuries and their development; secular monody in Latin

Chapter 22. Sequences

Sequence sources

An inventory of manuscripts:

H. Husmann (ed.): *Tropen- und Sequenzenhandschriften*, RISM B.v[1] (Munich and Duisburg, 1964)

Sequence manuscripts in facsimile:

R. J. Hesbert (ed.): *Le prosaire de la Sainte-Chapelle: manuscrit du chapitre de Saint-Nicholas de Bari (vers 1250),* MMS I (Mâcon, 1952)

Le prosaire d'Aix-la-Chapelle: manuscrit 13 du chapitre d'Aix-la-Chapelle (XIIe siècle), MMS III (Rouen, 1961)

Le tropaire-prosaire de Dublin: manuscrit Add. 710 de l'Université de Cambridge (vers 1360), MMS IV (Rouen, 1966)

G. Vecchi (ed.): *Troparium sequentiarium Nonantulanum: Cod. Casanat.*

Bibliography

1741, vol. 1, Monumenta lyrica medii aevi, series liturgica 1/1 (Modena, 1955)

Editions:

P. Aubry and E. Misset (eds.): *Les proses d'Adam de Saint-Victor*, Mélanges de musicologie critique II (Paris, 1900)

N. de Goede (ed.): *The Utrecht Prosarium*, Monumenta Musica Neerlandica VI (Amsterdam, 1965). A transcription of the manuscript Utrecht, University Library, 417

C. A. Moberg (ed.): *Über die schwedischen Sequenzen: eine musikgeschichtliche Studie*, Veröffentlichungen der gregorianischen Akademie zu Freiburg in der Schweiz XIII (2 vols., Uppsala, 1927)

Secondary sources

Origins:

P. Dronke: 'The beginnings of the sequence', *Beiträge zur Geschichte der deutschen Sprache und Literatur* (Tübingen), LXXXVII (1965), 43–73

H. Husmann: 'Alleluia, Vers und Sequenz', *AnnM*, IV (1956), 19–53 'Sequenz und Prosa', *AnnM*, II (1954), 61–91

B. Stäblein: 'Zur Frühgeschichte der Sequenz', *AfMw*, XVIII (1961), 1–33

The Notkerian sequence:

R. L. Crocker: *The Early Medieval Sequence* (Berkeley, 1977)

H. Husmann: 'Die St. Galler Sequenztradition bei Notker und Ekkehard', *AcM*, XXVI (1964), 6–18

W. von den Steinen: *Notker der Dichter und seine geistige Welt* (2 vols., Berne, 1948)

The Victorine sequence:

H. Husmann: 'Notre-Dame und Saint-Victor: Repertoire-Studien zur Geschichte der gereimten Prosen', *AcM*, XXXVI (1964), 98–123 and 191–221

Form:

G. Reichert: 'Strukturprobleme der älteren Sequenz', *Deutsche Vierteljahrsschrift für Literaturwissenschaft und Geistesgeschichte* XXIII (1949), 227–51 and music exx. at the end of the volume

Chapter 23. Tropes

Transcriptions of tropes

P. Evans: *The Early Trope Repertory of Saint Martial of Limoges*, PSM II (Princeton, 1970). Includes a transcription of the Proper tropes from Paris, Bibliothèque Nationale, lat. 1121 and a selection of other pieces

G. Weiss (ed.): *Introitus-Tropen*, vol. 1: *Das Repertoire der südfranzösischen Tropare des 10. und 11. Jahrhunderts*, MMMA III/1 (Kassel, 1970)

Texts and source studies

R. Jonsson (ed.): *Corpus Troporum*, vol. 1: *Tropes du propre de la messe*, part 1: *Cycle de Noël*, Acta universitatis Stockholmiensis: studia latina Stockholmiensia XXI (Stockholm, 1975)

Bibliography

O. Marcusson (ed.): *Corpus troporum*, vol. 2: *Prosules de la messe*, part 1: *Tropes de l'alleluia*, Acta universitatis Stockholmiensis: studia latina Stockholmiensia XXII (Stockholm, 1976)

G. Björkvall, G. Iversen and R. Jonsson (eds.): *Corpus troporum*, vol. 3: *Tropes du propre de la messe*, part 2: *Cycle de Pâques*, Acta universitatis Stockholmiensis: studia latina Stockholmiensia XXV (Stockholm, 1982)

G. Iversen: *Corpus troporum*, vol. 4: *Tropes de l'Agnus Dei*, Acta universitatis Stockholmiensis: studia latina Stockholmiensia XXVI (Stockholm, 1980)

A. E. Planchart: *The Repertory of Tropes at Winchester* (2 vols., Princeton, 1977)

Secondary literature

Origins of tropes:

R. L. Crocker: 'The troping hypothesis', *MQ*, LII (1966), 183–203

P. Evans: 'Some reflections on the origin of the trope', *JAMS*, XIV (1961), 119–30

R. Weakland: 'The beginnings of troping', *MQ*, XLIV (1958), 477–88

Genres:

C. M. Atkinson: 'The earliest Agnus Dei melody and its tropes', *JAMS*, XXX (1977), 1–19

D. Bjork: 'The Kyrie trope', *JAMS*, XXXIII (1980), 1–41

M. Huglo: 'Aux origines des tropes d'interpolation: le trope méloforme de l'introit', *RdM*, LXIV (1978), 7–54

K. Rönnau: *Die Tropen zum Gloria in excelsis Deo* (Wiesbaden, 1967)

Studies of the music:

N. Sevestre: 'The Aquitainian tropes of the Easter introit – a musical analysis', *Journal of the Plainsong and Mediaeval Music Society*, III (1980), 26–39

B. Stäblein: 'Zum Verständnis des "klassischen" Tropus', *AcM*, XXXV (1963), 84–95

Other matters:

E. Costa: *Tropes et séquences dans le cadre de la vie liturgique au Moyen Age*, Bibliotheca 'Ephemerides Liturgicae': subsidia XVII (Vatican City, 1979); two chapters appeared earlier in *EL*, XCII (1978), 261–322 and 440–71

E. Odelman: 'Comment a-t-on appelé les tropes? Observations sur les rubriques des tropes des Xe et XIe siècles', *CCM*, XVII (1975), 15–36

Chapter 24. Metrical and dramatic offices

Metrical offices

General:

R. Jonsson: *Historia: Etudes sur la genèse des offices versifiés*, Acta universitatis Stockholmiensis: studia latina Stockholmiensia XV (Stockholm, 1968)

Bibliography

Editions:

W. Arlt: *Ein Festoffizium aus Beauvais* (2 vols., Cologne, 1970)

M. J. Epstein: 'Ludovicus decus regnantium: perspectives on the rhymed office', *Speculum*, LIII (1978), 283–334

D. Stevens: 'Music in honor of St. Thomas of Canterbury', *MQ*, LVI (1970), 311–48. For the offices for St Thomas

G. Vecchi (ed.): *Uffici drammatici padovani*, Biblioteca dell'*Archivum Romanicum* I/41 (Florence, 1954)

H. Villetard (ed.): *Office de Pierre de Corbeil (Office de la Circoncision) improprement appelé 'Office des Fous'*, Bibliothèque musicologique IV (Paris, 1907)
Office de Saint Savinien et de Saint Potentien, premiers évêques de Sens, Bibliothèque musicologique V (Paris, 1956)

R. G. Weakland: 'The compositions of Hucbald', *EG*, III (1959), 155–62. For the offices attributed to Hucbald of Saint-Amand

The Passion

M. Huglo: 'Tradition orale et tradition écrite dans la transmission des mélodies grégoriennes', *Studien zur Tradition in der Musik: Kurt von Fischer zum 60. Geburtstag*, ed. H. H. Eggebrecht and M. Lütolf (Munich, 1973), pp. 31–42. Part of this article is a discussion of music for the Passion

Y. Rokseth: 'La liturgie de la Passion vers la fin du Xe siècle', *RdM*, XXVIII (1949), 1–58; XXIX (1950), 35–52

Deposition of the Cross

S. Corbin: *La déposition liturgique du Christ au Vendredi Saint: sa place dans l'histoire des rites et du Théâtre réligieux* (Paris, 1960)

The Quem quaeritis and Visitatio sepulchri ceremonies

D. A. Bjork: 'On the dissemination of *Quem quaeritis* and the *Visitatio sepulchri* and the chronology of their early sources', *Comparative Drama*, XIV (1980), 46–69

H. De Boor: *Die Textgeschichte der lateinischen Osterfeiern*, Germanistische Forschungen, neue Folge XXII (Tübingen, 1967)

C. C. Flanigan: 'The liturgical context of the Quem queritis trope', *Comparative Drama*, VIII (1974), 45–62

O. B. Hardison: *Christian Rite and Christian Drama: Essays in the Origin and Early History of Modern Drama* (Baltimore, 1965)

T. J. McGee: 'The liturgical placement of the *Quem quaeritis* dialogue', *JAMS*, XXIX (1976), 1–29

Chapter 25. Liturgical drama

Bibliography of liturgical drama

C. J. Stratman (ed.): *Bibliography of Medieval Drama* (Berkeley, Calif., 2nd edn 1972)

Bibliography

Collected editions of plays
Text and music:
F. Collins Jr. (ed.): *Medieval Church Music Dramas: A Repertory of Complete Plays* (Charlottesville, Virginia, 1976)
E. de Coussemaker (ed.): *Drames liturgiques du Moyen Âge* (Rennes, 1860; repr. New York, 1964). The 'facsimiles' in this book are, in fact, diplomatic transcriptions

Texts only:
W. Lipphardt (ed.): *Lateinische Osterfeiern und Osterspiele*, Ausgaben deutscher Literatur des XV. bis XVIII. Jahrhunderts, Reihe Drama v (6 vols., Berlin and New York, 1975–81)

The Fleury Playbook:
G. Tintori (ed.): *Sacre rappresentazioni nel manoscritto 201 della Bibliothèque Municipale di Orléans: edizione fototipica*, Instituta et Monumenta I/2 (Cremona, 1958). This includes an introduction by R. Monterosso on the transcriptions, which are mensural

Studies of liturgical drama
Musical:
D. Dolan: *Le drame liturgique de Pâques en Normandie et en Angleterre au moyen-âge*, Publications de l'université de Poitiers: lettres et sciences humaines XVI (Paris, 1975)
W.L. Smoldon: *The Music of the Medieval Church Dramas* (London, 1980)

Textual:
K. Young: *The Drama of the Medieval Church* (2 vols., Oxford, 1933)

Liturgical:
B.-D. Berger: *Le drame liturgique de Pâques du Xe au XIIIe siècle*, Théologie historique XXXVII (Paris, 1976)

Musical matters
The re-use of older material:
S. K. Rankin: 'The Mary Magdalene scene in the *Visitatio sepulchri* ceremonies', *EMH*, I (1981), 227–55

Musical differentiation of characters:
H. Wagenaar-Nolthenius: 'Sur la construction musicale du drame liturgique', *CCM*, III (1960), 449–56

Rhythm:
R. Weakland: 'The rhythmic modes and medieval Latin drama', *JAMS*, XIV (1961), 131–46

Instruments:
E. A. Bowles: 'The role of musical instruments in medieval sacred drama', *MQ*, XLV (1959), 67–84

Bibliography

Chapter 26. Non-liturgical Latin monody

The mediaeval lyric

General:
P. Dronke: *The Medieval Lyric* (London, 1968)
Poetic Individuality in the Middle Ages: New Departures in Poetry, 1000–1150 (Oxford, 1970)
A. Machabey: 'Introduction à la lyrique musicale romane', *CCM*, II (1959), 203–11 and 283–93

Planctus:
J. Yearley: 'A bibliography of planctus in Latin, Provençal, French, German, English, Italian, Catalan, and Galician-Portuguese from the time of Bede to the early fifteenth century', *Journal of the Plainsong and Mediaeval Music Society*, IV (1981), 12–52

Peter Abelard

Complete edition of the *planctus*:
G. Vecchi (ed.): *Pietro Abelardo: I 'Planctus'*, Instituto di filologia romanza dell'Università di Roma, testi e manuali XXXV (Modena, 1951)

Studies:
M. Huglo: 'Abélard, poète et musicien', *CCM*, XXII (1979), 349–61
A. Machabey: 'Les planctus d'Abélard', *Romania*, LXXXII (1961), 71–95
L. Weinrich: 'Peter Abaelard as musician', *MQ*, LV (1969), 295–312 and 464–86

Goliards

Carmina Burana:
B. Bischoff (ed.): *Carmina Burana: Facsimile Reproduction of the Manuscript Clm 4660 and Clm 4660a*, Publications of Medieval Music Manuscripts IX (New York, 1967)

Studies of the music:
W. Lipphardt: 'Unbekannte Weisen zu den Carmina Burana', *AfMw*, XII (1955), 122–42
A. Machabey: 'Remarques sur les mélodies goliardiques', *CCM*, VII (1964), 257–78

Notation of non-liturgical monody

E. Jammers: *Aufzeichnungweisen der einstimmigen ausserliturgischen Musik des Mittelalters*, Palaeographie der Musik I/4 (Cologne, 1975)

Bibliography

Part V. Monody in vernacular languages; instruments; the *ars musica*

Chapter 27. Troubadour and trouvère lyric

Editions

Comprehensive collections:

F. Gennrich: *Der musikalische Nachlass der Troubadours*, Summa musicae medii aevi, III, IV, XV (1958–65)

I. Fernandez de la Cuesta and R. Lafont: *Las Cançons dels Trobadors* (Toulouse, 1979)

H. van der Werf: *Trouvères-Melodien I–II*, MMMA XI, XII (Kassel, 1977–9)

A. Jeanroy, L. Brandin and P. Aubry: *Lais et Descorts français du XIII siècles* (Paris 1901, repr. 1970)

N. E. Wilkins: *The Lyric Works of Adam de la Hale* (1236–87), Corpus Mensurabilis Musicae XL (1967)

Anthologies:

H. van der Werf: *The Chansons of the Troubadours and Trouvères: A Study of the Melodies and their Relation to the Poems* (Utrecht, 1972). More than an anthology, a wide-ranging study of the music

J. Maillard: *Anthologie de chants des troubadours* (Nice, 1967)

J. Maillard: *Anthologie de chants des trouvères* (Paris, 1967)

S. N. Rosenberg and H. Tischler: *Chanter m'estuet: Songs of the Trouvères* (London, 1981)

A. Press: *Anthology of Troubadour Lyric Poetry* (Edinburgh, 1971). Texts and translations, no music

Studies

General background:

P. Dronke: *The Medieval Lyric* (London, 1968)

H. Davenson (pseudonym of H. Marrou): *Les troubadours* (Paris, 1961), 2nd rev. edn 1971)

General musical survey:

P. Aubry: *Trouvères and Troubadours* (New York, 1969, transl. from 2nd rev. French edn 1910). Includes numerous edns

Origins – contrasting ideas:

H. G. Farmer: *Historical Facts for the Arabian Musical Influence* (London, 1930, repr. 1970)

J. Chailley: 'Les premiers troubadours et les versus de l'école d'Aquitaine', *Romania*, LXXVI (1955), 212–39

Forms and styles:

H. H. S. Räkel: *Die musikalische Erscheinungsform der Trouvèrepoesie* (Berne, 1977)

Bibliography

W. Apel: 'Rondeaux, virelais, and ballades in French 13th-century song', *JAMS*, VII (1954), 121–30

H. van der Werf: 'The trouvère chansons as creations of a notationless musical culture', *Current Musicology*, I (1965), 61–8

J. Stevens: '"La Grande Chanson Courtoise": the chansons of Adam de la Halle', *Proceedings of the Royal Musical Association*, CI (1974–5), 11–30

Rhythm and performance:

H. Tischler: 'Rhythm, meter, and melodic organization in medieval songs', *Revue Belge de Musicologie*, XXVIII–XXX (1974–6), 5–23

B. Kippenberg: *Der Rhythmus im Minnesang* (Munich, 1962)

H. van der Werf: 'Deklamatorischer Rhythmus in den Chansons der Trouvères', *Mf*, XX (1967), 122–44

I. Parker: 'The performance of troubadour and trouvère song: some facts and conjectures', *Early Music*, V (1977), 185–207

Chapter 28. Monody in the German-speaking countries, the Iberian peninsula and England

Minnesang

Editions:

B. G. Seagrave and W. Thomas: *The Songs of the Minnesingers* (London, 1966): anthology with gramophone record

R. J. Taylor: *The Art of the Minnesinger* (Cardiff, 1968): complete edn of songs to *c.* 1300

Studies:

U. Aarburg: *Singweisen zur Liebeslyrik der deutschen Frühe* (Düsseldorf, 1956). Gives Romance originals for German *contrafacta*

J. Müller-Blattau: 'Zu Form und Überlieferung der ältesten deutschen geistlichen Lieder', *Zeitschrift für Musikwissenschaft*, XVII (1935), 129–46: on *Geisslerlieder*

Spanish songs

H. Anglès: *La música de las Cantigas de Santa María del Rey Alfonso el Sabio* (3 vols. in 4, Barcelona, 1943–64). Facsimile, transcription, and extensive discussion of notation and transcription, Spanish music to the 13th century and related music from other countries

I. Pope: 'Medieval Latin background of the 13th-century Galician lyric', *Speculum*, IX (1934), 3–25: songs of Martín Códax

English songs

E. J. Dobson and F. Ll. Harrison: *Medieval English Songs* (London, 1979): complete, though often heavily edited, edition of the small repertory, with extensive background discussion

Bibliography

Chapter 29. Italian poetry: *laude*

Laude spirituali

Sources:

P. Damilano: 'Laude latine in un antifonario bobbiese del Trecento', *Collectanea historiae musicae*, III (Florence, 1963), 15–57

F. Liuzzi (ed.): *La lauda e i primordi della melodia italiana* (2 vols., Rome, 1934)

G. Varanini, L. Banfi and A. C. Burgio (eds.): *Laude cortonesi del secolo XIII al XV* (2 vols., Florence, 1981). Useful survey by G. Cattin in vol. I, part 2, pp. 476–516

G. Varanini (ed.): *Laude dugentesche*, Vulgares eloquentes VIII (Padua, 1972)

A. Ziino: 'Frammenti di laude nell'Archivio di Stato di Lucca', *Cultura neolatina*, XXXI (1971), 295–312

Music:

H. Anglès: 'The musical notation and rhythm of the Italian laude', *Essays in Musicology: A Birthday Offering for Willi Apel*, ed. H. Tischler (Bloomington, 1968), pp. 51–60

R. Monterosso: 'Il linguaggio musicale della lauda dugentesca', *Il movimento dei Disciplinati nel settimo centenario dal suo inizio* (Perugia, 1962), pp. 476–94

Social background:

B. J. Blackburn: '*Te matrem dei laudamus:* a study in the musical veneration of Mary', *MQ*, LIII (1967), 53–76

A. Ziino: 'Testi religiosi medioevali in notazione mensurale', *L'Ars Nova italiana del trecento III* (Certaldo, 1978), 447–91

Strophic form and the *zajal*:

C. Terni: 'Per una edizione critica del "Laudario di Cortona"', *Chigiana*, XXI (1964), 111–29

Chapter 30. Musical instruments

Musical instruments

General:

J. Montagu: *The World of Medieval and Renaissance Instruments* (Woodstock, NY, 1976)

D. Munrow: *Instruments of the Middle Ages and Renaissance* (London, 1976)

Iconographical evidence:

J. W. McKinnon: 'Representations of the mass in medieval and Renaissance art', *JAMS*, XXXI (1978), 21–52

T. Seebass: *Musikdarstellung und Psalterillustration im früheren Mittelalter* (2 vols., Berne, 1973)

Bibliography

Pseudo-Jerome's letter:

R. Hammerstein: 'Instrumenta Hieronymi', *AfMw*, XVI (1959), 117–34

C. Page: 'Biblical instruments in medieval manuscripts', *Early Music*, V (1977), 299–309

Documentary evidence:

E. A. Bowles: 'The organ in the medieval liturgical service', *Revue Belge de Musicologie*, XVI (1962), 13–29

'Were musical instruments used in the liturgical service during the Middle Ages?, *Galpin Society Journal*, X (1957), 40–56

Chapter 31. The *ars musica* in the Middle Ages

Ars musica in the early Middle Ages

L. Gushee: 'Questions of genre in medieval treatises on music', *Gattungen der Musik in Einzeldarstellungen*, pp. 365–433

M. Huglo: 'Le développement du vocabulaire de l'*Ars Musica* à l'époque carolingienne', *Latomus*, XXXIV (1975), 131–71

L. Spitzer: *Classical and Christian Ideas of World Harmony* (Baltimore, 1963): derives from articles in *Traditio*, II (1944), 409–64; III (1945), 307–64

Scholastic writing on music during the thirteenth century

F. A. Gallo: 'Astronomy and music in the Middle Ages: the *Liber Introductorius* by Michael Scot', *MD*, XXVII (1973), 5–9

G. Göller (ed.): *Vinzenz von Beauvais O.P. (um 1194–1264) und sein Musiktraktat im Speculum doctrinale*, Kölner Beiträge zur Musikforschung XV (Regensburg, 1959)

H. Müller: 'Der Musiktraktat in dem Werke des Bartholomaeus Anglicus *De proprietatibus rerum*', *Riemann-Festschrift: gesammelte Studien zum 60. Geburtstag* (Leipzig, 1909; repr. Tutzing, 1965), pp. 241–55

Music in mediaeval education

N. C. Carpenter: *Music in the Medieval and Renaissance Universities* (Norman, Oklahoma, 1958)

L. Ellinwood: 'Ars Musica', *Speculum*, XX (1945), 290–9

J. Smits van Waesberghe: *Musikerziehung im Mittelalter: Lehre und Theorie der Musik des Mittelalters*, MgB III/3 (Leipzig, 1969)

INDEX

Abelard, Peter, 129–30, 131
Adam de la Hale, 134, 140
Adam of St Victor, 108–9
Admonitio generalis, 54
Aghios a theos, 44
Agnus Dei, in Gregorian chant, 93
Agobard (Bishop of Lyons), 54
alba, 134; *Phebi claro nondum orto iubare*, 129
Alcuin, Albinus Flaccus, 54
Al-Fārābi, 158
Alfonso X 'el Sabio' ('the wise'), 143
Alia musica, 81
alleluia, 10, 11, 16; in Ambrosian chant, 37; in Gregorian chant, 89; in Hispanic chant, 43; and sequences, 102–4; see also *jubilus*
alleluia prolixa, 43
Amalar (Bishop of Metz), 54, 102, 155
Ambrose, St (Bishop of Milan), 14, 15; and hymnody, 18–20; on *jubilus*, 11; and liturgical chant, 31–2; and liturgical pluralism, 38–9
Ambrosian chant, 31–8, 94; verbal melody, 35
Anastius I (Emperor), 25
Andoyer, Dom, 26
Andrew of Crete, St, 25
Anerio, Felice, 95
Anglès, Higinio, 143, 144, 152
antiphonal psalmody, *see under* psalmody
Antiphonale Missarum, 16; Ambrosian, 34; and Gregory the Great, 53; Pothier (Solesmes) transcription, 97
Antiphonale Missarum Sextuplex

(Mont-Blandin Antiphoner), 87, 102
Antiphonarium, see *Antiphonale Missarum*
Antiphonarium Officii, 16
Antiphoner, attributed to Gregory the Great, 50, 52; Carolingian rearrangement, 54
antiphons, 10; in Gregorian chant, 88
Apel, Willi, 29, 92
Apollinaris, Sidonius, 19
Aquileian chant, 39–40
Arnaut Daniel, 137
ars musica, 58, 79, 85, 157–61
Aubry, Pierre, 138, 144
Augustine, St (Archbishop of Canterbury), 17, 49
Augustine, St (Bishop of Hippo), 14; on *alleluia*, 11; and Ambrosian rite, 31–2; on hymns, 18–19; on *jubilus*, 10–11, 162–3; as music theorist, 80, 159; and vocal music, 155
Aurelian of Réomé, 81
Auxentius (Bishop), 19
Avenary, Hanoch, 9, 30

Bacon, Roger, 158–9
ballata, 148–9
Bangor Antiphonal, 42, 61
baptismal rites, 2–3, 5
Bar, 142
Barnabas (apostle), 5
Bartholomaeus Anglicus, 158–60
Basil, St, 22
Beatrice of Burgundy, 141
Bede, the Venerable, 50, 52
Behaim, Michel, 142
Benedict II (Pope), 52

239

Index

Index

dramatised liturgy, *see* liturgical drama
Durand, Guillaume (Bishop of Mende), 111, 114, 156

échoi, 25
Edict of Milan, 12, 13
Editio Vaticana, 63, 65, 71, 99–100
Eleanor of Aquitaine, 145
emboîtement, 70
Ephraim, St, 18
episema, 58, 66, 75–6, 99
Epistola ad Michaelem de ignoto cantu, 59
Eschenbach, Wolfram von, 142
Ethelwold (Bishop of Winchester), 120
eucharist, 15; in Gregorian liturgy, 88
eucharistic liturgy, 12; recalls Jewish tradition, 5–6
Exultet, 41

Faidit, Gaucelm, 145
Fasani, Rainerio, 147
Fenis, Rudolf von, 142
Ferretti, Paolo, 56
Fischer, Balthasar, 13
fractio panis, 93
fractus, 95
Francis of Assisi, St, 146
Franco-Roman chant, 46, 53–6
'Frauenlob', *see* Heinrich von Meissen
Frederick II of Sicily, 146
Frederick Barbarossa, 141
Friedrich von Hûsen, 142

Gajard, Joseph, 99
Gallican rite, 29, 45–7, 53, 54; influence on Roman liturgy, 55–6; and Mozarabic liturgy, 46–7
Garzo (poet), 148
Gautier de Coinci, 140, 143
Geisslerlieder, 143
Gelasius I (Pope), 16, 20, 50
Geoffrey of St Victor, 130
Germanus of Paris, St, 45
Gerson-Kiwi, Edith, 8
Getronius Filius, 123

Gill da Zamora, 154, 156; *Ars musica*, 185–9
Giovanni (*archicantor* of St Peter's), 27, 52
Gloria (in excelsis), 12; in Ambrosian rite, 35–6; in Gregorian chant, 92; in Hispanic rite, 44
Godric, St, 145
goliards, 128, 130–1
Gontier (canon), 96
Goussainville, Pierre, 48
gradual, 16; in Gregorian chant, 88–9
Graduale, Medici edition, 95; Pothier (Solesmes) edition, 97, 100
Greek chant, 23
Gregorian chant, 48–53; and Ambrosian chant, 38; classical repertory, 87–93; decline and renewal, 94–100; diatonic, 59; and duration of notes and neumes, 73–6, 95; and Franco-Roman liturgy, 55–6; mensuralist interpretation, 74–6; and modes, 84; and Old Roman chant, 26–31; and rhythm and neumes, 76–9, 94; syllabic time, 73–4, 78; use of MS sources, 68–9; verbal rhythm, 70, 78, 99–100; and words and melody, 70–1
Gregory the Great, St (Pope Gregory I), 15, 16, 48–53, 57, 89; and hymns, 20; welcomed liturgical variety, 17
Gregory II (Pope), 53
Grocheo, Johannes de, 156, 161
Guéranger, Prosper (Louis Pascal), 96
Guido d'Arezzo; on Boethius, 158; *Epistola de ignoto cantu*, 175–9; and *laude*, 148; and notation, 59, 84, 85, 87
Guiot de Provins, 141
Guiraut de Borneill, 137, 138

Hadrian I (Pope), 50, 54
Handschin, Jacques Samuel, 151
Hartmann von der Aue, 142

241

Index

Heinrich von Meissen ('Frauenlob'), 142
Henry (Duke of Friuli), 128
Henry II (German Emperor), 92
Henry of Anjou, 145
Heraclius (Emperor), 25
Hermannus Contractus, 95
Hesbert, René-Jean, 41, 87
hexachord, 59–60, 84–7
Hilarius (pupil of Abelard), 131
Hilary of Poitiers, 14, 18
Hippolytus, 10, 12
Hispano-Mozarabic rite, 35, 42–5
Høeg, Carsten, 24
Honorius (Pope), 50, 52
Horace, 128
hosanna, in Gregorian chant, 93
Houdard, Georges-Louis, 75
Hucbald of Saint-Amand, 58, 81
Hucke, Helmut, 29
Hufnagelnotation, 40
Hugh of Orleans (the Primate), 131
Huglo, Michel, 28, 84
Huizinga, Johan, 153
hymn to the Trinity (Oxyrhynchus papyrus 1786), 23
hymnody, 2–3, 17–20; in the Gregorian repertory, 93

Iam, dulcis amica, venito, 129
Iberian monody, 143–5; and rhythmic modes, 144
Infantas, Fernando de las, 95
Inguanez, Mauro, 122, 147
Innocent I (Pope), 39
instruments, accompanying troubadour songs, 133; in liturgical drama, 126–7; in liturgical rites, 152–6
introit, 15–16
Isidore, St (Bishop of Seville); Etymologiae, 169–75; and liturgical uniformity, 43; as music theorist, 80–1, 157–60

Jacopane da Todi, 109, 148, 152
James (author of epistle), 3
Jammers, Ewald, 28, 75
Jausions, Paul, 97
Jeannin, Jules-Cécilien, 75

Jena song-book, 141
Jerome, St, 14, 15, 39
Johannes Hymmonides, see John the Deacon
John, St, 2, 3
John (archicantor of St Peter's), 27, 52
John XXII (Pope), 95
John the Baptist, St, 5, 59
John Chrysostom, St, 22
John the Deacon, 50, 52, 53
jongleur, 133
Jubilate Deo universa terra, 90
jubilus, 10–11, 16, 33, 105; in Ambrosian chant, 37; in Gregorian chant, 89; in St Augustine, 162–3; and sequences, 102–3; see also alleluia
Julian of Speyer, 117
Jungmann, Josef A., 13
Justin (philosopher), 12
Justina (Empress), 18
Justinian (Emperor), 48
Justus ut palma, 89

kontakion, 25
Kyrie, in Gregorian chant, 91

lai, 140, 156
Lanquan li jorn son lonc en may, 137, 142
laudario, 148–9, 150; notation in, 150–1
laude, 147–52; and ballata, 149; decree on, 183–5; and modern tonality, 150; and modes, 150; and rhythmic interpretation, 150–2
laudes, 43
laudesi, 147; decree on, 183–5
Laurenzi, F., 130
Laus angelorum, 12
Leo II (Pope), 52
Leo XIII (Pope), 97–8
Leo the Great (Pope Leo I), 14, 16
Leon Antiphonary, 43
Lérins, 61
Li Geus de Robin et de Marion, 140
Liber Hymnorum, 103–4
Liber Pontificalis, 28, 50, 52

Index

Index

paired-line structure, 104–5, 107
Palestrina, Pier Luigi Giovanni da, 95
Paravi lucernam, 37
Parsifal, 140
pastourelle, 133–4
patchwork, *see* centonate composition
Paul I (Pope), 52
Paul V (Pope), 95
Paul the Deacon (Warnefrid), 51, 53, 54
Paul, St, 2, 4, 5; evidence for ancient Christian chant, 11, 17
Paulinus (Patriarch of Aquileia), 128
Paulinus of Nola, 19, 31
Peire d'Auvergne, 137
Pelagius II (Pope), 49
Pepin the Short, 52, 53, 54
Perceval le Gallois, 140
Peregrinus, 122
Perosi, Lorenzo, 98
pes stratus, 46
Peter, St, 2, 3, 4
Peter Martyr, St, 147
Philip II (King of Spain), 95
Pius V (Pope), 109, 116
Pius X (Pope) (formerly Giuseppe Sarto), 98, 100
plainchant (plainsong), 21–2; *see also* chant
planctus, 128–9
Planctus ante nescia, 130
Planctus de obitu Karoli, 128
Planctus Hugonis abbatis, 129
Planctus Mariae, 122, 130
Plato, 159
Pliny the Younger, 12
podatus, 41
polyphony, 73, 95, 101, 159
Pontificale Romano-germanicum, 55
Pothier, Joseph, 97–100
Pragmatica sanctio, 48
preces, 44, 47
Prologus in Antiphonarium, 59
Proprium Missae, 16, 36
prosa, 103, 105, 108, 111
Prosper of Aquitaine, 15, 19
prosula, 115
Prudentius Aurelius, 19

psallendum, 43
psallentes, 51
psalmody, 9–10, 13, 18, 91; alleluiatic, 9, 10; in Ambrosian chant, 31–2, 37; antiphonal, 10, 89; in Gregorian chant, 92; responsorial, 9–10
Psalms, 3, 10
pseudo-Aristotle, 159
pseudo-Jerome, 153
Pustet, Friedrich (publisher), 96–8

quadratic notation, 63, 66, 68, 70
Quem quaeritis, 112, 120, 121
Quoniam tu illuminas, 38

Raimbaut d'Orange, 137
Raimbaut de Vaqueiras, 134, 145
Raimondi (printer), 95
Ramis de Pareja, Bartolomeo, 59
Regino of Prüm, 81
Reinmar von Zweter, 142
Remedius (Rémi) (Bishop of Rouen), 52, 54
responsories, 88, 90
rhythm, 76–7, 81; syllabic, 70; verbal, 70, 79
rhythmic interpretation, in Gregorian chant, 76–9; in Iberian monody, 144; in *laude*, 150–2; in liturgical drama, 125; in non-liturgical monody, 130; in troubadour and trouvère lyric, 135–6
rhythmic modes, 125–6; *see also* rhythmic interpretation
Riemann, Hugo, 75, 136, 151
Riquier, Guiraut, 143
Rokseth, Yvonne, 151
Romanus Melodus, 25
Rudel, Jaufre, 136–7, 142
Rufinus of Aquileia, 14

Sachs, Hans, 143
Sacramentarium, 16; Gregorian, 50, 54
St Gall, 28, 94, 108; home of *scriptoria*, 61, 62; notation, 65–9
St Martial, 108, 112, 159

Index

Index